About the Book

This book takes the ancient concept of ~~practicing~~ and places it in the perspective of New Age metaphysics and spirituality. All can learn, with techniques of visualization and dance, how to create within their own circumstances the "magickal existence and spiritual life." This is a stressful time for all to be living, but control of our environment begins with control of ourselves. Herein, the techniques of the ancient Qabala are adapted to the New Age disciple to create a magickal existence.

Magick is simply a means to an end. It is the discovery that life is supposed to go right. It reveals our many levels of consciousness and instructs us in how to reach them, so that we can release the greatest creativity into our day-to-day lives. The purpose of any magickal process is not to attain "psychism" but to surpass our physical limitations by learning the creative possibilities that exist within those limitations.

This book shows that each of us has the capability of accessing energies and utilizing them. Its sole purpose is to stimulate within each individual—regardless of where he or she may be in their own paths—a greater realization of the Divine Creativity that exists within all life.

Ted Andrews' Imagick *is one of the most original and effective systems of kabbalistic pathworking that I have ever read. The book teaches how to work in the astral plane and how to activate astral energies safely. It blends the use of symbols with the use of colors, sounds and fragrances to release greater psychic energies. It carefully introduces the various Sephiroth of the Tree of Life and their corresponding archetypal images, and then expands this knowledge into stunning techniques for practical pathworking. But what is most exciting and groundbreaking in this work is the Dancing of the Tree of Life, especially the Imagickal techniques of Spinning the Tree into existence.* Imagick *is a truly enlightening reading experience and I strongly recommend it to anyone interested in kabbalistic practical magic.*

—Migene Gonzalez-Wippler

About the Author

Ted Andrews is a full-time author, student and teacher in the metaphysical and spiritual fields. He conducts seminars, symposiums, workshops and lectures throughout the country on many facets of ancient mysticism. Ted works with past-life analysis, auric interpretation, numerology, the Tarot and the Qabala as methods of developing and enhancing inner potential. He is a clairvoyant and a certified spiritualist medium.

Ted is also active in the healing field. He is certified in basic hypnosis and acupressure and is involved in the study and use of herbs as an alternative path. He combines his musical training with more than twenty years of concentrated metaphysical study in the application of "Directed Esoteric Sound" in the healing process. He uses this with outer holistic methods of healing, such as "etheric touch," aura and chakra balancing, and crystal and gemstone techniques, in creating individual healing therapies and higher states of consciousness.

Ted Andrews is a contributing author to various metaphysical magazines and has written numerous books, including *Simplified Magic*, *The Magical Name*, *Sacred Sounds*, *How to See and Read the Aura*, *Dream Alchemy*, and *Enchantment of the Faerie Realm*.

To Write to the Author

If you wish to contact the author or would like more information about this book, please write to the author in care of Llewellyn Worldwide, and we will forward your request. Both the author and publisher appreciate hearing from you and learning of your enjoyment of this book and how it has helped you. Llewellyn Worldwide cannot guarantee that every letter written to the author can be answered, but all will be forwarded. Please write to:

Ted Andrews
c/o Llewellyn Worldwide
P.O. Box 64383-016, St. Paul, MN 55164-0383, U.S.A.

Please enclose a self-addressed, stamped envelope for reply, or $1.00 to cover costs.
If outside the U.S.A., enclose international postal reply coupon.

Free Catalog from Llewellyn

For more than 90 years Llewellyn has brought its readers knowledge in the fields of metaphysics and human potential. Learn about the newest books in spiritual guidance, natural healing, astrology, occult philosophy and more. Enjoy book reviews, new age articles, a calendar of events, plus current advertised products and services. To get your free copy of *Llewellyn's New Worlds of Mind and Spirit*, send your name and address to:

Llewellyn's New Worlds of Mind and Spirit
P.O. Box 64383-016, St. Paul, MN 55164-0383, U.S.A.

About the Llewellyn Practical Guides to Personal Power

To some people, the idea that "magick" is *practical* comes as a surprise. It shouldn't!

The entire basis for magick is to exercise influence over one's personal world in order to satisfy our needs and goals. And, while this magick is also concerned with psychological transformation and spiritual growth, even the spiritual life must be built on firm material foundations.

Here are practical and usable techniques that will help you to a better life, will help you attain things you want, will help you in your personal growth and development. *Moreover, these books can change your life, dynamically, positively!*

The material world and the psychic are intertwined, and it is this that establishes the magickal link: that mind/soul/spirit can as easily influence the material as vice versa.

Psychic powers and magickal practices can, and should, be used in one's daily life. Each of us has many wonderful, but yet underdeveloped talents and powers—surely we have an evolutionary obligation to make full use of our human potentials! Mind and body work together, and magick is simply the extension of this interaction into dimensions beyond the limits normally conceived. *Why be limited?*

All things you will ever want or be must have their start in your mind. In these books you are given practical guidance to develop your inner powers and apply them to your everyday needs. These abilities will eventually belong to everybody through natural evolution, but you can learn and develop them now!

This series of books will help you achieve such things as success, happiness, miracles, powers of ESP, healing, out-of-body travel, clairvoyance, divination, extended powers of mind and body, communication with non-physical beings, and knowledge by non-material means!

We've always known of things like this . . . seemingly supernormal achievements, often by quite ordinary people. We are told that we normally use only ten percent of our human potential. We are taught that faith can move mountains, that love heals all hurt, that miracles do occur. We believe these things to be true, but most people lack practical knowledge of them.

The books in this series form a full library of magickal knowledge and practice.

Other Books by Ted Andrews

Simplified Magic
The Sacred Power in Your Name
How to See and Read the Aura
How to Heal with Color
How to Uncover Your Past Lives
Dream Alchemy
The Magical Name
Sacred Sounds
How to Meet & Work with Spirit Guides
Magickal Dance
Enchantment of the Faerie Realm

Forthcoming by Ted Andrews

The Healer's Manual
The Occult Christ
Animal Speak

Llewellyn's Practical Guide To

Imagick

Qabalistic Pathworking for Imaginative Magicians

Ted Andrews

1993
Llewellyn Publications
St. Paul, Minnesota 55164-0383, U.S.A.

FIRST EDITION
Second Printing, 1993

Cover art by Gabriel Berndt (Walter Holl, agent)

Library of Congress Cataloging-in-Publication Data
Andrews, Ted, 1952-
   Imagick : Qabalistic pathworking for imaginative
magicians / Ted Andrews.
   (Originally published as Imagick: the magick of images,
paths & dance.)
      p.   cm. — (Llewellyn's practical guide series)
   Includes bibliographical references.
   ISBN 0-87542-016-8
   1. Qabala. 2. Self-realization. I. Title. II. Series.
BF1623.C2A52   1989
135'.4—dc20
                                   89-13642
                                       CIP

Llewellyn Publications
A Division of Llewellyn Worldwide, Ltd.
P.O. 64383, St. Paul, MN 55164-0383

table of contents

Chapter Four (cont'd.)

Benefits of pathworking. Precautions concerning pathworking. Preliminary considerations. Group and ceremonial pathwork. Descriptions of the 22 Paths of Wisdom. Creating the Pathworking Journal. *Imagickal technique of "Temple to Temple Visitation." Imagickal technique of "Tales and Legends." Imagickal technique of "Creating the Life Adventure."*

Dedication

To Mary

with great Love and Joy

acknowledgments

Many thanks and much love is extended to Mary Younker for her sharing of time and energy and knowledge of dance and yoga for this work. When one works the paths, individuals of light cross our paths, bringing inspiration and joy. She helped keep alive the celebrational aspect of the spiritual path and has blessed my life!

Many thanks go also to all of those who have attended my classes and seminars. Their questions and desire to open and explore assisted my own growth and helped to synthesize the esoteric into the real world.

None of this would be possible without the support and assistance of the one who has chosen to share her path in life with me, Kathy Andrews. She is my teacher and my visionary in all!

The Labyrinth of Charms

There was no way to see. Each of the paths before him wandered and twisted so that he could see no more than 25 to 50 feet ahead. He paused. What to do? Which path should he take? Which would be the easiest?

He had been through so much already. Worlds had opened before him. Dragons had been slain, treasures discovered. He had lived ten lifetimes in this one, maybe even a hundred. He had done so much more than the average man or woman. Or had he?

The doubts assailed him. Old doubts. Old recriminations. Old shadows, which had been driven back by the many new lights he had discovered in his explorations, began pushing back. Had he done anything at all? Was there any real accomplishment? It seemed such a long time since he had first started, and yet in many ways he felt as if he were again back at the beginning.

The young man turned to look back from whence he had come. He stared at what he saw. Behind him was that same cottage with the same old man who had set him upon the path. The Master! The Master who had neither identified himself nor acknowledged that he knew anything about the young man's quest. And yet this old farmer had left the young man with a map—a map to the true treasures of the world, a map to the Tree of Life!

The young man turned from the three paths that lay before him, and walked back to where the old man stood. He sat himself down again upon the rock, just as he had done the first time he had encountered the old man. The old man smiled warmly, nodded at the young man and continued his weeding of the garden.

"I wish to thank you for putting me upon the path when last I saw you," the young man said softly.

Again the old man smiled, raised his eyes and spoke as if to some unseen companion, "He thinks I helped him." He chuckled softly.

"What am I to do now? Which path am I to take? I have followed the map you gave me. I have continued asking the questions. I have discovered many wondrous things. I have opened many mysterious abilities. But I know there must be more, and now my path divides. There are three choices, but how am I to know which is correct?"

The old man said nothing. He sat back upon his haunches and looked warmly and silently at the young man.

"You must be here to help me, or you would not have appeared at my time of questioning. So why do you not speak? My curiosity is not yet abated. I still have many questions. I still have dreams. There is so much to do. Which is the way to go?"

"Have you learned so little in all your travels? There is no pill that gives instant knowledge or awareness. Your knowledge, your understanding, has grown with each step you have taken. We are building for an eternity, not a lifetime, and an eternity of wisdom takes an eternity to acquire."

"But there is so much I can already do. Is that all for nothing? Is it all useless?"

The old man frowned and his voice grew scolding. "What you have learned, what you can now do, is only a tool! It can help in your times to come, but it is not the end in itself. You seek the spiritual, and yet you forget that what is psychic is not necessarily spiritual. What is occult or hidden is not necessarily uplifting, and what is desired is not necessarily useful. Build your universe one step at a time. Hold on to your questions, but remember that whichever path you take, you will encounter those situations that will provide the most growth and learning for you.

"Choosing is not losing opportunities. Opportunities are never lost. They always come back again. We learn from all situations, but that which appears easiest is most full of traps and snares. What is important is that *you* do the choosing, *you* do the acting, rather than being acted upon. That alone builds responsibility and it is from re-sponsibility that we get our greatest challenges, and our greatest rewards."

The young man lowered his head with humility and then glanced back up the road to the three paths before him. He looked back to where the old man sat. He was gone! The space was empty. He jumped up and looked back and forth, turning around and around as if it might all be a joke.

It was no joke. The old man was gone again. The garden was gone. The cottage was gone. It was as if nothing had ever been there. The young man shook his head in wonderment. He walked slowly back to where the road divided into three paths.

He felt he was starting over. It was like a labyrinth that wound round and round leading nowhere, leaving him where he started. It had all seemed so charming, so exciting, but was it all charm and no substance?

"All knowledge begins with you and ends with you. Remember that we learn from *all* situations. Follow your heart and you will learn to live in love. You are building for eternity."

The sound of the old man's voice echoed in his mind. It was soft and still; it quieted the doubts. It pushed back the shadows once more.

"Follow your heart and you will learn to live in love," the young man repeated the words. He smiled, and took a deep breath.

"As you—NO! As *I* wish!" he answered with a laugh, and he stepped forward onto his new path . . .

(to be continued)

chapter one

The Tree of Life and
the Path of Development

We need not be aware of the inner world. We do not realize its existence most of the time. But many people enter it—unfortunately without guides, confusing the outer with the inner realities and inner with the outer—and generally lose their capacity to function competently in ordinary relations.

This need not be so. The process of entering into the *other* world from this world and returning to this world from the other world is as natural as death and giving birth or being born . . .

Among physicians and priests there should be some who are guides, who can educt the person from this world and induct him to the other, to guide him in it and to lead him back again.

One enters the other world by breaking a shell—or through a door—through a partition—the curtains part or rise and a veil is lifted.

The outer divorced from any illumination from the inner is in a state of darkness—is an age of darkness.

—R. D. LAING
Politics of Experience

Magick is a divine process, and to enter into it without the appropriate reverence will lead to problems down the road. One of the most misunderstood terms in metaphysical and spiritual studies, "magick" is not some hocus pocus or form of prestidigitation; neither is it mere divination or pacts with spiritual or demonic beings of any sort.

Magick is a means to an end. It is mastery over life (and aspects of life) with the expression of that mastery into our everyday activities. It deals with recognizing and tapping into those levels of consciousness which we are normally unaware of and yet influence us greatly. Anyone who has mastered some aspect of his life can be seen as a magician. Being able to handle conflicts with patience, tolerance and

1

insight can seem quite magickal to many people.

Magick is discovering that the Divine already exists within us. It is discovering that life is supposed to go right, and discovering how to make it right. People receive answers to their prayers, they experience miracles and magickal happenings in their lives, and then they proclaim, "The most *amazing* thing just happened!" The truth is that *prayers are supposed to be answered. Miracles and magick are supposed to happen!* It would be truly amazing if they did *not* happen! It is only our own doubts, fears, self-recriminations, our own sense of unworthiness and our refusal to look beyond our limited perspectives that delay and hinder the manifestation of a magickally wonderful existence.

It is the destiny of Western man to conquer matter. This is the quest for the spirit, a search for our innermost part, the point of our greatest reality. It is not a path straight up to some Divine Light from which there is no return, nor should there be expectation of having problems and trials of life dissolved in some blinding light of spirituality. It is man's destiny to bring out the *spirit* in matter so that the "kingdom of heaven" manifests. It is man's duty to spiritualize matter, not to escape from it. It is the search for the way to bring the spiritual into one's day-to-day life.

All of the ancient teachings and scriptures utilize similar terms and phrases to indicate this magical process. "Gateways," "doors," "the outer court," "the inner court," "temple," "Holy of Holies," "the quest," "the pilgrimage," and many other such terms are part of the ancient mystery language in which were veiled the teachings that could assist one in manifesting a higher destiny, a more magickal existence. This mystery language related to stages of development and training, to an interior unfoldment of spirituality within one's life.

Every civilization and religion has had its magickal teachings. The phraseology may have changed and the symbols readapted, but only to conform to the needs of the times. "What is extraordinary, however, is that there are more similarities than differences in the methods used by the secret traditions to change the consciousness of their respective practitioners." (*The Templar Tradition* by Gaetan Delaforge; Threshold Books; Vermont, 1987.)

In the West, this unfoldment of the Mysteries is most often referred to as the "Quest for the Holy Grail." This quest serves two distinct and yet related purposes:

1. It is the search to discover and to awaken our true spiritual essence, our innermost self.
2. It is the quest for our spiritual path in this lifetime, the best way to express our true essence during this incarnation.

These ancient Mysteries have always been available to those willing to put forth the time, energy and patience to find them. For most people they have assumed a supernormal and supernatural caricature. There are a number of reasons for this. For the unenlightened and the "unawakened" person, the whole idea of an occult life is either completely baffling, mysterious, ridiculous, intimidating, or all of these. They have been and still are considered "mysteries" because they add much greater knowledge to an individual when discovered, and greater knowledge gives greater power which in turn requires greater *responsibility*. For the mundane or the profane individual, the procedures for unfolding higher levels of consciousness and abilities are "mysterious," beyond the reach of the uninitiated. They are still called Mysteries because for eons the teachings were zealously guarded against outside intrusion to prevent a profaning of the energies. It is the profaning that draws the attention of masses and fuels the superstition, fears and narrowmindedness of the average individual. The ancient teachings that lead to the manifestation of a higher destiny, the magickal existence, can so completely transcend all customary experience and states of consciousness that an individual's center of perception and balanced thinking can be seriously disturbed. Unless an individual is well-grounded and has a well-founded base of experience in the spiritual sciences to fall back upon, there can be disruptions and abuses of the energies.

The idea of occult or magical teachings being referred to as Mysteries is still appropriate today, as many of the ideas and teachings are still somewhat unnatural to the average person in his or her present stage of development.

In every person the qualities essential for accelerating their growth and spiritual evolution is innate, but even if this is recognized, there is still needed a system or a means of releasing them. Such a system should be easily understood, and if based upon an older Mystery Tradition, it should be living and growing, adaptable to the modern aspirant. The system should also be capable of awakening inner potentials without overwhelming the student in the process and, finally, it should enable the student to experience the universal energies to which we have access within our lives. The ancient mystical Qabala fulfills *all* of these requirements.

Be it the mystical Qabala, as in the case of this work, or any other system, certain reminders must be stressed. *All* mystery systems, metaphysical philosophies, and religions are nothing more or less than systems of props whose sole object is to support and steady the mind and consciousness while it prepares for higher evolution. When we set out to consciously bring the force of divine energy into play within our world and our lives, *we must learn to direct and control it in full consciousness!*

The potential to accelerate and awaken our own divine manifestation lies within each of us. It is for this reason that above the portals of the ancient mystery schools was the phrase "Know Thyself." *Knowing thyself* constitutes the first stage of training in any true system of magick. It requires an impersonal approach to all of our desires and beliefs that we cannot bring ourselves to face. It is not always a pleasant task because it involves a purging or stripping away of the veils of pretense; those that we have placed about ourselves as well as those that society has placed about us. *It is a process that is often repeated.* It may even require that we retreat from time to time from active exploration, but we always return stronger and further along than if we had continued to force the growth. In many ways it is similar to the stripping process we go through at death, but occurs through the fulfilling of our life obligations in a creative and positive manner.

We can be our own worst enemy in this process. We either can't or won't make the most of our opportunities. We refuse to deal with our obligations and our hardships in a creative manner. We may resort to quick methods that ultimately create tremendously damaging difficulties down the road. (This could be anything from emotional imbalances to a misuse of one's energies by beings that could use an individual to hinder the progress of others, preventing them from becoming channels of light.) We may just halt because the process is too great and demands too much effort. There are *no* shortcuts to true spirituality. Metaphysics and magick are not fast food. It is not quick and easy.

There is prevalent today a major misconception concerning the path to higher spirituality, be it a magickal path or a mystical path. Many assume that if they are not working actively in the field of metaphysics, they cannot be truly making progress. If not ostensibly demonstrating psychic ability or learning, they are not growing. As a result, there now exists a preponderance of individuals trying to teach and work, and yet they do not have the depth of knowledge and experience to do so in the safest and highest manner.

It was to prevent such things from occurring that the ancient mystery schools required an active life aside from the spiritual studies. It is also why most required silence in the first two or even ten years of their concentrated study. They recognized that through the fulfilling of daily obligations in a creative manner we are propelled along the path. It is not the demonstration of psychic ability or book learning that unfolds our potential. In fact, quite often it can hinder, especially in the early years of learning and training. Rather than concentrating and focusing the energy, we dissipate it by using it to "teach" or do psychic work. The need or desire to be out front, displaying, is part of what ultimately must be purged away.

It is through the daily trials and tests that we begin to unfold our sleeping potential, enabling ourselves to identify and then lay down the outworn forms and patterns so that the newer and higher can come through. For most people this will involve simply opening the hearts of those they touch on a daily basis through a smile, a kind word or the meeting of obligations. They may not be demonstrating their knowledge or acquiring the attention that so many others seem to receive; and this does not imply that they are less evolved. It can imply that they may not have to learn how to be out front. They may have come to learn other lessons, and on a soul level they may truly be further along "the path" than those who are demonstrating publicly.

This is the *Quest for the Holy Grail.* For many, the form of the quest will take shape by working and teaching within the field of metaphysics as we know it today. For others, it will take the form of simply living their daily lives in a creative manner, and being a positive influence in the lives of those they touch. The form of the quest does not matter because all who go forth, in whatever manner, will achieve their true aim. Unfortunately, not all have the wisdom to see this.

In more ancient times, the path was under the strict guidance of a teacher. The spiritual pupil in our times must win for himself or herself the higher initiations through his/her own inner activity, as well as the conditions for initiation and for heightened consciousness. Nowadays, the guidance and support we receive from those around us during our periods of strain, testing, and temptation, and even the changes in circumstances, provide clues to the ancient teachings that only took place within the temples. These will ultimately take the place of admissions to various levels of temple teachings within the New Age.

The modern student must be able to take the life knowledge, instructions, and meditative content of his or her life, judge it independently, and then decide how the specific steps in esoteric learning should follow. If unable to carry through this necessary self-observation, judgment and obligation that is based upon it, then obviously more preparation is necessary before proceeding. This process begins by recognizing that no one knows better for you than you and the divine spark within you. Regardless of credentials, titles, degrees, or "abilities," the decisions concerning your life and the ensuing responsibilities and consequences are yours alone! This demands the development of secure perception and cognition; not only in the physical world but in the supersensible, nonphysical world as well. This presupposes careful self-observation, discrimination and judgment of one's own soul processes.

All who intend to accelerate their soul growth will find themselves tested continually upon the probationary path along three lines:

1. *Discrimination* — One must be able to discriminate and discern reality from illusion, the false from the true, when to act, how to act, where to focus energies, when not to focus energies, who to believe, whom not to believe. The individual must be able to test to determine half-truths. Discrimination is at the base of the Qabalistic Tree of Life, in that level of our consciousness known as Malkuth. It thus must be the basis of all our studies in the physical and nonphysical world. Connecting with the supersensible states of consciousness and those beings that exist there does not make one omniscient and omnipotent. It demands even greater testing and discrimination because it is fluid, changeable and unfamiliar, and the expressions of energy from that realm span the spectrum of positivity and negativity as greatly as does our own physical world.

2. *Test of the Teacher* — This is that testing of the individual to be able to discern complete and truthful teachings and their sources. There are many expressing "knowledge" on how-to-do, but it does not mean that the methods are necessarily appropriate or beneficially creative, regardless of their

effectiveness. Any time greater knowledge becomes more accessible, there is not only the opportunity to use it for benefit, but there is also ample opportunity for it to be misused. Many of the ancient methods of accelerating growth are no longer appropriate for modern man's energy and evolvement. The ancient methods have to be adapted to modern man.

There occurs with greater accessibility of knowledge and ancient wisdom an influx of teachers, many of whom do not have the appropriate depth of background and schooling in the entire field of esoteric science. Without an in-depth background in the spiritual sciences, it is difficult to discern what teachings to pass on and to what degree. Thus, there are many teachers in the metaphysical field who become tools for beings who desire to mix truth and lies, creating webs of entanglement that ultimately will trip students up and set them further back on the path than if they had left well enough alone. Sometimes the "teacher" becomes such a tool consciously, but this also occurs unconsciously. There is a tremendous karmic responsibility involved that can have far-reaching repercussions.

If an individual is misled because of another's teachings, the teacher is responsible to that individual but also to every other individual that student in turn affected and touched as a result. An excellent example is found in those who use techniques of candle magic to draw a love into their lives. Rather than use it to allow the universe to bring the ideal, many still attempt to manipulate and draw a specific individual into their lives. If this individual was not "supposed" to become a part of the manipulator's life, then the manipulator is responsible to that individual, but also to every other individual whom that person was supposed to connect with but did not get the chance to.

At some point within the student's growth process, there will be an encounter with a "teacher" who may have tremendous knowledge, but who may not be working for the benefit of the Divine. In spite of the "knowledge" that could be attained, it is important to discriminate and back away. With any knowledge that comes, seeds of half-truths and deception also come. These will ultimately trip up the individual. It is here that the words of St. Paul hold the strongest: "Test all things and hold fast to that which is True!" Accept nothing on blind faith, and remember that when you sit to be taught anything, you are opening yourself to being influenced by the teacher. This influence is often very subtle, but it is always very powerful. *Test, discriminate what comes through and remember that no one knows better for you than YOU!* In this way, your teachers become mediators and assistants for your own bridge-building to higher evolvement.

3. *Uncontrolled Fancy* — This is the test of your ability to discern the *maya* and illusions of energy manifestations that affect us when we begin to open up to more ethereal realms. This may affect us on the physical, but it especially affects us when operating upon and working with those planes of life and energy with which we are unfamiliar. Visions, channelings, insights can be nothing more than uncontrolled fancy, a manifestation of your own imaginings to provide a stroking for the ego. Not delving deeply enough, accepting blindly without testing and failing to be objective in the process of self-observation all lead to manifestations of uncontrolled fancy. What may come through as spiritual insight may be little more than a fanciful manufacturing to verify what you already know or to justify your own viewpoint. Imagination is important in unfolding our higher potential, but it must be a controlled and creative imagination and not just uncontrolled fancy. Sometimes the difference is difficult to detect, but this is why continual self-observation is essential in all work in the spiritual sciences. There is no fast and easy method. Those that are true require persistent effort, and that effort will be rewarded.

Manifesting a magickal existence, a higher destiny, requires a genuine search for knowledge, as well as a striving to fulfill the obligations of life. It demands a new, *fully conscious* union with the spiritually creative, supersensible world. This cannot be fulfilled by mere clairvoyance or demonstrations of "psychic powers." Remember that what is psychic is not always spiritual. What is occult or metaphysical is not always uplifting, and what is appealing is not always useful to us. The finger pointing at the Sun is not the same as the Sun! This also cannot be fulfilled by soul experiences induced with drugs. A tremendously heightened sense of responsibility must be experienced when setting foot in the spiritual realm.

The purpose of all growth, training and initiation is to render oneself more useful to the service of humanity. The Piscean Age is passing and the Aquarian is being ushered in. It is the age of the water carrier, the dispenser of the waters of life. It is the age of independent man. It is the age to recognize and carry our own burdens and to develop our own discrimination. It is the time to awaken and test three aspects that comprise our divine spark: love, wisdom and power.

The purpose of our spiritual studies is not psychic power, but the ability to look beyond the physical limitations, to learn the creative possibility that exists within limitations while at the same time transcending them. It is to help us rediscover the wonder, the awe and the power of divinity and to learn how that power lives within us.

Part of what the New Age will do is to allow us to look into ourselves for our answers and for our own magick and miracles. Not from books or from teachers—although they serve their purposes—but from the well of truth and light that lies within! Rather than searching for some light to shine down upon us, we must look for the Light within to shine out from us!

THE NEW AGE QABALA

As we become more fully enmeshed within the New Age, it will become even more important to expand our awarenesses and our consciousness, to more fully tap our own inner resources, to align ourselves with the highest possible energies. We must utilize all aspects of our being and awaken the energies within them to do this. We must utilize our *body, mind, soul* and *spirit* if we want to take full advantage of the energies pouring onto the Earth plane during this age. It will no longer be enough to develop just one aspect of ourselves.

The New Age will utilize all aspects of our self. It will involve integrating both the higher and lower, in fully conscious, uncon-ditional love. For this kind of consciousness to manifest will require a cleaning out of those aspects, characteristics and qualities that can be detrimental. We must be able to confront and transmute our lower tendencies, our shadow selves—a process which the ancients called "meeting the dwellers on the threshold."

We must begin to purge these negative aspects if we are to most fully create the magickal existence from this life or from any number of past lives. If we intend to accelerate our growth, we must also accelerate the cleansing of the past. It is to this end that the use of the mystical Qabala finds its purpose for the New Age aspirant. The mystical Qabala, as was introduced and elaborated in *Simplified Magic: The Beginner's Guide to the New Age Qabala* (Llewellyn Publications, St. Paul, MN, 1989), is a system of spiritual unfoldment that will reveal an individual's highest creative and magical energies, as well as the greatest weaknesses, fears and negativities.

The magickal process known as pathworking, explained in this book, is a powerful technique to bring to our awareness just what needs to be cleansed and just what can be used to bring light. It is a process that will assist us in crossing that "threshold" to higher and more divine energy.

These meditations and techniques are not for the "psychic dabbler," and if used simply to experience some "psychic thrills" will bring a rude awakening. The effects of these techniques are both subtle and real, and if an individual is not prepared to deal with his/her life and self head on, he/she should avoid them. They deal with very real and powerful energies which instigate very real and powerful conditions, decisions, choices and experiences within the physical and may "force" a spiritual, alchemical change in one's life.

On the other hand, a balanced use will create tremendous rewards. The techniques and meditations described in this book only start the process. They serve as a catalyst, and energy, once in motion, must either be controlled and experienced or it will disrupt. These techniques will start the process of meeting the shadow selves, but one meeting does not always cleanse the old and integrate the new. Each time we meet a shadow self, we have the opportunity to open ourselves to even more energies and more of our innate gifts and abilities. It is like cleaning the attic of our lives. The techniques bring about a period of strong self-evaluation. You will be forced to take a look at the people, the circumstances and the situations as they relate directly to who you are and what you are doing with your life. It can stimulate a very emotional time, *but whatever is cleaned out will be replaced by something much more beneficial to you and where you are going.*

Work with the Qabala only provides the deep inspiration. Its sole purpose is to stimulate within you a greater realization that you are a microcosm of the universe. For that purpose, the tools and instruments and robes and temples often associated with the magickal life are not needed. The Aquarian Age is the age of mental energies. It involves utilizing new forms of mental energies, the energies inherent within us all. Working with the Qabala in the New Age needs nothing more than an open mind and an expanding awareness in order to stimulate higher forms of consciousness. The extremities and the symbols are used only to help form a bridge to higher levels of awareness.

The Qabala is rich in mystical and magickal symbolism, but these symbols are the tools for the New Age! Learning to utilize the symbols to link our consciousness to other levels and planes and beings is what the mystical Qabala and New Age magick is about. By learning to link them, we have the opportunity to allow those energies to affect and alter our lives to where we become living, loving examples of the highest and best. We become living beings of light. This and this alone constitutes a true alchemical change. It is this alone which opens the door to awakening to one's own Higher Self, or Christ consciousness.

This is a very magickal time to be living. It is a powerful, dynamic, growing time for individuals and the planet, a time that many can use to bring the ancient energies and myths to life within a new scenario. It is a time of greater energy and stress. We are at the cusp of a New Age, a time that provides opportunity for tremendous change. Because of greater awareness of other planes of life surrounding us becoming more intrusive into the physical, we have the opportunity to tap into a much greater energy. We also have the increased necessity to discriminate in all aspects of spiritual unfoldment. It is a time of the tearing down of the old and the building up of the new, and if it is to be constructive, then new understandings must arise.

There is occurring a wider revelation of the ancient Mysteries, and for those who begin to consciously focus their spiritual energies, opportunities to take higher initiations will arise. There is unfolding more compatible and cooperative work with the elemental and devic beings of Nature. There is occurring a blending of consciousness with higher beings. A blending of mysticism, physics, biology, engineering, etc. is occurring, along with a dissolution of the glamour associated with the esoteric traditions. New sources and kinds of energy, and new methods of healing (more in alignment with Nature), are occurring daily, as is an increase in awareness and rapport with all life forms, including the plant and mineral kingdoms.

If we are to take the fullest advantage of this wonderful time, there must occur some changes in consciousness unfolding. There are new laws and energies governing the raising of consciousness. This includes a greater understanding of the laws of manifestation: Love, Transmutation and the Expression of Truth. The intensified New Age energies projected and awakened on a planetary level can only flow through individuals where effort is made through living application.

In the past, individuals and groups received energy without giving back to the source in return. With the New Age, this will not be possible. The more powerful energies cannot enter where the laws are not obeyed. Individuals and groups must respond appropriately in order to return the energy to its source, completing the cycle of circulation, or an imbalance will occur.

The New Age aspirant must learn to work with the intensified energies, while also giving of their own, to increase the flow and the power. Energies from cosmic or nonphysical sources must be properly discerned, discriminated, grounded, used and returned. There must also be individual preparation and purification. This includes a greater in-depth knowledge of the spiritual sciences. Surface and superficial techniques and learning will not maintain an individual. Attempts to do so will result in a breakdown of energies at some point: physically, emotionally, mentally or spiritually. Energies will not be able to be utilized entirely for personal benefit, only for the realizing and externalizing of mankind's heritage of expanded consciousness.

This is why the New Age Qabala is the effective means to use. It involves the study of man from all aspects. It involves man's conscious improvement. It involves processes for the realization of our ultimate perfection. It involves a spiritual discipline aimed at expanding human consciousness to give birth to an entirely new awareness. It comprises a philosophy of life and a personal ethic by which to live. It requires a turning to individual growth and concentrated unfoldment, purification and consecration. The individual must utilize systematic self-knowledge and self-mastery. It also embodies the best of the ancient sacred traditions and the best of modern science, integrating them in a creative and synthesized manner. It gives an understanding and an experiencing of the universal and personal forces. It shows our weaknesses, while it tests our courage. It awakens our strengths, while it tests our ability to discriminate at all times. It is a growing, living system that adapts itself to the individual.

THE TREE OF LIFE

The ancient, mystical Qabala is one of the most ancient of all the mystery traditions. There exists much argument over its true origin. Almost every major civilization has utilized aspects of the Qabala. In essence, the Qabalistic Tree of Life is a diagram to the treasures of the universe—magickal and material. It is a symbol rich in rewards to those who have found the keys to unlocking it.

On one level, it depicts how the universe itself was formed. (See the diagram on page 14.) The universe formed through nine stages of manifestation—a condensing and compacting and channeling of divine energy to manifest in a tenth stage encompassing all of the material universe. This can be compared to the process of condensing steam into water and then into ice. It is still two parts hydrogen and one part oxygen, but it has condensed itself into solid matter. *We are spiritual, divine energy densified into physical matter so we can operate and learn upon the Earth plane.*

This process of manifestation into material being is known as the "path of the flaming sword," but there is much more to this diagram than meets the eye. It reflects more than just the process the universe underwent in coming into being, and it also represents a map to man's evolution.

Each stage in the process of manifestation also represents a level of consciousness to which we each have access. There are predominant energies available at each level as well as specific beings to which we can attain contact when we learn to bridge our normal consciousness to those subtler levels. The diagram gives the traditional title for each of the levels of consciousness, known traditionally as sephiroth (singular is sephira). The translation of these from the Hebrew reflects the character of the energy at that particular level.*

In the diagram on page 15, our normal waking consciousness is represented by Malkuth (The Kingdom of Earth). When we can

---

* The Hebrew associations are utilized within this book predominantly. It must be remembered though that the Qabala is not strictly of a Hebraic origin. There have been many Qabalas, including Egyptian, Chaldean, and Christian or Catholic.

The Qabala of today is not even strictly Hebrew. In reality, the Qabala we utilize for magickal expansions of consciousness is a compilation and integration of many Qabalistic systems.

The Hebrew version is more in line with the true Western Mystery Tradition because the Western world is predominantly Christian, with the Jewish faith as its foundation.

Other sources will use different correspondences. This is something that each student must decide for him/herself. Find the system of correspondences that is most comfortable for you, that you can visualize and respond to most easily. There are many ways of expressing the same ideas. Part of our responsibility requires that we find that which most fits us as individuals.

NOTHINGNESS—Primal Point from which we came and to which we return, beyond understanding.

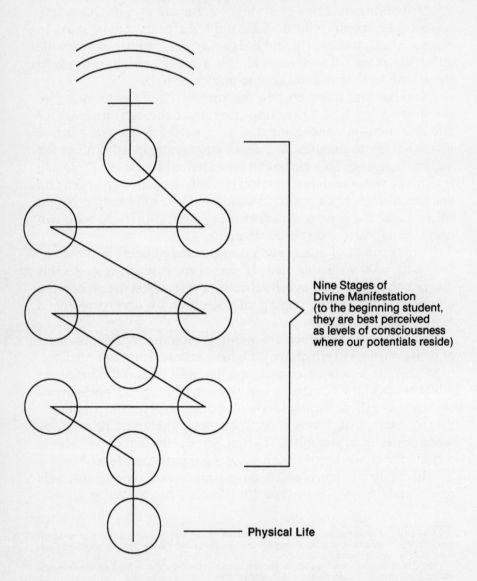

Nine Stages of
Divine Manifestation
(to the beginning student,
they are best perceived
as levels of consciousness
where our potentials reside)

————— Physical Life

The Path of the Flaming Sword is the path that Divine Spirit took through nine stages of manifestation before finally densifying and manifesting into physical life as we know it.

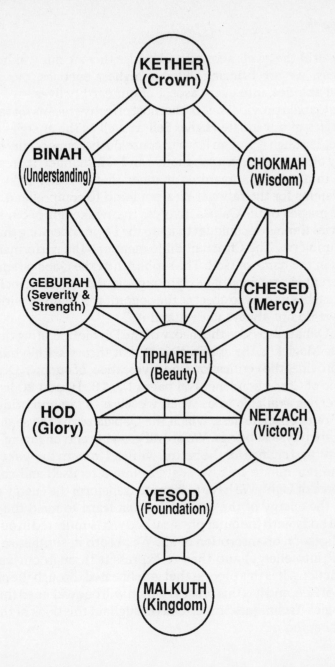

The ten sephiroth (the ten levels of consciousness) within the map of the Tree of Life and the titles that reflect the character of the energy found at that level.

15

awaken all of the levels above it and bridge them to our waking consciousness, we are bringing out our highest energies, our innate magickal abilities, into every aspect of our earthly lives.

The Qabala provides one of the most effective means for tapping the energies of our innate Higher Self as well as the energies of the universe. Through it we can learn to consciously connect our essence with any other essence in a productive and safe manner. It presents a method in a rational, organized manner that is easier than many other systems for the rational Western mind to comprehend.

The magick of the Qabala involves the awakening of our supernal energies through techniques that tap the Divine operating throughout the universe. The Christian Bible mentions the performance of miracles in the name of God. The sephiroth of the Qabala represent the different expressions of God throughout the universe, including man. It teaches us how to observe the operation of divinity within us, even if we do not always understand it.

The Qabala provides the theory of the Divine operating through all of life. Magick is the application of that theory within our own lives. It provides the verification, and vivification, of our own Divinity. The Table of Correspondences on pages 17, 18, 19 and 20 lists the basic energies available to us when we learn to tap and bridge the levels of our consciousness, which the Qabala terms the sephiroth.

We are physical beings. We are all growing and changing. If we are to grow and change for the better, we need to learn to awaken and transform our innate creative energies into a focused and concentrated force of Light. We have to learn to transform the energy of the inner to the energy of the outer. We must learn to meld the inner magickal body with the outer physical body. It is reflected in our process of digestion or absorption of air. We absorb it, synthesize (converting it into energy) and then re-express it through our various daily functions. It is this process that is delineated through the plan of the Tree of Life, and it is this process which will be awakened through the "Imagick Techniques" described throughout this book at the end of each chapter.

Sephira	Divine/God Force Available	Archangel Most Accessible	Angels Most Accessible	What Can Be Attained By Tapping These Levels of Consciousness
MALKUTH	ADONAI HA-ARETZ (Lord of Earth) The most direct influence over our physical and material affairs.	SANDALPHON (Prince of Prayers) Answers our prayers; intercedes w/Holy Spirit; works with formation of all life.	ASHIM (Blessed Souls) The saints and angels assisting Sandalphon with mankind.	Greater ability to discriminate in life; to overcome inertia; can be used for problems of physical health of self or others; all affairs of the home; greater self-discovery; knowledge and contact with the elemental life forms and the beings of Nature; a vision of the Holy Guardian Angel (our Higher Self); to discover things hidden within the physical universe.
YESOD	SHADDAI EL CHAI (Almighty Living God) That aspect of the Divine which helps us to know that God is in all things.	GABRIEL (Angel of Truth) Guards the gateway to other levels of consciousness; brings gift of hope.	CHERUBIM (Angels of Light & Glory) Keepers of Celestial (Akashic) records; knowledge of workings of universe.	Understanding that there is a divine plan; to overcome idleness; greater sense of true independence and confidence; greater intuition and psychic ability; mental and emotional health; dreamwork of all kinds; understanding and recognition of the tides of change; true work with omens; an increase in understanding of the lunar effects within your life.
HOD	ELOHIM TZABAOTH (God of Hosts/ Wisdom/Harmony) That aspect of God which oversees scientific knowledge; evolution of world.	MICHAEL (Prince of Splendor & the Great Protector) Brings gift of patience; protects when knowledge creates psychic dangers.	BENI ELOHIM (Sons of God) Transmit God consciousness into minds of men through greater knowledge; awaken need to "know God."	Awakens greater truthfulness; revelation of any falsehood or deception about us; awakens greater energy for communicating; energy for wheeling and dealing; knowledge of magic; for overcoming dishonesty within one's self; stimulate greater prosperity through greater knowledge; enhances any scientific or educational endeavor; can release information and awareness of how Mercury is affecting your life astrologically.

DIAGRAM 3 — TABLE OF CORRESPONDENCES The energies and powers and beings available by touching the ten levels of consciousness (sephiroth) within the Qabalistic Tree of Life.

Sephira	Divine/God Force Available	Archangel Most Accessible	Angels Most Accessible	What Can Be Attained By Tapping These Levels of Consciousness
NETZACH	JEHOVAH TZABAOTH (God of Hosts) Divine aspect which helps us win over hosts of our emotions (expressing them in positive manner).	HANIEL (Love and Harmony) Patron of the arts; assists in all creative activities; brings inspiration.	ELOHIM (Gods/Goddesses) Protectors of religion; guard leaders of people; inspire right decision (energies of ancient myths).	Awakens sense of unselfishness; understanding and energy in relationships; all love relationships; awakens sexuality and can release awarenesses for those problems; greater contact with the elements of Nature (fairies, etc.); increases creativity and artistic energy; awakens love and idealism; can be used to overcome impurity on all levels; can awaken greater understanding of the astrological influence of Venus in our lives.
TIPH-ARETH	JEHOVAH ALOAH va - DAATH (God Made Manifest Through the Mind) Christ aspect; Divine works through minds to create world and life.	RAPHAEL (Brightness, Beauty, Healing and Life) Ministers all kinds of healing energies; Healer of God.	MALACHIM (Virtues/ Angelic Kings) Chief bestowers of grace and valor upon mankind; workers of miracles and wonders upon the Earth.	Awakens a greater and higher sense of devotion; awakening of Christ Consciousness; can stimulate energies of glory and fame; should be tapped for all matters of healing; stimulates energy of life and success; contains energy to bring harmony to any matter on any level; awakens glimpse of universe unfolding; victory over adversity; vision of beauty in everything; the true energy of the rainbow; overcomes false pride.
GEBURAH	ELOHIM GIBOR (God Almighty) That aspect of God which cuts away what is no longer useful so new growth can occur.	KAMAEL (Prince of Strength and Courage) Defends/protects weak and wronged; slays dragons of life.	SERAPHIM (Flaming Ones) Powers; assist in stopping those who would overthrow/ upset world and our lives.	Manifests a vision of natural forces and understanding of their use; utilized to overcome cruelty/destruction; awakens energy, courage, strength; stimulates energy for tearing down old forms; change of any kind; awakens critical judgment; attains information on enemies and discord; stimulates greater understanding of astrological influence of Mars within our lives.

DIAGRAM 3 (continued)

Sephira	Divine/God Force Available	Archangel Most Accessible	Angels Most Accessible	What Can Be Attained By Tapping These Levels of Consciousness
CHESED	**EL** (**God, the Mighty One**) The Divine aspect that helps us realize the universe is ruled with glory, magnificence, and grace.	**TZADKIEL** (**Prince of Mercy**) Protector of Abraham and all teachers; he guards the gate to east winds; brings mercy.	**CHASMALIM** (**Brilliant Ones**) Dominations; manifest majesty of God in all men and through all worlds; awaken self-majesty.	Awakens a greater sense of obedience to the higher; provides energy for financial gains and opportunities; draws justice to one's self; awakens the abundance within the universe for all; stimulates greater prosperity; facilitates hearing the inner call; essential to the Quest for the Holy Grail; helps bestow peace and mercy into our lives; overcomes hypocrisy/bigotry; awakens higher understanding of influence of Jupiter in our lives.
BINAH	**JEHOVAH ELOHIM** (**Perfection of Creation**) The Divine aspect that brings understanding to process of life situations.	**TZAPHKIEL** (**Prince of Spiritual Strife Against Evil**) Confront/ overcome/learn from situations of life. (Keeper of Akashic records.)	**ARALIM** (**Strong and Mighty Ones**) Help sustain us through strife to achieve understanding; rule over Mother Earth with us.	Greater understanding of our sorrows and burdens; any mother-type energy or information; can reveal our relation to Mother Nature at all times; understanding on all levels; stimulates strength through silence; helps us understand anything secretive; helps us learn how restrictions and limitations operate in our lives; stimulates realization that nothing is separate from us.
CHOKMAH	**JAH (JEHOVAH)** (**Divine, Ideal Wisdom**) That aspect of God which oversees all starry heavens, and how they play within us all.	**RATZIEL** (**Prince of Hidden Knowledge & the Concealed**) Helps us to understand how heavens and universe operate on all levels.	**AUPHANIM** (**Whirling Forces**) Assist in the spiritual experience of "Vision of God Face to Face."	Awakens greater personal initiative; instills devotion beyond piety; awakens a pure source of energy (life-giving energy); stimulates the energy to put things in motion; can unfold any father-type information; opens a realization of one's hidden abilities; stimulates the wisdom to use our knowledge properly; will unfold an understanding of the working of the zodiac within our lives.

DIAGRAM 3 (continued)

Sephira	Divine/God Force Available	Archangel Most Accessible	Angels Most Accessible	What Can Be Attained By Tapping These Levels of Consciousness
KETHER	EHEIEH (I Am That I Am) At this level the force of God is simply there; our most spiritual, divinely pure aspect; almost incomprehensible.	METRATON (Greatest of Archangels) To sustain mankind; gave man the Qabala so we can regain our true destiny.	CHAIOTH ha-QADESH (Holy Living Creatures) Love, light and fire in most spiritual senses help us understand Qabala and our evolutionary process.	Awakens true creativity; can reveal any final ending and beginning information; stimulates the energies of transition and change; sheds light upon the inner spiritual quest and its causes and attainment; a source of tremendous spiritual energy to amplify and intensify any aspect of our life and evolution; reveals awareness that God is an ever-present fact, always was and always shall be a Divine Companion for all of creation!

DIAGRAM 3 (continued)

*** While the previous book, *Simplified Magic: The Beginner's Guide to the New Age Qabala*, focused primarily upon the techniques necessary to activate these levels of consciousness, this book will define specific techniques for bridging and linking these levels of our consciousness to our normal, waking state. If we wish to stimulate a magickal existence and truly build the magickal body, we need to create a flow of energy from each level with an open and accessible channel to all from our normal, waking consciousness.

IMAGICK TECHNIQUES: Awakening the Tree

Using the Plan of the Tree of Life as his guide, the magician invokes the lower gods or archangels, as they are named in another system, desirous of mingling his own life with and surrendering his own being to the greater and more extensive life of God.
—Israel Regardie
Foundations of Practical Magic
(Aquarian Press Limited; England, 1979)

Imagick is a process of using visualization, meditation and imaging in conjunction with specific physical activities to tap and bridge the various levels of our consciousness and of the universe with our normal state of mind. It must be understood that mere intellectual studies of the correspondences will not generate any magickal changes, and neither will a mere arousal of the energies. It is not enough to touch the various levels; we must also bring them into our day-to-day lives if we are to achieve our hopes, dreams and wishes. The Imagick Techniques, and especially the pathworking techniques described throughout this work, are powerfully effective. They build a bridge between the inner worlds and the outer world in which we operate. They serve to link them, creating a flow that augments our energies, abilities and potentials in all areas of our lives.

There have always been certain laws and principles that govern manifestation, life, and existence on both the physical and non-physical planes of life. Whether these are referred to as natural laws, the universal laws, or Hermetic principles, each civilization has taught the workings of the universe through them to their aspirants. Two of these in particular are what are focused upon and utilized through the techniques of pathworking and imagick, as described within this work. These are the Principle of Correspondence and the Principle of Cause and Effect shown in the table on page 23.

The Principle of Correspondence, according to Hermetic philosophy, states: "As above, so below; as below, so above." Simply, it tells us that there is always a correspondence or link between the phenomena of the various planes of being and life within the universe. All the planes affect the others. We cannot do something on one level without it affecting us on another. What we do on one level will play itself out on other planes as well—in a corresponding energy. The ancient Hermeticists use this principle in particular to pry aside the obstacles that hid the spiritual or unknown from physical view and observation.

DRAWING UPON THE SUBCONSCIOUS

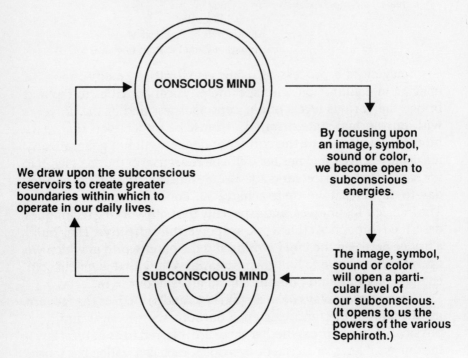

CONSCIOUS MIND

By focusing upon
an image, symbol,
sound or color,
we become open to
subconscious
energies.

We draw upon the subconscious
reservoirs to create greater
boundaries within which to
operate in our daily lives.

SUBCONSCIOUS MIND

The image, symbol,
sound or color
will open a parti-
cular level of
our subconscious.
(It opens to us the
powers of the various
Sephiroth.)

THE SEVEN HERMETIC PRINCIPLES
as taken from *The Kybalion:*

1. THE PRINCIPLE OF MENTALISM:
   "The All is Mind; the Universe is Mental."

2. THE PRINCIPLE OF CORRESPONDENCE:
   "As above, so below; as below, so above."

3. THE PRINCIPLE OF VIBRATION:
   "Nothing rests; everything moves, everything vibrates."

4. THE PRINCIPLE OF POLARITY:
   "Everything is dual; everything has poles; everything has its pair of opposites; like and unlike are the same; opposites are identical in Nature but different in degree; extremes meet; all truths are but half-truths; all paradoxes may be reconciled."

5. THE PRINCIPLE OF RHYTHM:
   "Everything flows, in and out; everything has its tides; all things rise and fall; the pendulum swing manifests in everything; the measure of the swing to the right is the measure of the swing to the left; rhythm compensates."

6. THE PRINCIPLE OF CAUSE AND EFFECT:
   "Every cause has its effect; every effect has its cause; everything happens according to law; chance is but a name for law not recognized; there are many planes of causation, but nothing escapes the law."

7. THE PRINCIPLE OF GENDER:
   "Gender is in everything; everything has its masculine and feminine principles; gender manifests on all planes."

The Principle of Cause and Effect, according to Hermetic philosophy, states that every action we take will have its particular effect not only in the physical, but on other planes as well. If we take focused and concentrated action—physical, mental or spiritual—it will have its effects within our lives.

Through particular symbols and images we can set energy in motion on higher, more subtle planes of life, which will in turn trigger a corresponding action or effect upon the physical plane. Learning the symbols and images and how to use them for their various effects to create specific "magickal" occurrences is what this book entails.

Psychology has the task of interpreting symbols and images. Magick lives through them. The symbols and images should energize our awareness on many levels, along with our perception, and thus change our world. The symbol or image reflects an inner world or subtle dimensional energy, and so the first area of change is usually oneself.

All images are magickal in that when an individual uses the image as a symbol of spiritual significance, it takes on a magickal significance. The greater the significance that we attach to the image, the greater the power it will have within our lives, and the greater "magick" it will hold. Even though any image or symbol can be imbued with great energy, some images are best for "magickal" purposes. It may be that they have been used for centuries and thus imbued with tremendously powerful thoughtforms, and it could be that they are very primal and thus are more purely connected to the energy they reflect; or they may more intimately reflect the archetypal energy at its source. As R.J. Stewart stated, "An archetype is a matrix or key image which gives shape and direction to energies arising out of the primal source of all being." (*The Underworld Initiation,* page 92, Aquarian Press, Northamptonshire, publisher, 1985.)

If the images and symbols we utilize are to be effective, there are specific steps to take in stimulating their primal energies:

1. We must first be conscious of them as reflecting primal energy, and go beyond our usual logic in working with them and in drawing associations and conclusions about the energies released by the image. We begin by simply reflecting upon the outer surface of the image, its outermost (and often most obvious) significance. As we explore and work with the image, such as through the techniques of this work, we delve more into the cosmic spiral of energy of its arche-

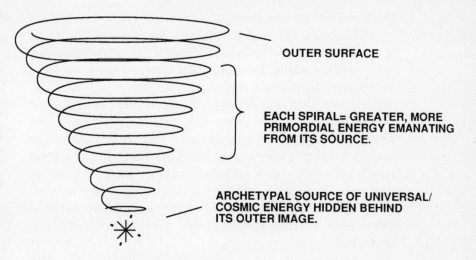

OUTER SURFACE

EACH SPIRAL= GREATER, MORE PRIMORDIAL ENERGY EMANATING FROM ITS SOURCE.

ARCHETYPAL SOURCE OF UNIVERSAL/ COSMIC ENERGY HIDDEN BEHIND ITS OUTER IMAGE.

type. This releases more of its primal power to the outer physical world.

2. We then begin the process that immerses us more deeply into the energy of the image or symbol. This is sometimes referred to as the Magickal Action or Magickal Process. It is the journey or the pathworking that brings to the surface more of the archetypal energy hidden behind and operating through the image. This can be done through meditation, creative visualization or specific physical activities. It is in this process that we begin adopting and absorbing the energies as our own. We bring them into being within our lives. One aspect of this is the creating of the magickal body, which will be explored in greater detail elsewhere.

3. After the magickal working, we need time to contemplate and reassimilate the experience and what it is teaching. This may take one day or one week of assessing, though it is what assists us in delving deeper each time. We no longer deal with surface reflections of the energy. Each time we repeat steps one and two, we will have even more to reflect upon. This part involves contemplation of our inner reaction to what we experienced through the exercise, and an analysis of events in day-to-day life following the exercise. This is how the effect of the very potent but more ethereal energies upon

the physical realm is determined.

This inner reaction and contemplation should not be shared. It is strictly individual. Sharing it with others can result in dissipating the energy that was accessed. It can set up barriers through comparisons. Yes, there will be some experiences that will be shared, but on the whole, most should not.

4. The grounding of the energies and the exercises into the physical realm is very important. This more than anything else is what separates and distinguishes these techniques from nightly dreams or fanciful imaginings. They may all touch the same energy, but unless they are grounded, taken out of that ethereal mental realm, they will not work efficiently.

The post-exercise process—inner reaction and outer assessment (Step 3) initiates the grounding, but even it is not necessarily enough. Something more physical is needed. Remember that these techniques will be used to bridge the various levels of consciousness. Always start with a physical activity (prayer, posture, etc.), move to reflection, and then on to the Imagickal Pathworking Technique. This is then followed by contemplation of the experience and the grounding of the energy through a physical activity:

a. The writing of it and reactions within a journal.

b. A closing prayer or dedication of the activity and the energy released from it to work in your life.

c. The acting out, in a form of pantomime or such, the lesson or experience of that which is being released. If you are trying to release energy that will bring more choice into your life, this would require choosing to involve yourself in some new activity or endeavor in your life within 24 hours of the exercise. This sends a message to the universe that you are going to utilize all the energy that you have activated. It lets the subconscious know that you intend to utilize and act upon any energy that is released so it can feel free to release it in as great an abundance as possible.

The techniques described and outlined throughout this work need not be held to the letter. We have a responsibility to adapt them to our own unique energy system. To confine the Qabalistic Tree of

Life and all of its energies, attributes and potentialities to specific manifestations and uses only serves to limit how effective it can be for us. As we become used to these techniques and to linking the various levels of our consciousness through them, we will want to adapt them more specifically to our own lives. We will have to separate being from just *reading* about being.

The symbols and images are chosen to deliberately alter our awareness, to create a scene different from our day-to-day life. This is necessary if we are to break down the personality, which is essential for true "magickal growth." We are trying to rid ourselves of those aspects which block or hinder the energies of our true individuality. We are attempting to change directions within our lives. First inwardly, and then outwardly. "As above, so below." We are cleaning the bridges, the links between our various levels of consciousness, and all of their energies. We are forcing ourselves to look at the disrepair of our bridges. We always have some flow from other levels, but the magickal path requires that we more consciously set about increasing that flow in a controlled and directed focus. The imagick techniques and the pathworkings awaken us and test our ability to use those bridges—that increased flow of energy—that connect our highest, most divine aspect to our physical, day-to-day lives.

IMAGICK TECHNIQUE #1: Planting the Tree of Life

Awakening the Tree of Life and all of its inherent energies is essential to a magickal existence. It requires that we more consciously stimulate our perceptions in physical and non-physical environments. This technique is very powerful for growing new states of awareness and for the blossoming of newer, stronger potentials. Some may consider it just another form of "sympathetic magick," but it requires much more.

The tree is an ancient symbol. It represents things that grow, fertility and life. To some it is a world axis, and to others it is the world itself. Its roots are within the Earth, and yet it reaches toward the sky. It is a bridge between the heavens and the Earth; the mediator between the two worlds. This is most appropriate with the Qabala and for the entire unfoldment process. We are trying to bridge one level of our consciousness with the next, just as a tree bridges the heavens and the Earth.

Think òf all that is done with trees. They bear fruit from which we gain nourishment. They provide wood for the building of homes and the making of paper—a means by which knowledge and communication occur. As children we climb trees, finding enjoyment in reaching new heights and new challenges. The leaves fall in the autumn, only to re-emerge again in the spring, reflecting the continual cycle of change and growth, dying only to be born again. We rake the leaves in the fall, gathering what has occurred in the previous months; then they are burnt or used as a mulch for future plantings.

The tree, as the Tree of Knowledge, has been associated with Paradise and Hell. In Greek mythology, it was upon a tree that the Golden Fleece hung. The Christian cross was originally a tree. Buddha found enlightenment while sitting under a tree. Druids recognized energies in various trees. Every civilization has its stories, myths and legends about the Tree of Life.

The tree also serves as a barrier, often used by farmers as a windbreak or fence. It served as the boundary, whether separating one piece of land from another or one world from another. The tree also provides shade.

Trees have always been imbued with certain magickal or spiritual attributes. Our superstition of "knocking on wood" was started to make sure no spirits were in the tree before it was cut down and utilized by man. In German folklore, one particular group of spirits, known as the *Kobolde*, inhabited trees. The trees in which these sprites lived were cut down and carved into figures so that the tree sprites would have a place to live. These carvings were then shut up into wooden boxes and brought inside the home. Only the owner was allowed to open it. If anyone else did, there was untold damage. Thus children were warned never to go near it, and jack-in-the-boxes were fashioned to scare the kids and remind them not to touch the real boxes.

We also have the family tree. This tree has its roots with our ancestors, both familial and spiritual. All that we are lies in the roots of the tree, and thus, all of our ancestry can be awakened through the Tree. The technique at the end of chapter 2 reveals ancestors and past lives that have helped create and nurture the "tree" we are now.

The process of awakening your own Tree of Life and all of its inherent energies begins with the fully conscious planting of an actual tree. This may be a tree that you plant outside, or one of many trees that can grow indoors. It is important that it be an actual tree.

The kind of tree is individual; each tree has its own energies and distinct properties. The list on the following page outlines just a few. Doing your own research, reflecting upon it and deciding before the purchase or transplanting of the tree is the same as preparing the soil. Our consciousness is being prepared for the awakening of the energies of life.

You are making a conscious choice of the energies. You do not have to know all that this tree will reflect. That will unfold as it grows and you nurture it, but you should be fully aware of its significance. Do you want a fruit-bearing tree? Do you wish to bear a lot of fruit in your own life? Take into consideration that most fruit trees only bear fruit seasonally. It doesn't mean that growth isn't occurring at other times, but there may be particular times throughout a year's span in which the tree will not be producing. Also, all trees bear fruit in their own unique way. Learn about the trees before you pick. Perhaps you can start with the kind of tree you have always felt closest to. Go out into Nature around trees and meditate on which would be best for you. Don't choose a tree simply because it seems to have more "magickal" associations. It may not be true for you.

Plant the tree, indoors or outdoors, where you will see it every day, a reminder that as it grows and blossoms and becomes a bridge, so will the tree within you. "As above, so below. As below, so above."

If the tree is planted indoors, at some point you may want to transplant it outdoors so that it can grow free and uninhibited. If so, you may want to choose another tree for use indoors. As you care for the tree, do it in full conscious awareness that you are also pruning and watering your own tree, your self, enabling it to take firmer root and to reach out for the heavens. When you utilize any of the techniques of the Qabala, be it from the author's previous work or from this book, have the tree placed in the area in which you do the exercise or, as in the case of a tree planted outside, take a few moments prior to the exercise to bring to mind your tree, what it represents, and how much you have helped it to grow. This strengthens the techniques and exercises, making them much more focused and concentrated. Just as trees are often planted on hillsides to prevent soil from eroding, this prevents the energy that is stimulated from eroding away or being dissipated.

After the exercise, contemplate this while pruning your tree, giving it some water or turning the soil over. This grounds the energies, bringing the inner experiences into the physical life. Although it seems "mysterious," it is very powerful!

Inevitably, there are some who will say, "I can't make anything grow." "Every time I plant something, it dies!" This is a process to bring change into one's life. Death is change. Death is always a companion of life. It is part of the cycle: birth, death, re-birth. If one is unable to deal with this aspect, he or she will have difficulty with all aspects of the Qabala, and it can be a sign that at this point the Qabalistic method of unfoldment is not for that individual.

On the other hand, keep in mind that the tree is an outer reflection of an inner energy. If your tree dies, it does not mean that you are going to physically die. What it can mean is that an aspect of yourself that is no longer vital has been changed. Discrimination is needed here. Maybe the tree that you chose was not the best one for you to start with. Some people choose a particular tree because of its extensive "magickal" associations, but many trees are difficult to grow. Maybe it died because the individual was trying to do much more than they were capable of at this point. Start simply. Allow your tree to grow at the rate that is best for you. One of the tests that all undergo is the test of patience. If you wish to force the growth, this can impair judgment. When you plant a seed, that seed needs time to germinate, take root and then work its way up through the soil. Unfortunately, many will assume that nothing is happening until they see the plant working out of the soil. Things do happen in the time and the manner and the means that are best if you allow it.

If the tree does die, give it back to the Earth, thank the universe for its presence within your life, if only for a short period, and then get another. And another, if necessary. If you wish to truly bridge and unfold your highest capability, persist. Everything that you try and grow within your life—successful or not—adds to your life experience on a soul level.

THE MAGICAL TREES

Tree	Associated Energy, Symbology and Magic	Associated Sephira
Ash	Might; immortality; a universal source of life; Norse gods held council under it; Odin sacrificed on it.	Tiphareth/ Geburah
Aspen	Resurrection; calms anxieties; releases energy to enter subtler planes of life; soul fearlessness; communication.	Hod/ Tiphareth
Apple	Tree of knowledge; Fruit of Avalon; magickal powers; home of Unicorn; all healing energies; promotes happiness.	Netzach/ Tiphareth
Beech	Awakens soul quality of tolerance; aids contact to higher self; can be used for all patterns of growth.	Binah
Birch	Staffs of birch used by shamans to awaken energy to pass from one plane to another.	Yesod/ Netzach
Cedar	Protective; healing to imbalances of emotional or astral level; healing.	Yesod/ Tiphareth
Cherry	Tree of phoenix; openness in consciousness; realizing insights; threshold of new awakening.	Netzach/ Chesed
Cypress	Healing; understanding of crises; awakens comfort of home and mother.	Binah
Elm	Lends strength; aids overcoming exhaustion; tree of intuition; Inner call of Nature spirits and elf contact.	Binah/ Malkuth/ Netzach
Elder	Mysteries of all burial rites; contact with the Mother Goddess; protection and healing.	Netzach/ Malkuth/ Binah
Eucalyptus	Oil used in ancient mystery schools to clean aura during growth; protective; healing; stimulates third eye.	Chokmah/ Chesed/ Yesod

Tree	Associated Energy, Symbology and Magic	Associated Sephira
Fig	Sacred tree of Buddha; releases past life blockages; links conscious with subconscious with correct perspective.	Chesed/ Tiphareth Hod
Hawthorne	Fertility; creativity; growth on all levels; sacred to the fairies.	Netzach
Hazel	Magickal tree; as in all fruit trees, the fruit is hidden wisdom; hazel twigs make powerful dowsing instruments.	Hod
Holly	(Technically a bush, but with all power of trees); protection; awakens love and overcomes hate; birth of Christ within.	Tiphareth
Honeysuckle	Energy that helps learn from past; stimulates energy of change; sharpens intuition; opens psychic abilities.	Yesod/ Chokmah
Lemon	Cleansing to the aura; draws protective spirits; good for purification at time of Full Moon.	Yesod/ Tiphareth
Lilac	Spiritualizes the intellect; mental clarity; activates the kundalini; draws good spirits.	Binah/ Chokmah/ Netzach
Maple	Balances the yin and yang; draws money and love; grounding to psychic and spiritual energies; chakras in feet.	Chesed/ All on the Middle Pillar
Magnolia	Energy to locate lost ideas, thoughts or items; activates heart chakra; aligns heart with higher intellect.	Tiphareth (aligned with Daath)
Mistletoe	Sacred tree of Druids; female energy; all lunar aspects of universe; protects children or the child within.	Yesod/ Binah

Tree	Associated Energy, Symbology and Magic	Associated Sephira
Oak	Sacred tree of Druids; represents male energy and all solar aspects of universe; strength; endurance; helpfulness.	Tiphareth/ Geburah
Olive	Tree of peace and harmony; restores peace of mind; regeneration; enables the touching of inner guidance.	Tiphareth
Orange	Assists in rising on the planes and astral projection; brings clarity to emotions.	Hod/ Tiphareth
Palm	Tree of peace; protection of an area or group; leaves prevent evil from entering an area; Christ energy.	Tiphareth/ Geburah
Peach	Awakens realization that immortality can be attained, but only in legitimate ways; calms emotions; artistic.	Netzach
Pine	Sacred tree of Mithra; Dionysian energies; calms emotions; awakens true occult Christian salvation; understanding.	Geburah/ Netzach/ Binah
Sycamore	Sacred tree of the Egyptians; used to draw Hathor; brings life and gifts; nourishment, beauty, female energies.	Netzach/ Yesod
Walnut	Hidden wisdom; power for transition; catalytic energy; freedom of spirit; following one's path; laws of change.	Chokmah/ Chesed
Willow	Healing; removes aches; flexibility in thought; realization of links between our thoughts and external events.	Yesod/ Chesed

IMAGICK TECHNIQUE #2: "Entering the Tree of Life"

Most of the Imagick Techniques to follow use very dynamic symbols to awaken the energies of our consciousness. When utilizing any of these techniques, it is always good to reflect upon the symbols prior to the actual working. It is not necessary to memorize or keep the symbology constantly in mind, but reflection upon it prior to the exercise does sow seeds so that the effects can be more tangibly experienced.

The symbology of the Tree has already been discussed. With this technique one sets up and manifests the energy to become the actual living Tree of Life, replete with all of its energies and potentialities. In most tales and myths the treasures searched for were always guarded and protected by some kind of beast, serpent or dragon. This guardian had to be overcome in order to obtain the treasure.

The guardians encountered were representative of various energies and levels of consciousness, and they need to be examined from a variety of perspectives. The guardian in this technique serves many purposes, as everything in our life does. A guardian prevents us from entering where we do not belong. In such cases and at such times in our life, it is beneficial to be prevented from entering where we are unfamiliar and could easily hurt ourselves. It is for this reason that many individuals have difficulty opening up to the psychic energies that lie within us all. They just are not balanced enough to handle what could be released in the most appropriate and creative manner. Yes, we can force an awakening of our energies, force an entrance to other realms. In this case, we are in essence slaying the dragon or guardian, rather than working with it as we should.

The guardian at the Tree which opens other dimensions to us can also be likened to our own higher self. It is that aspect of ourselves that truly is the magickal aspect. It already knows what we wish to know, and it already has obtained what we wish to obtain. It serves as a guide, so that we can integrate the knowledge from this Tree of Life more easily into all aspects of our normal, waking consciousness.

The guardian is also our lower self. It holds our fears, doubts and angers that prevent us from achieving and fulfilling our highest and greatest goals at all times. It is this aspect that must be met by all upon the path to higher consciousness. To some, it can be looked upon as that which the ancients called the "Dweller upon the Threshold":

that which must be met and transmuted before the threshold to higher consciousness can be crossed.

The guardian can also be viewed as that which prevents too quick and strong of a transference from the other realms. It serves to close the doors behind us so that we are not intruded upon and can remain in full conscious control. More of this aspect and an Imagick Technique for activating protection from the more ethereal realms is given in chapter 7.

Any one or more of these aspects of the guardian can be in play at all times within our lives. We have to be able to always recognize and control and direct it. We are trying to take greater control of our lives through a life of imagick: doing the acting, rather than being acted upon.

This exercise is one that opens the doors and is one that should be used in conjunction with the pathworking or Imagick Technique described later as the "Temple to Temple Visitation." If utilized regularly, it is one that will assist you in being able to adopt an altered state of consciousness at will and in full awareness. It provides a safety feature to the other exercises; if something goes astray within the imagickal or pathworking process, you can return to the safety of the temple within the Tree by simply visualizing it. It is a place of safety, security and warmth which allows for a comfortable awakening of perceptions and innate energies.

Rite of Preparation

There are, of course, preparations that should be made prior to any magickal exercise or working. It is always best in any form of meditation to remove any possibility of interruption from any source: people, phones, etc. Next, it is important to set the correct atmosphere. Everything should be done deliberately and in full consciousness, and this holds particularly true for the creating of any magickal space, be it for meditation or for other magickal practices. Two of the most effective means of creating an energy that facilitates accessing various levels of consciousness are candles and fragrances. (The chart on page 95 will provide information for the most appropriate choice for your purpose.)

With the atmosphere having been set, make yourself as comfortable as possible. For some, an upright posture is best, while for others reclining will work. Reclining positions are often discouraged because it is a position we use daily in the sleep process. Assuming that position while using meditative techniques may result in too great of an altered state of consciousness—sleep itself. You can use various breathing techniques and progressive relaxation (focusing on each part of the body in turn, sending warm relaxing thoughts to that part of the body) to facilitate the inducing of an altered state of consciousness. The more relaxed you are, the easier it will be to visualize and focus your attention upon the exercises themselves, thereby eliciting the greatest effects. This being accomplished, it only remains to visualize the scenes described and allow the images to work in the manner in which they are designed.

Entering the Tree of Life

You stand before an ancient oak tree. Its massive branches and trunk dwarf you, and its bark is twisted and gnarled like the skin of some giant, ancient entity. The upper portion of its roots are exposed like the twisted limbs of a mythological serpent. You know they must extend into the heart of the Earth itself. As you stand under its lower branches, staring up its length, it seems to extend forever, bridging the Earth with the heavens themselves. You feel small and insignificant next to it, and it is as if the tree has chosen to ignore you in your slightness—an appropriate metaphor for your life to this point.

You circle the tree clockwise, amazed that any tree could be this large. If ever a tree could house gnomes and elves, this one surely could. As you return to the front, you are greeted by a small opening into the trunk itself. You stare in awe and amazement. Was the tree acknowledging your existence after all?

You step forward gingerly, cautiously. A loud groan erupts. Earth sprays the air as it cracks open around you. The roots break free of the Earth, dancing serpentine between you and the opening. You leap back in fear. The roots are no longer roots at all. They are the appendages of a hydra-headed beast guarding the entrance into the Tree of Life.

"What is it you seek?" it roars in a distorted chorus.

You stare, unable to speak. Your throat tightens. Your breathing is rapid.

"What is it you seek?" it demands a second time.

You cannot answer. You do not know how to answer.

"What is it you seek?" it demands for the third and final time.

Your mind races, knowing there must be a correct response.

"I seek . . . I seek to know that I may serve?"

As if from some primordial remembrance, the words come forth. Though spoken softly, timidly, they echo with an ancient power. The twisting, dancing hydra freezes. The long serpent necks of the beast draw back, parting before the entrance to the tree. They curl up and around to form an archway before the entrance. The heads touch, nose to nose, forming an ancient image that was vaguely familiar. You bend slightly and step cautiously under the upraised heads and into the blackness of the opening.

The darkness envelops you like a warm cloak. The air is thick, and as you breathe deeply, forcing yourself to relax, your eyes begin to adjust. You reach out with your hands, touching the underside of the tree, just inside the doorway. You are surprised at how warm and soft it really is. You can feel the life blood flowing through the tree itself.

You step forward, your eyes beginning to discern the dim shapes inside. You see that you are in a circular orifice. In the center is a large stone altar. Upon it rests a lamp whose light grows brighter and brighter to reveal all of this inner temple. The floor is pitch black and its ceiling is stark white. The walls are engraved with sigils, glyphs, and writings from every civilization and religion in the world, past and present. Most are incomprehensible, but some you recognize, even though you do not understand their full significance.

Upon the altar rests a bowl of water, a piece of flint and steel, a plate with salt and a fan. At the foot of the altar lie three baskets in the shape of cornucopias. In the first, wheat, corn and other grains overflow. In the second are cut and uncut rocks, and gems of every color and value. Next to it the third basket fills the room with its exotic fragrance of oils and powders.

In the center of the altar sits the lamp, which now burns a crystalline blue. Its light fills the temple and warms every aspect of your being. It burns eternally within this inner temple. Beneath the lamp is a large circular talisman, carved into the altar itself. Around its outside are the insignias of all the names of God throughout history. On the upper curve of a second, inner circle of the talisman is inscribed your name. On the lower curve of that same circle is your name a second time, in ancient script. This is your name as it was when you first entered the mysteries of the inner temple. It is your soul name.

You begin to understand. This is *your* temple. This tree is *your* Tree of Life! The scriptures upon the wall are the teachings of wisdom which you can open to yourself by working from this temple to other temples within your own consciousness.

Encircling the room are ten statues, ten of the ancient magickal images. Behind each is a doorway leading to another level of consciousness. These are doorways to other temples and other learnings. You are filled with the joy of having returned home. You have found the way to bring light to the outside world.

As the realization flashes through your mind, the floor begins to tremble. The temple vibrates and roars! Two stone columns burst through the floor on either side of the altar. One is of blackest ebony, and the second is silver-white crystal. They lodge themselves permanently, and peace returns to the temple.

Now it is complete. The pillars of balance are within the temple, and now within your Tree of Life. The pillars of balance are now accessible to your outer life. The magic of the tree is now active and alive. The eternal light shines brightly; it reflects off the pillars, chasing all shadows from the temple. The entire room brightens, taking on a crystalline clarity.

As the temple brightens, a fire ignites upon the front edge of the altar itself. It is so intense that it burns into the stone. You watch in awe as it burns across the edge, inscribing the altar and your heart with the words of the Divine:

"BEHOLD! THY SOUL IS A LIVING STAR."

As the flame fades, leaving its message permanently within the temple, you feel rejuvenated, alive for the first time in what seems ages. You know that *all* is truly available to you now. Nothing can be denied you. You are now heir to all the wonders, magick and light within the universe. By again entering into the Tree of Life, you have declared your right to your divine inheritance.

You step to the altar, bowing slightly but with reverence. You give thanks for the return to the path. You bend and reach into the basket of grains. You place some into your pocket to take with you to the outer world. It will ease the hungers that confront you there. You take from the second basket a small crystal attached to a necklace. You fasten it about your neck, there to remain a part of you and to remind you of the wealth that is your divine spiritual and material inheritance. You draw an oil from the third and anoint your forehead and your heart. You re-dedicate yourself to manifesting the light in your life and in the lives of those you touch.

You step back from the altar and bow a second time. As you do, the baskets shudder and spill out more of their contents, a final reminder that nothing is lacking in the universe for those who will truly work to manifest a higher destiny.

You turn from the altar toward the entrance. You can see the outer world through the open doorway. You know that you now carry with you the ability to light it even more.

You step from the tree and turn to look at the entrance. The hydra-headed guardian raises slightly from its sleep. It moves to block the entrance to the tree and then again sinks down into its peaceful sleep until next time. The hole is no longer there; it is just a solid tree trunk. You smile. You know that it is never truly sealed from you. You now know the words that will open it forever!

At the end of the Imagick Techniques and pathworkings, it is a good idea to do some actual work with the tree you are physically growing: water it, turn the soil up around it, etc., while you reflect upon the experience. Stroke the leaves gently, but do something physical with it to ground the energies of this ethereal experience into your physical life. This will help these energies work more effectively for you.

chapter two

The Invisible Level
of Consciousness

We live in a time in which supersensible knowledge can no longer
remain the secret possession of a few but must become common
property of all those in whom the sense for life in this age stirs as a
need of their soul existence.

—Rudolph Steiner

If man wishes to climb the Tree of Life and ascend to greater
heights, he must have a disciplined inner schooling, a schooling that
will enable him to attain a knowledge of the divinely creative worlds
and the beings that belong to them. Careful preparation is necessary
in order that the potentials within us all can be realized.

In the modern Qabalistic schooling, this is accomplished through a
sephira referred to as DAATH. Daath is not an original concept of the
Qabala. In fact, early Qabalistic texts speak of ten and only ten
sephiroth on the Tree of Life. Daath is mentioned only in conjunction
with either Chokmah or Binah. Today's modern student of the occult
and metaphysics must look upon it as a separate level of consciousness in its own right, one which acts in ways quite different from the
other ten.

It has been called the invisible sephira, hidden within the Great
Abyss that separates the bottom seven levels of consciousness from
the three supernals. As seen in the diagram on page 42, it bridges the
seven lower levels of consciousness (those to which we have easier
access) to the three higher levels—those which are more difficult to
work with and manifest within our lives. When we can bring the
three upper levels to play in our lives, along with the seven lower,
then we are living the Tree of Life, and we greatly accelerate our
movement in the process of manifesting a higher destiny. It is this
eleventh sephira, known as Daath, that assists us in this process.

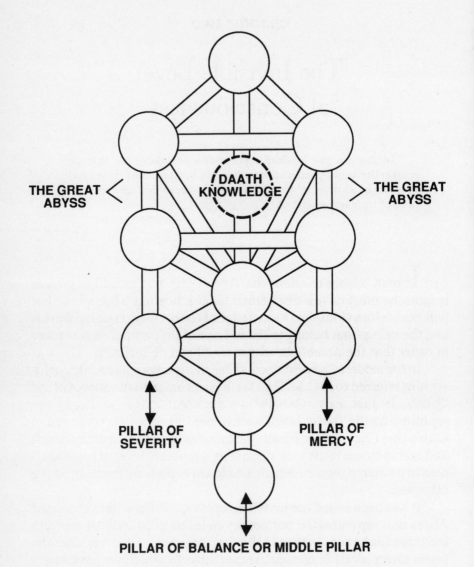

THE GREAT
ABYSS

DAATH
KNOWLEDGE

THE GREAT
ABYSS

PILLAR OF
SEVERITY

PILLAR OF
MERCY

PILLAR OF BALANCE OR MIDDLE PILLAR

Daath Becoming Visible on the Qabalistic Tree of Life

Daath, or higher knowledge, becomes the bridge to heightened consciousness and higher initiation for the modern spiritual student.

In more ancient times the mystical knowledge was hidden from the general public. Man was not fully grounded in his thought capacities. Today, mystical and metaphysical knowledge is more available to the general public, particularly in the Western world. This knowledge is a reality, and is only hidden today in that it lies behind and influences all of the other ten sephiroth. Today there is knowledge about all aspects of mysticism as reflected within the sphere of life.

We have more knowledge of the workings of Nature and the Earth than at any other time in history. We are breaking into the mysteries of Nature that have previously been hidden. The once theoretical and invisible atom is today a scientific and physical reality. The world in which we live is being truly unveiled. This is knowledge of Malkuth, or Daath influencing man in Malkuth.

We are coming to understand the psycho-structure of the human mind in ways never before comprehended. This is knowledge, or Daath, influencing modern man at the level of Yesod. The scientific realms are aligning with the alchemical teachings of the past; science and magick are not as distant as once believed (again Daath or knowledge, working through Hod).

Knowledge of every aspect of man is plentiful today. Knowledge of every aspect of the Tree of Life is more available to the general public than ever before, and the opportunity to use it to accelerate the development of our sleeping potential is greater. The information, the key to knowledge of the mystical, is there for us today. *Daath is a reality!* Meditation on the knowledge inherent within each sephira will yield great benefits to the spiritual student.

Because of this greater knowledge, there is also greater responsibility. In more ancient times, the awakening to higher levels of consciousness, and the aligning of them with day-to-day consciousness, was overseen by a master or teacher. The ancients recognized that opening the higher planes would stimulate the *siddhis* or psychic energies that would have to be balanced and expressed properly within the physical realm. These siddhis are the energies of our true spiritual essence that work through our lives whether we are aware of them or not. They bind and flow through our subtle bodies to our physical lives, all from our *spiritual essence*. When stimulated or awakened through study, spiritual and occult exploration, our spiritual essence becomes more closely aligned with our physical being, releasing greater amounts of its creative energies into our physical lives.

We must remember that we are more than a physical being. We are multidimensional and we have subtler bands of energy surrounding and interpenetrating our physical vehicle. These bands are referred to as our *subtle bodies* (see the chart on page 80). They bridge our true spiritual essence to our physical vehicle so we can have consciousness within it. It is that spiritual essence that we are trying to awaken more fully within our lives. When we "raise our consciousness," we stimulate the spiritual essence to release greater energy to be expressed within the physical. These bands will be explored in greater detail in the next chapter. Any stimulation of these, through strong emotion, spiritual discipline, new knowledge, etc., will cause a release of energy from our spiritual essence into our physical lives to manifest in the way we direct. The energy is released, but our conscious will must direct its expression.

The ancient masters and teachers recognized particularly that concentrated study in the spiritual sciences and living with a spiritual discipline held even greater potential to release this energy into our physical life. This energy could be destructive or be expressed in an inappropriate manner if there were not the proper moral and mental background and training. It could overstimulate the individual in a variety of ways, leading to physical, emotional, and mental imbalances.

Because of the prominence of information and knowledge available today, man does not need a teacher to open the other worlds. There is however the same responsibility: the spiritual student must win for him/herself the conditions necessary for higher initiation and consciousness. This requires even greater time, care and responsibilities in the development process. It demands a *fully* conscious union with the spiritually creative worlds, and this cannot be fulfilled by mere clairvoyance or psychism of any kind. Today's path to manifesting a higher destiny requires a genuine search and use of knowledge. It requires greater depth of study of the spiritual sciences.

There is much information available in all of the spiritual sciences, but the student must be familiar with previous spiritual investigations. There must be complete and independent testing of these by the individual, who also needs an ability to draw correspondences, similarities and assimilations, and must discern/discriminate the truth from the half-truths and the illusions from reality. Otherwise, such information will only serve to create entanglements that will trip the student and set him/her further back on the path than if s/he had left well enough alone to begin with.

It is dangerous to enter the spiritual worlds with a thinking that has been strengthened only through meditation or through a gathering of information and psychic energy. There must be an in-depth study and *knowledge* of the entire path of esoteric or spiritual schooling, in order to truly heal and intensify the soul activities and to balance the events of one's own life with the universal life process. It is to aid in this that Daath is so active today, not only within an individual's consciousness, but also within the consciousness of the entire universe. Daath in the Qabalistic Tree of Life will open the entire school of esoteric learning.

Our minds and our knowledge can be a gateway to other dimensions. It has been said that we enter the Mysteries through the sphere of the mind, but only so we can worship at the shrine in the heart. Western man has grown increasingly rational in his thinking processes during this past century, and many times this colors his higher feeling aspects. Today we need to learn to link the mind with the heart—Daath with Tiphareth—higher knowledge with Christ consciousness.

It is significant that Daath falls within that area of the Tree of Life known as the Great Abyss. Knowledge has brought light to many of the fears and superstitions of humanity; it has served to move us through the abyss of our darkest doubts and superstitions in every area of life. Knowledge sheds light upon both the natural and supernatural worlds.

Many times in the process of unfoldment true spiritual energies and heightened initiation does not occur until we are able to tap more fully those levels of consciousness which are closer to pure energy, those that we associate with Binah, Chokmah and Kether. We may manifest tremendous potential from the others (tremendous psychic, emotional and mental energies), but until we tie or link the upper levels to them more fully, even the lower levels will have limits within our lives. This is what makes Daath so critical to the path of spiritual evolution. It becomes the bridge. It is what effects the true alchemical transmutation on a soul level. It is the crossing of the abyss that is reflected in the Biblical story of Elijah, who "saw God and was no more." He accessed the energies available on the other side of the abyss, and it effected a permanent change in consciousness. The old no longer exists, for something new is created.

Daath or knowledge helps us to work from all of the levels of consciousness associated with the Tree of Life. As our knowledge of the energies available to us at each level grows, we are propelled along our own unique path. It is because of Daath that we are able to work on each of the individual levels and awaken their corresponding energies, thereby increasing our understanding (Binah) of our own purposes in this life and the wisdom (Chokmah) to act upon that understanding. Thus we may touch the highest aspect of our own divine consciousness (Kether).

There is significance to Daath being placed upon the Middle Pillar of the Tree of Life diagram. Knowledge can balance us, but knowledge misused will result in misplaced force or imbalance within our lives. The idea of "a little knowledge being a dangerous thing" is apropo. Our fears and doubts, and even our inbred, societal superstitions that are represented by the abyss can cause us to use our knowledge inappropriately. Being represented upon the Middle Pillar reminds us of the need to balance information and knowledge with appropriate discrimination (Malkuth), independent testing and work (Yesod), and appropriate devotion (Tiphareth), if we are to touch the crown of our Divinity (Kether).

Universally, Daath operates and effects the awakening of the energies of all levels of our consciousness. The more we know about a particular level, the more we can use it to benefit ourselves. It also works from the microcosmic aspect. Daath can be linked to the throat chakra within the individual human (see the diagram on page 47). The throat chakra is very important for the modern spiritual aspirant.

The throat chakra is linked to the neck area of the body and to the function of the thyroid gland. It is the center of will and of creativity becoming active within our lives. It holds the secret of generation and regeneration. In it lies the ancient magickal teaching of the power of sound, i.e., "In the beginning was the Word." We know that the aspect of God associated with the heart of the Tree of Life and with the energies of our own heart chakra is called in Hebrew *Jehovah aloah va Daath*, or "God made manifest in the sphere of the mind." Our thoughts create much of our life circumstances. When we give voice to our thoughts, either appropriately or inappropriately,

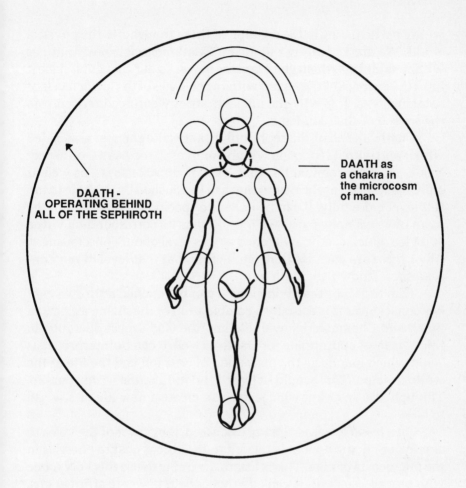

DAATH -
OPERATING BEHIND
ALL OF THE SEPHIROTH

DAATH as
a chakra in
the microcosm
of man.

Daath in the Microcosm of Man

Daath not only works to release knowledge of each of the levels of consciousness in man, but also serves as a separate consciousness as well, wherein universal knowledge of all the spiritual and esoteric sciences can be attained. On a lesser level it also corresponds to the throat chakra, the center of will and creativity within man. It is a center of cornucopia, because through proper use and understanding of it we can learn to manifest all we need from any of the other levels of our consciousness.

we are participating in the creation of those thoughts in the physical world. We are activating the innate Daath consciousness that lies within us all and which gives greater power to our thoughts, since it links the energies of the higher with the energies of the lower levels of consciousness. It is why the ancients strictly enforced reticence in the speech of their students.

Daath, like all of the sephiroth, has specific energies associated with it and with its function within our lives. It too has a God aspect that is most predominant at that level of consciousness, as well as archangelic and angelic beings that can be touched by learning to tap this level more fully. It can be linked to specific energies within the more physical universe as well. It also has its corresponding virtue and vice which can be awakened at this level of our consciousness. All of these are energies that can be found at that level of our consciousness known as Daath.

That aspect of the divine which can be touched at this level of our consciousness is actually a combination of the divine aspects of Binah and Chokmah. Jehovah Elohim, the God aspect operative in Binah, is most appropriate for Daath as well. It can be interpreted as "God which manifests the perfection of creation and the life of the world to come." This would fit Daath and its function within our life. Through Daath, or knowledge, we can create a new life or a world to come.

On a lesser level, as already discussed, the power of the voice to create our circumstances is related to the throat chakra energies in the microcosm of man. This is Daath. Learning to use this holy name with proper visualization can add tremendous power to affirmations, mantras, and other words of power. It can literally empower the throat chakra for greater manifestation.

Prior to tapping the level of Daath, the spiritual student is still in a process of "becoming." The student is still awakening to the other levels of consciousness and learning to integrate them. When one learns to fully unite Daath with the others, when knowledge operates fully and consciously with each of the other levels and is capable of integrating present life with universal life, then the aspirant enters into true discipleship and is thereafter involved in the process of "being." There is no further activity in "becoming," for the soul now has access to all that was, is and will be. It does not mean that the soul can employ it all, but it would have access to it.

Unfortunately, many New Age "aspirants" attempt to "be"

before they have learned to "become," and it does trip them up eventually, resulting in imbalance. Knowledge is worthless unless it can be integrated into one's life and essence in a balanced and creative manner. This is why the process of "becoming" is so critical to the spiritual student. Through it is learned integration of all levels of consciousness. This is why the techniques of pathworking are so powerful. They assist in integrating all levels so that "becoming" will lead to "being."

Through Daath we realize we only have to be all that we are, but part of the learning process requires that before we can have such a realization we must do much, learn much, act much, and integrate it *all*. Those that touch a level of energy or knowledge and try to "be" according to that energy without the proper training, background or integration of lesser energies (which build to empower us and strengthen us for the "being" process) are liable to short-circuit all of their energies. It is comparable to running high voltage through low-voltage wires. It will melt the wires.

The process of "becoming" is time consuming, and many people do not wish to put forth the time and energy necessary for the true flow of knowledge. But it is this process that enables the wires to carry the more intense voltage without short-circuiting the system— in this case, the consciousness of the human being.

There are quick ways of "rending the veil" to open up higher energies and levels of consciousness, but if the wires cannot carry the load, the current will be distorted or closed. It will even burn itself up. Today, channeling is very popular, and there are quick methods for learning to do it, but unless the channels have been cleaned, cleared and properly prepared, the communication can be distorted and misinterpreted. The channel can also become a tool for those who would mix the truth with half-truths to mislead individuals. Such beings, physical and non-physical, do exist and require constant watchfulness.

Often, those with just a little knowledge feel they are constantly in control when in reality they are not; and frequently such realizations do not occur until it is too late. Even if the techniques have been "learned" in previous lives (which many channelers credit for their facility at the process), it still requires proper training to awaken them in the safest and most beneficial manner. That takes time. Through the techniques within this book we can learn to clear the paths between the various levels of our consciousness and begin the process of integrating them, so that we can move past "becoming" and into "being."

Learning to work at the level of consciousness known as Daath will awaken the virtue of detachment. This is detachment from the desires that we all have. The person that learns to tap this level can go about his/her business with a detachment that will not allow him/her to be distracted, and which can serve to cut a person off from the mainstream of people and society.

> The Daath powers in balanced function, of course, give the type of person with a mission or sense of destiny who will have sufficient detachment to cut his way through any obstruction to his aims, at no matter what cost, and who has absolutely no concern for what danger the future may have in store, such is his faith in his powers and acceptance of destiny.
>
> —Gareth Knight
> *Practical Guide to Qabalistic Symbolism*

This aspect of Daath can work against us, creating a kind of misguided fanaticism. It is misguided in an individual if other virtues from the Tree of Life are not integrated. Such virtues would be devotion to God, humility, love for fellow man and a sense of charity. The detachment is from the lower aspects of the personality, not from mankind itself.

By tapping that level which opens up higher knowledge, we can awaken a true confidence in the future. We are able to see across the abyss of our day-to-day lives. We come to "know" that there truly is a better life for us, one that we are capable of creating.

If unbalanced, the energy of Daath can create or stimulate a further activation of vices within our day-to-day lives. We become lost in our own misery. The future holds nothing for us. We doubt everything. Because of this, we stop trying. Apathy takes over in many areas of our lives. We put the blame on everything and everyone but ourselves. Our lives become stagnant. We are afraid to move. A fear of the future locks us into place.

Daath can also awaken an imbalanced sense of pride. A "know-it-all" kind of attitude begins to prevail. No one can tell us anything. We know better than anyone else. We do it all better than anyone else. This breeds an imbalanced form of detachment, an isolation due to an antagonism toward anyone else displaying any knowledge. It stimulates a fear that others may think someone else knows something we do not.

Daath is located in the abyss, the center of our deepest subconscious, a place where our deepest fears and inner demons may exist. Tapping Daath places us right in the midst of them, where we have little choice but to deal with them. It is for this reason that Daath is also known as a sphere of justice. Justice involves confronting and dealing with what must ultimately be faced.

At this level we can have knowledge of all deeds, past and present, revealed and brought to full consciousness. This can be severely disruptive to the soul and to the mind. It disrupts the conditions, if only temporarily, with an intensity that can be difficult to rebalance. Here we learn and face true Cosmic Law. We see what we have done, and we know it must be balanced. For those who have lived many, many lives, karma can be frightening. It is for this reason that many of the more ancient esoteric schools cautioned students about past-life exploration. It had the potential of releasing energies that have already been balanced and it can open wounds that have already healed. It can also release the balancing of karma and its manifestation with an intensity and in a quantity that only serves to create agony for the soul.

Daath can open a Pandora's box of past-life karma. The technique at the end of this chapter is one that is adaptable for working with past lives through Daath, but even with it, caution is recommended. The old saying holds very true: "Be careful of what you ask, for you may get it!" Once we have tapped Daath, we *do* get what we ask.

There is no archangel in particular who has ever been assigned to Daath. Usually, the archangels of the four cardinal points are assigned and accessible through this level of our consciousness. Raphael is for the East, Michael is for the South, Gabriel is for the West and Auriel is for the North. This is appropriate, because learning comes to us from all directions, if we learn to recognize it. These beings can help us to learn from all things within our world. Invoking their aid before any work on the level of Daath surrounds us with protection and enables us to use the knowledge with less chance of an imbalance within our physical lives. On another level, since all of the archangels serve as teachers for the different sephiroth, or levels of consciousness delineated within the Tree of Life, any archangel can work through Daath. Teachers disseminate knowledge, and Daath is the sphere of knowledge. Any teacher we work with helps us to activate the Daath level of our consciousness.

Working with the archangels are a group of angelic beings, similar to the seraphim of Geburah. Gareth Knight describes them as having the appearance of "silvery grey serpents with golden darting tongues." Personal experience reveals them as being very similar to this appearance. It must be realized that there will be some differences, because they will interact with our own energies in a uniquely individual manner. They are very serpent-like, casting a silver-like flame or light about them. Their eyes have appeared very mist-like, shifting like the mist upon a lake in the early morning. This is appropriate, in that our knowledge is always shifting our perceptions into new forms and waves.

On a more mundane level, the energy available to us through Daath is astrologically comparable to the energy of Sirius, the Dog Star. In Egyptian mythology, the name of Sirius is traced to the god Osiris, and it was considered the resting place of the soul of Isis. In fact, the Isis mythology can be most easily used in awakening the energies of Daath within ourselves. Osiris and Isis are both attributed to Sirius and thus to Daath; Isis is the Supreme Feminine (Binah) and Osiris is the Supreme Masculine (Chokmah), and their union occurs in Daath. The technique of using myths and tales to tap the levels of our consciousness is explained in greater detail in later chapters.

In astrology, if Sirius is well placed, it denotes or can contribute to wealth, fame, honor, etc., within one's life. All of these are things which greater knowledge can lead to within our own lives. The world is a world of abundance, an abundance that we all can share in if we *know* how. Through Daath we can come to *know*. Not only is it a conjunction of Binah and Chokmah but it also unites Geburah and Chesed, or Mars and Jupiter—energy and abundance.

The colors that best reflect the energies of Daath within our own consciousness are grays and lavenders. Gray is like a cloud which hides knowledge behind it. Some fragrances that are effective in creating an atmosphere that facilitates touching this level of our consciousness are lilac, bay oil, wisteria and the more common, universal fragrances of sandalwood and frankincense. Using candles of the appropriate color and the corresponding fragrance for the sephira facilitates touching it. This technique is described in great detail in the predecessor to this work: *Simplified Magic: A Beginner's Guide to the New Age Qabala.*

Associated with this level of our consciousness is a magickal image which, like the archangels, is a teacher of the energies of this level. It is usually depicted as a man with two faces, each looking in opposite directions. This is appropriate; unless knowledge is used correctly, it will result in either looking toward or using it only where we have already been, which is involution of the energy. We can use it instead to go beyond where we were, across the abyss to higher evolution. It is also a reminder that knowledge must always be balanced. This image can be used to open up for us, after the proper preparation, a vision across the abyss—a vision of the new life to come which brings hope, fulfillment and a strong sense of will and destiny.

All images can become magickal because they have the capability of helping to open up energies and levels of consciousness never before fully touched. The symbols and images of Daath are vague at best, because the energies they open are fluid and changeable. Each new bit of knowledge changes all that was learned previously, and changes our perspective of the world. In essence, it then changes the world. Learning to change it to work creatively is what we attempt to do with the techniques of imagick. With Daath the images and dreams are empowered with the potential to become the reality and knowledge of the material plane. They are given life, and they open up the cosmic spiral on the Middle Path of the Tree of Life.

Most people today upon the spiritual path are operating with astral-plane powers. Daath is that level of consciousness that can open the mental plane for us. During the Piscean Age we have all had the spark of Divine stimulated within the heart chakra. As we move into the Aquarian, the abilities and planes associated with it will become more accessible to each individual. In the process of evolution, one is not considered an initiate of a particular plane until all the energies of the previous plane are mastered, and all the energies of the lower cannot truly be worked with until the plane above it has opened its doors.

The Aquarian Age is an age of mental energies and mental-plane powers, with all the energies of the astral becoming available to us. It is knowledge that opens up this plane. By the end of the Aquarian Age, many souls will be considered initiates of the mental plane. They will have mastered the astral-plane energies, and asserted their control over them. This control is closely connected to the will of the throat chakra.

Daath is being opened for many souls, and thus greater phenomena are being activated and manifested more quickly than at
other times. It is comparable to the flow of air. In a closed vacuum,
little occurs. If a door is opened, the air begins to move. In the New
Age, the door to the mental plane is opened, which allows greater
movement upon the astral plane. The air and energies can now circulate. Knowledge of the past is no longer lost to us, but we must conduct the search with all of the necessary precautions. This will allow
greater freedom of movement upon the astral, with all of its inherent
wonders. There are dangers too, because freedom and flow must be
disciplined, or they will create imbalance.

In the Western world, particularly in the United States, this is
significant to the karma we all participate in. We are here in this
country to learn the proper lesson of freedom, and true freedom can
only be attained with proper discipline; otherwise it is unbalanced
force. Many examples of unbalanced freedom can be easily brought
to mind. We share the effects, just as we all share the causes, either
directly through commission or indirectly through omission. Freedom unbalanced leads to anarchy and deterioration; pornography is
one small example of unbalanced freedom.

Knowledge, Daath's true power, can upset all previous conditions of the body or the mind. With the implanting of the divine
spark within the etheric energies and heart of mankind at the onset of
the Christian era ("the giving up of the ghost"—the implantation of
the Christ into the etheric band around the Earth so that with each
incarnation it can grow stronger), man now has the capability to handle
the new energies, if he wills. With Daath, there is often as much to
unlearn as there is to learn, and any lack of control will manifest disruption and imbalance of an intensity that has major repercussions,
physically, emotionally, mentally and spiritually. There are no
shortcuts. Through imagick we can open the energies of Daath and all
of the sephiroth, and learn to integrate them and ground them so that
we can learn all of our lessons.

The first lesson of all knowledge is that nothing is insignificant.
Everything has importance and consequence within our lives. Recognizing this and working with this is what Daath and imagick and
pathworking are all about. Learning to utilize and incorporate all of
our energies at all times, in full consciousness and responsibility, is
the Great Work of "becoming" more than human. It is what leads to a
human "being"!

IMAGICK TECHNIQUE: The Temple of Knowledge

The symbols and images within this exercise have been chosen carefully to elicit the strongest and safest effect from that level of consciousness known as Daath. It would be best to familiarize yourself with the meditation and its symbols prior to the working. Contemplating them and their significance will help to trigger an even stronger response. The sigils for the archangels of the four quarters are given below, as is a brief symbol explanation of some of the other important images within the meditation and imagickal working.

The effect of this meditation is very powerful and subtle. It manifests into your day-to-day life energies that must be dealt with and transmuted. It works very gradually. The first time the author utilized this specific technique, the effects were felt for several months. Emotions and thoughts arose that had to be dealt with; numerous individuals commented or inquired about his change in energy. It was not recognized as negative or positive, just obviously different. Knowledge of the self is one of the benefits of this level of consciousness, but knowledge can be painful. It can reveal the thorns that need to be removed. The removal hurts, but in the long run, it is not so painful as allowing a thorn to remain, becoming infected and festering.

This particular imagick technique is not one that should be done too frequently. Initially, at the very least, leave a month after working it so you will be able to discern what effects it is having. Knowledge has been given as the cause of the fall of mankind from grace, as depicted in the story of Adam and Eve eating the fruit from the Tree of Knowledge. Knowledge has its consequences. If we are to utilize knowledge to its utmost, we must be willing to take that responsibility.

When we touch the level of Daath, that knowledge, especially when it concerns aspects of ourselves that we would rather ignore, can become disruptive to the personality. It can show our darker aspects, bringing them out so that we can face them and transmute them. Daath within our own consciousness and within the universe is very direct. It does not sugarcoat; and it takes time to re-assimilate and integrate that knowledge and increased awareness in the most beneficial manner.

At the same time, though, anything that is cleaned out through greater knowledge of the self is replaced by something much more beneficial. It opens up levels within Daath that can release higher knowledge for propelling us along the path to a higher destiny. We can learn to use that level of our consciousness to enhance the learnings in every other area of our lives. We can learn to read from the Holy Writ, or the Book of Knowledge of the universe.

If knowledge—or rather misuse of knowledge—was the cause of the fall of mankind, then knowledge must be transmuted and be utilized to take us back. This is why man was given the Qabala, and this is why Daath is so important. There is a principle of healing in homeopathy that applies here and within our lives: "Like cures like." Very simply, it means that to treat an individual a small dose of a substance can be used which in a large dose would actually produce effects similar to the patient's disease.

Again, this provides clues to working with Daath. It needs to be done in small doses, first so that the system can assimilate it, and second so that it can do so without imbalance occurring. Too much too soon would merely serve to create the same kind of fall that has been experienced before, individually and universally. There would arise an inability to handle the knowledge in the most appropriate and beneficial manner. What is or seems to be beneficial for the individual can be disruptive to everything beyond him or her.

If knowledge is to be used correctly, we must be able to discern how it affects us as individuals and how it affects everyone and everything else in the universe. Everything is connected. Nothing can be treated as distinctly separate. Not realizing this, or treating it too lightly, is what causes the sharp, serpent bite of knowledge. Knowledge can be painful, especially since it cannot be used to interfere with the free will of others. To do so is to draw upon ourselves some strong repercussions.

One of the symbols associated with the Daath level of our consciousness is that of the pentagram. Daath is the heart of the pentagram, with points touching Kether, Chokmah, Binah, Geburah and Chesed. It links the lower sephiroth with the three supernals in the Tree of Life. It is a geometric shape which activates the higher energies of an individual so that there is dominion of the spirit over the elements, reason over matter. It activates the throat chakra, that energy center in the human body associated with Daath. Although this is also a symbol that can be related to Geburah as well, it is more appropriate to Daath.

The pentagram, or five-pointed star, is the sign of the microcosm.

It is a symbol of humanity with his arms and legs extended and his head touching and adoring the creator. At the heart of the microcosm is Daath—knowledge which helps us realize that all of the energies of the universe (macrocosm) play within us.

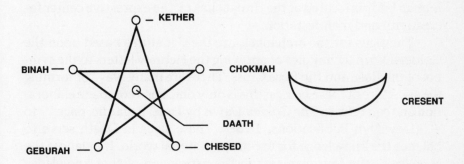

The crescent is also a symbol for Daath. The moon symbol is more strongly related to Yesod, but Daath is a deeper level of Yesod. They both reflect energies of the subconscious, with Daath supplying the knowledge of how to more appropriately utilize them. In one way, it can be seen as the higher energies of Yesod playing within our lives. The energies and potentials of that level of consciousness known as Yesod can be taken to a higher, more spiritual degree: Daath.

The crescent is a geometrical shape which creates a vortex of energy that will enhance healing of emotional imbalances and problems of expression. Through greater self-knowledge we can face and transmute our lower emotions, freeing ourselves for greater creative expression within our lives. The crescent awakens the feminine energy of the soul: the intuitive, receptive aspects. It is through the female that the Christ consciousness can be born. The female is the intuitive, illuminated and enlightened soul, the only kind of soul that can give birth or manifestation to the Christ consciousness. Knowledge, innate within us all, has the potential to illumine and enlighten so that we can give birth to the Higher Self. The crescent is a figure that is also related to Nada Yoga, or the dynamic and creative use of sounds and mantras. Again the reflection of Daath in the human body is located at the throat chakra, the expressive center for creativity and manifestation.

The sigils for the archangels are the signatures based upon the Golden Dawn techniques of applying the Hebrew letters to the symbol of the Rose and the Rose Cross. There are many ways of forming the signature of these beings; this is only one. For a complete elaboration one can refer to *The Golden Dawn* by Israel Regardie, pages 9 to 47 (Llewellyn Publications, 1986). These sigils in Daath serve to balance the knowledge for use in the material world. It balances the energies of the four elements in the expression of that knowledge within our life. Any meditation and work in Daath should utilize the sigils or other symbols and images associated with the four archangels of the quarters, if only for basic protection and grounding of energies that can be awakened at this level of our consciousness.

RAPHAEL — The Eastern Quarter —

GABRIEL — The Western Quarter —

MICHAEL — The Southern Quarter —

AURIEL — The Northern Quarter —

Entering the Temple of Knowledge

You stand outside the ancient Tree of Life. As always, its immense size astounds you. It grows larger and more impressive with each visit. This time you see the entrance, but the guardian is also there. The ground erupts, and it raises its serpent heads, eyeing you coldly. It shows no familiarity. It simply knows its tasks and fulfills them.

"What is it you seek?" it roars.

You know the answer now, but today the words have more significance than before. Today you enter the Temple of Knowledge.

"I seek *to know* that I may serve."

The guardian parts, making way for you to enter the Tree.

Knowledge has done so much good and yet caused so much pain. You wonder as you enter into the familiar darkness of the Tree. Humans know so much about the physical world, and so little about the others. Humans can be arrogant. No one knows more or better than they! Fanatics have always believed they knew better than the ordinary person. History books are filled with such individuals and the chaos they created. Knowledge is a responsibility, and it requires discernment at all times.

You remember something once read, but now barely remembered: "Be ever watchful!"

You are anxious, as you wait for your eyes to adjust to the inner darkness. It is the first day of school as far as you are concerned. There is anticipation and anxiousness. The Temple of Knowledge is something you have looked forward to for some time. To be able to finally know! What peace it will bring. To have the knowledge of all the ages at your hands; what joy!

A dim light begins to grow. You wait, your breath becoming more rapid in anticipation. You remind yourself to be patient. Your eyes widen, and your shoulders sink in disappointment. This could not be the Temple of Knowledge. The light grows to reveal a stone-gray, empty room.

You had come expecting the magnificence of the Libraries of Alexandria, and you find an empty room. No books. No scrolls. No writings or marks of any kind, except for an insignia carved into the upper part of each of the four walls. Each is different, but they tell you nothing. It makes no sense, and you are filled with disappointment.

There is not even an altar in this temple—if indeed it is a temple at all. Near the back sits a small pedestal. It is wooden. Its base is in the shape of a pentagram and three rods extend upward out of it to a crescent-shaped surface. Upon this crescent surface sits a large leather-bound volume. On either side of the middle rod of the pedestal are two carved snakes, resting in a circular coil on the pentagram base.

As you step to the pedestal, the book is at chest level—heart level with you.

"We enter the mysteries through the sphere of the mind, but only so we can worship at the shrine in the heart."

You turn, looking for the source of the words that ring in your head. You are not sure if they are your words from some deep level of your consciousness, or the words of some being that you have not yet discovered.

"It is good that you are puzzled, for the asking of the question is the beginning of the answer."

The words ring again. Again you look about, searching the shadows, but there are no shadows! There is dim lighting at best within this room, *but there are no shadows!* It is as if they have been chased away. There are no blacks or whites—only grays!

You turn slowly back to the pedestal and the book. Above the book burns the dim lamp that provides the only light within the room. The lamp is shaped like a pine cone. It must have significance, but this eludes you at the moment.

You examine the book. It is closed, wrapped in a leather binding that is strapped and locked. You reach out gingerly to touch it. Your hand caresses it lightly. You feel the texture and your hand traces the image of a man with two faces which has been burnt into the leather. The faces look off into opposite directions. As you touch the image, the lamp grows brighter.

You fumble with the latch, and it pops open. You lean forward, preparing to open the volume. You lay it wide, like wings across the pedestal top. There on the top of the first page is your name!

You stare with utter surprise and disbelief. You fail to notice in your surprise that the coiled snakes have come to life. They slide upward, crisscrossing and intertwining around the middle rod. Their heads search around the outer edges of the book, peering over the top as you lean forward to read what is written about you in the Book of Life.

As you lean forward, the twin serpents strike. Each bites you on the temple behind the eyes. You jump back, drawing your hands to your face, feeling the sharp pain pierce your entire head. The book snaps closed. You watch as the serpents draw back, receding down the middle rod to settle back into non-existence at the base. The pain in the temple recedes. All that is left is a strange tingling to remind you what has happened.

"The first bite of True Knowledge is always the hardest to bear and catches one off guard."

You look about the room in amazement. Everything is brighter, more distinct. The bites cleared your eyesight. The insignias on the walls begin to glow, casting the grays back and filling the temple with crystalline white light. The temple begins to shake and vibrate as if to collapse upon itself. You fall to the ground, covering your head in fear. The temple roars! And then fades into nothingness.

You lie upon the floor. You have no idea how long you have been there. You shiver and realize that you are now naked. You draw yourself up, confused and bewildered.

"All knowledge has its price—its pain. By enduring it, one can strip away the old, tear down the foundations so that new life and light can enter in forever. Knowledge brings light only when balanced with love. Knowledge and love breeds *truth*, and the Truth shall set you free!"

The voice fades again. You are shaken. All is quiet, but something is different. Why does the room feel so strange? Why is it so much more crystalline? You pause to listen for the voice.

Nothing. Silence is your answer.

You turn to leave. You glance back once more to the pedestal. The pine cone lamp brightens in response. The book lays itself open for you. A soft breeze moves through the temple, flipping the pages of the book. You smile weakly, still shaken. You begin to understand. The Book is now open to you forever. It is there for you to read from. It holds the past, the present and the future you have yet to create.

You move to the outside entrance of the Tree. You step through the opening, allowing the warm sun to fill every pore of your body with healing. You feel more alive and more in control than ever before. The future is something to look forward to, not run from. You know it is there for you to create in any manner you decide.

You glance at the guardian as it rests quietly. You nod. Maybe now you can rest more quietly as well, secure in the knowledge that awaits you!

Take time after this exercise to work with your actual living Tree. Read or learn more about your particular tree, expand your knowledge about it in some way. Find out what you can do to make it grow even more for you. This will ground the energies of this exercise and empower them for you.

This exercise is a guide. Do not worry about remembering all of the details. We must use our own input and insight and allow the basic imagery and symbols to adapt themselves. Each will have their own variations, but it is best at first to hold as closely as possible to format so that the basic territory and energy can become familiar. Then we can begin to use it more freely.

There will be different responses, but if we hold to the basic imagery, we stay grounded and can release its energy in our own unique manner. One does not want to hold too strictly to the script. Once Daath has been opened, we can go back and read from the Book. This can open up knowledge on anything we wish to learn. Every reading does have its accompanying bite. Sometimes it is more vicious than at other times, depending upon what knowledge is being revealed and whether or not it can be easily misused. *The bite is our reminder that all knowledge has its price!*

The time frame in which to work this technique and see results varies. It could take a month to fully begin to recognize the effects this technique has caused. For some, it may happen quickly. It depends on various factors: concentration, ability to visualize, state of relaxation, etc. The ancient mystery schools taught their students to "Know Thyself." This is the kind of energy released through this working. It releases energy to stimulate and awaken aspects of ourselves that we do not know, at least not as well as we should. It serves to manifest conditions in our lives that put us into a position to look at ourselves, for good and bad.

One does not have to wait a month before going back to this level to read from the Book. The month period is a guideline, so that you can determine how strong an effect it will have in your life. This requires self-examination. Have your emotions been more charged and volatile since the working? Have new situations arisen, good and/or bad? How are you relating differently to people in your life or they to you since the working? Are there certain things that are upsetting you more since the working? Have you started any new learning situations? Have there been new people drawn into your life since then? What kind of people are they?

Examine every aspect of your life. Remember that knowledge throws light upon our shadows. It forces us to look at things from a different perspective. Self-knowledge is most important. Unless we become aware of those aspects of our own personality that limit us, we can never clean them out and replace them with those energies that can benefit us. This exercise sets the energy in motion to bring out new learnings and perspectives in all areas of our lives. This happens as a result of this exercise in both subtle and obvious ways. Thus, we need some time to assimilate, or we may bring on too many new learning circumstances too quickly, and that disrupts rather than transmutes.

Each must use his or her own judgment. Remember that the Qabala will show us our greatest strengths and our greatest weaknesses. That can be quite troublesome in our lives if it is allowed to be, particularly when working with Daath. There is always a craving for more knowledge. She who has much, always wants more. He who has access to much, wants it always opened and augmented, even at the risk of imbalance. There are times to seek and use knowledge, and there are times to leave it alone. Each must use his own counsel in this choice. The autonomy of the spiritual student must be unqualifyingly recognized. "Free will" is the greatest gift humanity has received, that all life has received, but this free will has its responsibilities and our choices always have consequences. If we refuse to acknowledge such, we will find ourselves and our lives in great turmoil. We must come to know how these levels of consciousness affect our lives, and we must keep in mind that with each tapping of a level of consciousness—especially in Daath—the energy will intensify the effects.

chapter three

Touching Even
Greater Power

This is an age in which psychic phenomena will increase to such
a degree that past techniques of dealing with them will become
obsolete. Only those who develop the ability to penetrate into the
deeper mysteries will be able to help people who are exposed to such
psychic experiences.

—H.P. Blavatsky
"Theosophical Forum"

Many methods, techniques and combinations exist for awakening psychic energy. Many of these, however, do little more than just
that. They simply awaken, and for many people this is comparable to
stirring up a hornet's nest. There are almost as many methods and
uses for energy as there are individuals practicing them. Energy
unused or misused becomes disruptive, and energy is only used correctly when it is used for the service of humanity—and this includes
ourselves. The energies we awaken are spiritual energies and thus
should be used for spiritual purposes, which help us to integrate our
true spiritual and most divine aspects with our normal physical life
and consciousness.

Traditionally, there have been two predominant methods for
drawing out power: *meditative* and *ceremonial*. The meditative
techniques are plentiful. They include symbology, visualization,
creative imagination, pathworking, mantras, yantras, etc. We must
remember that for any meditational method to work to its fullest
capacity within our lives, we must concentrate, not upon the problem, but upon the spiritual unfoldment and development that will
come of it. In this way we keep ourselves grounded, and we increase
our awareness of the universe and our divine connection to it and all
that exists within it as well. It opens the door for all the energy we

need. This book presents a method for utilizing meditative techniques that grow and intensify the spiritual life expression. They can be adapted to the ceremonial method, but that is not dealt with to any degree within this book.

With every meditation, with every imagickal working, regardless of its particular purpose, you are planting a *seed thought*. In essence, this phrase means that if you place a magickal or mystical idea or image into your visualizations with a strong intention (i.e., recognizing that the process is a reflection of the divine within you), and if that image is built clearly, and then if you consign it to your unconscious mind, it will begin to increase in energy of its own. If you repeat the process every day, if only for a few moments, this magickal idea, image or working will build a bridge to the divine that will energize your entire life, increasing your creativity and your expression of life while in the physical.

Most "occult" techniques, such as a truly effective meditation, are very simple. Most of them depend upon capacities that can be developed by any intelligent man or woman, providing enough time and effort is expended. The training can be difficult and can take a long time, but *everyone* can achieve some results almost immediately. The techniques are based upon three fundamental abilities that must be developed: visualization, concentration and creative imagination. This will then lead to higher forms of inspiration and a fully conscious intuitive perception of the spiritual realm and all its manifestations of life.

Visualization is the ability to create a mental picture and to hold it steady within the mind for a reasonable time. The picture should be as clear as things seen in physical life. It should be made as life-like as possible in color and fragrance, etc., just as it would be in real life. A simple exercise is to visualize an orange, clearly seeing its shape, size and color. Feel the skin on it, and feel it as you press your finger into it to begin to peel it. Notice the fragrance as the juice squirts out. Then create the image of its taste.

Concentration is the art of holding the image that you have created within your mind without the mind wavering or wandering to other things. One should have a concentrated focus strong enough to hold one image to the exclusion of all others.

The third fundamental ability is creative imagination. This is enabling the mind to create images and scenes associated with the meditative seed thought or image. These created images should be in three-dimensional form. They are like a highly concentrated day-dream or actual dream, in which the individual becomes completely absorbed within the framework of the unfolding scenes, losing awareness of the ordinary world around him.

Creative imagination, or imaginative cognition, is a key to opening the doors to true spiritual energies and beings. The creative imagination and its proper development will open the spiritual background of physical life. We begin to see the spiritual essences and energies surrounding and interplaying with the physical world at all times. True, consciously developed and balanced imaginative experience is the expression of an objective, supersensible reality. Energy translated from the supersensible realms to the sensible ones of physical life must take the form of images in order for man to begin to recognize and work with them. At their core lies archetypal energies which we cannot even yet dream of. This relation between the archetypal energy and its translation to us within the physical will be explored later within this chapter.

What we consider imagination is a reality in some form on levels beyond the normal sensory world. With creative imagination, we create a new awareness, a new kind of experience in color and form, in relation to this world. It is through this ability that we empower and utilize symbolic pictures. They do not specifically reflect anything external. The soul learns to empower the symbol and then permeate it in order to gain entrance into the soul-spiritual realms. One builds up the energies and significances of the pictures and images, imbuing them with relevance to the spiritual path. Then we learn to assume a union with them. In this way, we can practice making transitions from the picture to its supersensible origins. By means of repeated use, we open a bridge through that image to a new soul power within our lives.

This in turn triggers higher forms of inspiration and intuition. It begins to unveil the macrocosm working within our day-to-day lives. It begins to give us an understanding of the conditions of our lives and the spiritual laws that govern it, along with the spiritual hierarchies who inhabit it. After the door is opened through the imagination, we begin to explore through inspiration, having direct spiritual perceptions themselves rather than just images which must be translated. This will reveal beings who rule in the supersensible world of forces.

To establish this more direct contact, we must first of all develop the use of concentrated creative imagination, which is what this text helps one to do. Secondly, there must be a greater knowledge of the entire school of inner, esoteric learning which enables one to distinguish the true from that which only appears to be true. We must also learn to exclude all thoughts and images of the physical world for definite periods of time, and be able to extinguish by our own resolve those very same pictures and images that we used and created to open the doors for us. When we can do this, we can connect with our own spirit-soul being, or higher self.

At a certain point, one uses images just as a carpenter would use nails, hammer and saw. Images become only tools with which we build to the spiritually creative worlds and to those same energies within ourselves. This means that we must be able to construct a "passive, reflected thought," transform that thought through our creative imagination into a living, empowered energy and be able to extinguish it through a complete and strong effort of the soul.

When we can accomplish this, then we can become full citizens of the macrocosm. We then have the means to open the doors to the cosmic channels, and to act and communicate in all of the spiritual realms, while working with all grades of spiritual beings. It is here, and at this point only, that one develops an objective and conscious identification with the spiritual beings. This demands a strengthening of the moral powers; otherwise we will be unable to translate the spiritual perceptions into concepts of ordinary consciousness. Only through stages can we see how the spiritually divine laws are playing upon us at all times. Only when such perceptions are ingrained into our physical consciousness can they be retained and then brought forth to enhance the physical life.

These abilities are simply ways of changing the focus of our attention from the physical world to the various realms of the spiritual. Metaphysicians and occultists believe that the real powers and motivations of man lie within these inner worlds, which are not normally available except through dreams. The use of the imagick techniques enables us to gain access to these realms in a deliberate and willed manner. These methods of visualization, concentration and creative imagination make it possible to bring through to the conscious mind the wealth and experience of the inner man and world, thus enriching our ordinary consciousness, increasing our potentials, broadening the mind and enhancing life. Repeated use of the techniques in this book and similar ones elsewhere will build roadways between the outer and inner worlds and make available all of the hidden powers' potential to humanity.

The symbols associated with the Tree of Life provide the tools to open the various doors to the realm existing around and beyond our physical environment. The Tree provides a system of using the images so that we can learn to explore and tap those realms without getting lost. The images and symbols become our guideposts; they have been used this way successfully by many people for many centuries. The paths have already been laid out for us, with markers to prevent our getting lost. All we then need do is learn to read the markers and walk the paths in order to link our own unique energy with the universal energy that becomes available to us in this process. The system of the New Age Qabala enables us to awaken the energies and pull back the veils that separate the physical from the non-physical realms, so that we can learn how best to express those energies within our lives.

A physically and spiritually creative person is one who can process information in new ways. A creative individual *intuitively* sees possibilities for transforming ordinary data and experiences into new creations. New ways of utilizing the ancient teachings enable us to make new discoveries about our different states of consciousness and provide great illumination that liberates our highest and most creative potential.

Inside each of our skulls, we have a double brain with two ways of knowing and learning. The dualities and different characteristics of the two hemispheres of the brain have a dynamic role in the development and utilization of altered states of consciousness for releasing higher abilities into our day-to-day lives.

Each of the hemispheres gathers in the same sensory information, but they handle that information in different ways. One hemisphere, often the dominant left, will "take over" and inhibit the other half. The left hemisphere analyzes, counts, marks time, plans and views logically and in a step-by-step procedure. It verbalizes, makes statements and draws conclusions based on logic. It is sequential and linear in its approach to life. In the Western world, the left hemispheric approach to life is predominant.

On the other hand, we have a second way of knowing and learning. This is known as right-brain activity. We "see" things that may be imaginary—existing only in the mind's eye—or recall things that may be real. We see how things exist in space and how parts go together to make a whole. We understand metaphors, we dream, and we create new combinations of ideas. With the right hemisphere, we tap and use intuition and have leaps of insight—moments when everything seems to fall into place, not in a logical manner. The intuitive, the subjective, relational, holistic, time-free mode is the process of the right hemisphere.

One of the marvelous capacities of the right hemisphere is imaging, *seeing an imaginary picture or symbol with the mind's eye!* The brain is able to conjure an image and then look at it. These images reflect our sensory information and data—past, present and future. It is for this reason that symbols, visualization and creative imagination are a part of developing higher potential. They assist us in accessing that part of our brain and mind which bridges into deeper levels of consciousness. Learning to use the right brain to tap and access levels of consciousness in a balanced and fully conscious manner, to bring it out and then to use it in some aspect of our daily life, involves "hemispheric synchronization." We use *both* sides of the brain to access greater levels.

The Qabala assists us in this. It provides an organized system of images to access and connect deeper levels of our consciousness to our normal waking consciousness. It is a system (left brain) of image and symbol usage (right brain). It is a safer and easier process when we begin to consciously control and work for our higher unfoldment through such a system. Other, more atavistic methods of unfoldment allow our inner fires and energies (the kundalini) to rise just like a serpent, moving this way and that until it reaches the top. When we control the inner energies, direct them and focus them consciously, we are doing what Dr. Rudolph Steiner referred to as "grabbing the serpent of wisdom by the neck." We are choosing and directing the movement of energy within us. We do it consciously and with full responsibility. We learn to make the energies work for us when we wish and how we wish!

Unless controlled, this serpent energy (energies of our deeper levels of consciousness) must meander, because we have not cleared a path for it to move and become directly active within our lives. Through many lives we have accumulated much debris in the form of negative thoughts, wrong ideas, imbalanced feelings, etc. This debris has accumulated on the various bridges from the subconscious to the conscious mind, and thus the flow of creative energy from the subconscious is hindered and impeded. Our energies must meander, winding around like a serpent, finding their own atavistic path into our normal day-to-day life expression. Through the controlled and concentrated use of various images and symbols, we can clear out the debris that locks the bridges to other levels of our consciousness and thus enable that inner creative energy to flow freely and directly for explicit expression within our lives (refer to the diagram on page 72).

The key to learning to empower your life through meditation is to set up the conditions that cause a mental shift to a new way of processing information—an altered state of consciousness. Through meditation and related techniques described within this book, we can learn to delve into parts of our mind too often obscured by the endless details of daily life. Through the images and symbols and through such physical activities and exercises as are described in chapter 6, we create a mind-set that begins the process of seeing things anew. We begin to see underlying patterns, and we develop the ability to more fully access greater potential and release it into our waking consciousness. We release creative solutions to problems and add energy and animation to our lives.

To achieve results and to tap deeper levels of consciousness and greater potentialites, we need only the ability to shift our awareness, and control and maintain it for the time and purpose necessary. Controlled and active meditation is a learned skill! And as with all learned skills, it does require practice and an increasing reinforcement and complexity in relation to the energies we wish to access. The Qabala provides the key to setting the process in motion. The more we use it, the more energy, power and magic it brings forth into our lives.

The human mind is the most powerful instrument in the three "lower worlds" in which man operates: the mental, astral and etheric/physical planes of life. We must remember, though, that our mind is not located in the physical vehicle or brain. Yes, there is an intimate connection and relation between the mind and the brain and its activities, but we must remember that the mind is the seat of our consciousness. As such, we need to learn to control it, if we are to control fully all of the vehicles in which it operates.

We are comprised of more than just physical energies and a physical body. We have subtler bands of energy that operate and integrate with the physical being and all of its functions. These subtle bands of energy give us access to consciousness of other planes and realms; thus if we wish to control our learning of these other dimen-

Conscious Mind

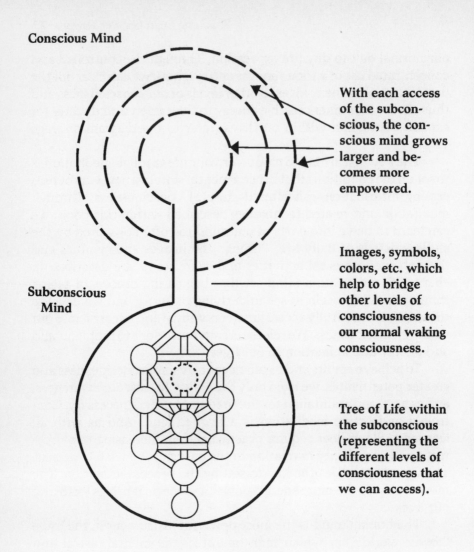

With each access of the subconscious, the conscious mind grows larger and becomes more empowered.

Subconscious Mind

Images, symbols, colors, etc. which help to bridge other levels of consciousness to our normal waking consciousness.

Tree of Life within the subconscious (representing the different levels of consciousness that we can access).

Tapping Our Hidden Levels

By focusing upon specific images, symbols, colors, sounds, fragrances, etc., we can open up specific levels of our subconscious energies. The symbols and images, when utilized through such techniques as imagick and pathworking, enable us to draw upon our subconscious reservoirs to create even greater boundaries within which to operate in our normal waking lives. The symbols reflect other realities. By working with them more consciously, we bridge all aspects of ourselves, which in turn opens higher understanding, greater mysticism and access to all realms and times.

sions, be they the astral, mental or spiritual planes and dimensions, we must control and direct the energies of our mind, which affects and operates in all of them. By learning to control and discipline the mind, we control and discipline our higher capacities and achieve the kind of results and effects within our life that we desire, whether they be greater abundance or fulfillment or greater clairvoyance. It is a lack of discipline and a lack of the understanding of how the energy-releasing process operates that is the cause of the basic failure to accomplish what we set out to do in life. It is *absolute control* that we must strive for and learn, especially in the beginning.

Working in the Astral Plane

In the beginning of our unfoldment, we operate predominantly in what metaphysicians and occultists refer to as the *astral plane*. It is that dimension or realm that is closest in vibration to the physical plane (the etheric being included as part of the physical by the author). Many terms have been given to the exploration of other planes—particularly the astral. These include astral travel, astral projection, scrying in the spirit, rising on the planes, etc. The terms are not necessarily synonymous. In reality, they are different techniques for opening up to that dimension known as the astral plane. One is neither better nor worse than any other, although some are more difficult to learn and to use.

The one commonality among them is that they basically involve two steps:

1. Energizing the astral body, stimulating its energies through accessing other levels of consciousness, and
2. After energizing, learning to utilize it as an independent vehicle for consciousness expansion.

Working with various symbols and images, meditational techniques start the process of energization. It takes such energizing and work to develop these techniques into conscious use as an independent vehicle. It must also be understood that there is just as much to manifest within our lives through intense energizing as through trying to focus on the utilization of these techniques as a separate vehicle of consciousness.

Many individuals try the second step before the first one has occurred. This will ultimately lead to imbalances—physical, emotional, mental and/or spiritual. This is comparable to attempting intricate gymnastic movements without proper training and loosening up. It will result in injury that could prevent participation of any substantial degree throughout the rest of this incarnation or even into others. We live in a kind of "fast-food" society, and people like their metaphysics the same way. What is fast is not always best. The techniques within this work and its predecessor enable an individual to energize all the subtle bodies and integrate them more effectively without great risk of imbalance within their lives. The methods have been utilized and practiced by many others. The groundwork has been laid.

The astral plane is a very fluid, changeable realm of existence. Unless we are able to discriminate (the virtue developed through Malkuth of the Tree of Life), we will find ourselves blown hither and yon by all the energies and manifestations that exist upon it. The Qabala, with its intricate set of symbolic signposts, enables us to explore with the least danger of delusion and deception occurring. The proper use of these symbolic signposts requires practice and persistence.

With the proper tools and techniques, we can train ourselves to control all of our energies and begin to operate in those planes of life that are visible as well as invisible. To attempt to do so without proper preparation is comparable to putting "new wine into old skins." The skins can easily rupture and split, spilling the wine. By working with the energies in a controlled, disciplined manner, we can rebuild or re-energize ourselves, so as to handle the new energies available to us upon the astral plane.

When we first begin working with the astral plane and all of its inherent energies—which is what we do with the Qabala—much can come to us that will benefit us. First, this plane shifts our attention from the physical world and its problems to the magnificence and wonder of the divine, which operates in other ways and dimensions around us. This alone diminishes the problems. Once we have experienced other realms, we cannot deny the reality of a Divine Force operating within the universe or within us. And most importantly, it places us in touch with three of the most powerful forces operating in the physical and non-physical universe:

1. Thought or action by imagination. This is what opens the higher realms and levels of consciousness to us. It is what

enables us to make contact with those beings who can serve as a Teacher to us and give us greater assistance within our lives.

2. The Force of light and an increased awareness of how light manifests to bestow wisdom, love and bliss.
3. The Force of sound and contact with it that helps us to realize that *all* that the Supreme Being is and does in all worlds manifests through the creative expression of *sound.*

These three forces are predominant within the astral plane, if we access it in a controlled and balanced manner. The other more ethereal planes have their own unique expressions and gifts, but for most individuals, the astral and its many dimensions will provide many lifetimes of exploration before mastery occurs. We must pass through the astral to touch even more ethereal planes, and the Qabala is a system that can lead us to ever more ethereal and spiritual energies (refer to the diagram on page 76).

Traditionally, students are taught of the seven planes of existence: divine, monad, atmic, buddhic, mental, astral and the physical (which includes the etheric). This work does not propose to deal at any length with these, as there are other works more suitable for such studies. It must be remembered, though, that at each of these levels or planes we have access to energies and awarenesses that we did not have access to at the others. Each plane manifests life and energy in its own unique and distinct form. Each plane interpenetrates and affects the physical, whether we are aware of it or not. Because we are comprised of many bands of energies that resonate with these planes of life, we can train ourselves to tap and utilize the energies of the more subtle, ethereal realms to affect the physical realm in which we predominantly operate.

These three lower bodies which we operate in seem to have the strongest effect upon us. By learning control over them, we open access to the use of our higher bands of energy, thus giving us access to higher planes of existence. This is especially important in the process of manifesting a higher destiny for ourselves. If we cannot bridge through to our spiritual bands of energy, they will begin to atrophy, thus cutting us off from a life source that lies within our highest spiritual consciousness. This atrophying can manifest as a hastened aging process. This is why working with any system of spiritual unfoldment is necessary for our overall health and well-being. It

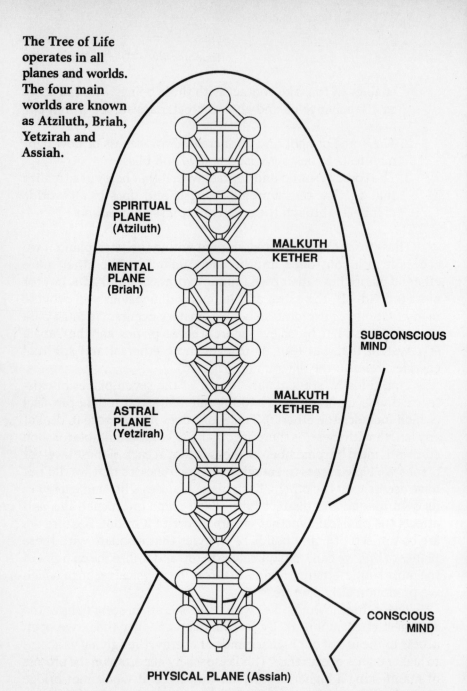

The Tree of Life operates in all planes and worlds. The four main worlds are known as Atziluth, Briah, Yetzirah and Assiah.

SPIRITUAL PLANE (Atziluth)

MENTAL PLANE (Briah)

ASTRAL PLANE (Yetzirah)

MALKUTH
KETHER

MALKUTH
KETHER

SUBCONSCIOUS MIND

CONSCIOUS MIND

PHYSICAL PLANE (Assiah)

The Tree of Life operates upon all planes. As we learn to work and manifest the energies on one level, we can go deeper to tap the energies of the next. All are available to us and can be utilized through basic tools and techniques.

triggers the Law of Correspondence, as discussed earlier. If we work for our development and energizing on any level, even if only the physical or astral, it will affect our more spiritual aspects. "As above, so below; as below, so above." This is not to imply that the astral or physical planes are not spiritual, but rather it is to demonstrate that by working on them, we can open the faucets to allow even finer and greater energies down through them into our lives.

The *mental body* has one of the most subtle and powerful effects upon man in the physical. At the heart of the Tree of Life, in that sephira known as Tiphareth, operates the aspect of God known as *Jehovah Aloah va Daath*. This translates into "God made manifest in the sphere of the Mind." In this is the ancient recognition that our thinking process is at the heart of all that manifests within our physical lives. All of the masters at one time or another spoke of controlling the mind, controlling our thoughts. Controlling the thought process is a major factor in stepping out on the path to higher evolvement. This is why with the Qabala one uses specific symbols and techniques. We control the thoughts through specific images.

The ancients recognized that thoughts create energy manifestations that will manifest within the physical and must be accounted for—good or bad. *All energy follows thought!* This means that wherever we put our thoughts, the energy begins to form, and upon the mental plane of existence and life those thoughts are being set in motion and played out. This is why the master whom we call Jesus warned his followers that if they merely looked upon another with lust or adultery, it was the same as having committed these sins. We exist and operate simultaneously on all of these planes, but we are just more focused upon the physical; so we tend to ignore the others. One of the purposes of imagick and pathworking is to make us aware that we are operating and living upon other planes as fully as upon the physical. We are multidimensional and thus our responsibilities become such. The more we know, the more we are held responsible!

It is our mental body and its action in the form of our thoughts and words upon the mental plane that most strongly sets the pattern for what we experience in the physical. It forms the matrix or blueprint of what is to manifest within our lives. It is on this level that the *ego* can manifest most strongly and can block access or awareness of access to the four higher planes and the operation of our energies upon them.

The *astral body* is that band of energy interpenetrating the physical and through which feelings and emotions are expressed and experienced. The interplay of desire is felt within this body, and it is because of this body that pairs of opposites are experienced so that we can learn to balance them: pleasure and pain, fear and courage, love and hate, etc. Most people in the physical operate very strongly through this body—usually in a very atavistic or uncontrolled way. They are blown back and forth, being swept along with whatever feeling is stimulated at the moment. As a result, this lack of control wears out the energy, and draws entities and lower energy forms from the less evolved levels of the astral plane to play upon the individual's energy system, physical and otherwise, which leads to obsessions and in some cases possessions.

As long as we are in the physical, we will have an astral body. This is to help us learn the lessons on the nature of polarity: how to bring opposites into balance, and how to express feelings impersonally and unconditionally. The astral body acts as a bridge or medium between the physical and mental—the brain and the mind. For the mental plane to open fully to us, we must clean out the debris of hindering and negative feelings that block the bridge of the astral.

Much psychic phenomena, especially of the seance room, manifests through the energies of the astral plane operating in the astral body of the individual. "Astral power" and psychic ability can be developed and used by anyone. The development of it requires no more higher morality than does the development of greater physical strength. Neither does the development reflect high moral character any more than having great physical strength reflects it. The psychic and astral energies exist within us all, but it is latent, or manifests in an atavistic manner. We either ignore it, refuse to acknowledge it or refuse to develop it. It is a skill that is learned.

Attainment of "astral" power as an end in itself leads to what in the East is referred to as the *laukika* method of development. The abilities and powers obtained are only for the present personality, and because true spiritual safeguards are not employed, it is extremely likely that the powers will be misused. If we are to instill the ability on a soul level for eternity, we must follow discipline and will, and use them with discretion and discrimination. They manifest to help us grow in our path. Working upon the astral and the awakening of its energies simply helps us to extend our consciousness beyond the astral to other, higher planes. We do it to assist our overall growth.

That and that alone should be the purpose. Any other uses will have pitfalls and can incur some strong karmic responsibilities.

Miscellaneous Astral Phenomena:

1. Mediumship (not a power but a condition)
2. Apportation
3. Materialization
4. Precipitation
5. Clairvoyance (many forms, but not all)
6. Clairsentience
7. Levitation
8. Spirit Lights
9. Firehandling
10. Transmutation of metals
11. Production of fire
12. Psychic Healings
13. Spirit Communication (many forms, but not all)
14. Slate writing
15. Other

Almost all of the astral phenomena involve an increased sensitivity to the vibrations of the astral plane and require learning to direct and handle them. They can be developed in full consciousness. They are not, however, an end in themselves. They are secondary "gifts" to assist us as we open ourselves to higher planes of consciousness and being.

The astral body has three primary functions. It makes physical and non-physical sensation possible. *All* feelings come through the astral. It serves as a bridge between our mind and physical matter, and it can act as an independent vehicle of consciousness and action. As mentioned earlier, there are two stages of development that occur within the astral body and its related energies. The first is a point of transmission—an increased sensitivity (clairsentience) that assists the second stage, which is the strengthening of the use of the astral body as an independent vehicle upon the astral plane itself. Without employing the first stage, we can make ourselves the target of all feelings and emotions and entities that exist or have been created for positive and negative purposes. When we work with imagick and the Qabala we are learning to strengthen ourselves so that we can control whatever energies we encounter.

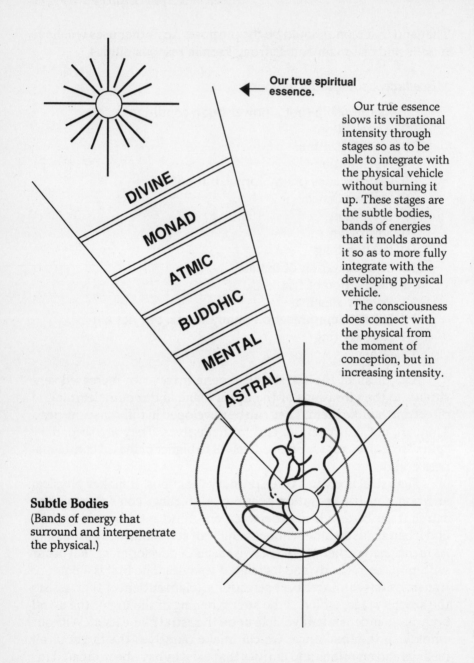

← Our true spiritual essence.

Our true essence slows its vibrational intensity through stages so as to be able to integrate with the physical vehicle without burning it up. These stages are the subtle bodies, bands of energies that it molds around it so as to more fully integrate with the developing physical vehicle.

The consciousness does connect with the physical from the moment of conception, but in increasing intensity.

DIVINE

MONAD

ATMIC

BUDDHIC

MENTAL

ASTRAL

Subtle Bodies
(Bands of energy that surround and interpenetrate the physical.)

The Incarnational Process

The *etheric body* is the densest of the subtle bodies and is usually considered part of the physical body. It vitalizes, energizes and protects the physical vehicle. It aids in integrating our more subtle, spiritual energies with the physical body and with the energy field of the Earth, enabling us to operate more fully and more consciously in physical life. Because the astral interpenetrates all matter, feelings and emotions have a direct effect upon the physical body. The mental body's energies—although they also interpenetrate—have the greatest effect upon the etheric part of physical existence. We have mental matter or energy in rhythm within us, which is how, for example, thoughts affect our health. Although affected by the astral, it is the mental energies that stimulate the astral to create an effect upon the etheric and physical body. Our thinking creates emotions. Our thoughts and feelings while in the physical are nearly inseparable.

The etheric forms around the physical anytime between birth and puberty, most often between the ages of four and eight. Until it forms entirely, the astral plane plays directly upon us. It is not filtered out. It is for this reason that many of the so-called "imaginary" playmates of children are not really so "imaginary" after all. That plane of existence has not been filtered out. Until the etheric forms, the child is still drawing energy more directly from the more ethereal realms—and continues to do so until it is able to focus upon the physical life. Once formed, it anchors the consciousness to the physical, because this is where it needs to be focused to learn and do what it came to do during this incarnation. It filters out the play of other more subtle energies from the physical.

As we grow and mature, we again try to reopen our energies to the more subtle realms. We begin the process of extending our consciousness back through the etheric to activate the energies operating on the astral, mental, etc. Lying between the etheric and the astral bands of energy is what is often called an atomic shield, a thin layer of atoms that filter astral energies from physical consciousness. Because the astral can be so strongly affective upon our being, this shield serves as a filter for most of the strongest feelings and emotions that could play upon us.

When we begin the process of development, we try to loosen the shield, stretching it for more flexibility in order to stretch our consciousness beyond it to the astral and further. This needs to be done carefully. It is comparable to warming up before any strenuous exercise, preventing injury. If the shield becomes torn or bruised or

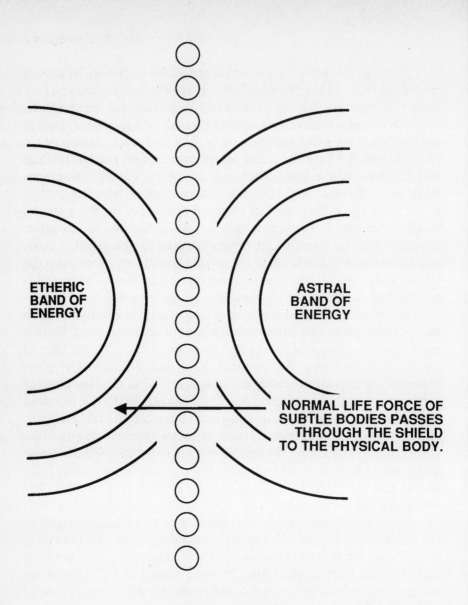

ETHERIC
BAND OF
ENERGY

ASTRAL
BAND OF
ENERGY

NORMAL LIFE FORCE OF
SUBTLE BODIES PASSES
THROUGH THE SHIELD
TO THE PHYSICAL BODY.

The Atomic Shield

Lying between the etheric band of the physical body and the astral body is a thin shield. Because the astral can so strongly affect us, the shield serves as a filter for the strongest emotions and feelings that could play upon us. Stress, poor health, emotional/mental trauma, or premature psychic development can wear it down, tear it or puncture it, resulting in a variety of problems.

injured due to a lack of "warming up" or preparation it opens us to a continual influence by astral-plane energies which we cannot necessarily prevent. This brings back the reason for the two stages discussed earlier in activating astral energies. First, there *must* be an energizing in a controlled and directed manner. Stress, poor physical health, emotional and mental trauma, premature psychic development, abuse of drugs or alcohol, etc. can wear this shield down, tear it, or puncture it, resulting in a variety of physical, emotional, and spiritual problems.

The exercises and tools within this work and in its predecessor enable one to develop greater flexibility and control of our psychic and spiritual muscles. The symbols and images that will be discussed may seem complex, but we must keep in mind that the Qabala is a technique for life animation upon all levels. By following a specific course, we can rediscover the universe. The images and symbols enable us to build up correspondences between all levels of our consciousness. At first, working with them may seem tiresome, but as we use them, they become automatic and work for us. They become our guides and our shields, helping us to make our discoveries and use them with the greatest safety.

The Astral Doorways

The ancient Qabalists knew that if someone tried to explore the subtler dimensions, he or she could open him/herself to a wide barrage of energies that might not be controlled. They explored the universe in a directed manner, using the Tree of Life diagram as their map. They applied specific images to the map as road markers that led from one level of consciousness to the next, assisting the individual in finding his or her way. The images, the symbols and the colors all help the spiritual explorer in several ways:

1. They prevent our getting lost among the subtleties and ever-changing energies of the astral plane.
2. Familiarity with the symbols and images and their particular correspondences creates a built-in safety line to ground us and bring us back to our normal state of consciousness. This is particularly important when we encounter our fears or become lost, or when we are not yet prepared to face whatever may lie ahead upon the path.
3. They help us to clear the pathways between the different

levels of our consciousness, so that there can be an open flow into our normal, waking consciousness that can be turned off and on at will. It is comparable to cleaning out clogged pipes. Our own pipes may be stopped up with misconceptions, misinformations, fears, doubts, limitations (self-imposed and otherwise), etc. By working with the various symbols and images associated with the Tree, we shake loose the debris—the dead limbs and leaves—to restore to the Tree greater freedom to stretch and grow fuller and taller. We open the flow from one level of our consciousness to another in a controlled and directed manner.

Many times our spiritual "muscles," just like our physical muscles, will atrophy if we do not use them. The symbols and images serve to exercise our spiritual muscles, stirring up the circulation of energy, stretching them and strengthening them. They restore the flow of blood, so we can begin to use these spiritual muscles once again.

4. The images and symbols also help us to access specific forces and energies within ourselves and the universe. They open doors to ever-deepening levels of consciousness. The images, symbols, colors, etc. are all ways of controlling specific aspects and manifestations of this energy within our lives.

The techniques in this work enable one to access the various levels of our consciousness as delineated in the Tree of Life. They are geared to bridging all of the levels of consciousness to each other and to our normal, waking consciousness. In order to utilize the techniques, it is necessary to familiarize oneself with the basic symbols of the sephiroth, as well as the symbols and images that can be used to bridge them, i.e., the paths on the Tree. It is also necessary to understand how they operate, so we can use them to our greatest benefit.

At first the symbols and images may seem too intricate and complicated, there being so many symbols associated with the energies of the Tree of Life. The initial work may seem cumbersome. This is why this work focuses predominantly on the more basic symbols which reflect the energies of the levels of our consciousness and the paths that link them together. Eventually, their use will grow and their correspondences to each other will increase, and then the Qabala itself will become the teacher to you. It will show you and teach you aspects of the universe beyond any physical teaching, but for that point to be reached, initial preparation and practice are necessary. We must learn to use the symbols and images we do know to begin energizing ourselves, so that when the time arrives for even greater perception and learning to be released to us, we will be able to handle it without short-circuiting ourselves in the process.

Symbology is the language of the unconscious; each of us at some time will need to learn more about it and how to use it to our fullest capability. If we intend to step out on the path of controlled and higher evolution, we must become aware of the power and significance of symbols within all aspects of our life and being.

To understand symbols is to understand ourselves—including our deep-rooted and instinctive actions and capabilities. It helps us to understand what our beliefs, superstitions and fears are based upon. Symbols open up to us levels of our being that we have either ignored or been unaware of. Symbols form the bridge that enables us to cross from the rational to the progressive and intuitive levels of our being. Symbols lead us from the limited regions of the conscious mind to the unlimited regions of the subconscious mind. Learning to use them is necessary if we intend to become more active in utilizing all of our capacities. We all receive symbols through our dreams. We are the receiver of the communication, but communication is receiving *and* sending. We must also learn to send to the subconscious, and for this to occur we must learn to use specific symbols and images for specific responses. This is what the Qabala teaches us to do.

Symbols like the Tree of Life operate on many levels: mundane or physical, the emotional or astral, the mental and the spiritual. We must learn to use them accordingly. By starting and learning to work with them from the astral level—that level closest to our normal waking consciousness—we can eventually extend their usages to their ultimate and truest energy form—*the archetype.* The archetype is the primordial source of the symbol. It is the energy, the true, pure energy that the symbol or image only reflects. This is similar to the way the Moon only reflects the light of the Sun. In and of itself, the Moon is not a source of light, but its ability to reflect enables us to see more clearly at night.

Symbols take the abstract, pure archetypal energy and manifest it to us through the image. Ultimately it will lead us back to its source. It leads us back to *our* source. It helps us to merge the finite with the infinite.

Symbols and images can have universal meanings and reflections,

The Basic Archetypes of Carl Jung

Archetypes	Characteristics and Symbols of Archetypes
Self	• deals with energy of the ego/individual • sacred symbols include temples, homes, books, star, egg, weeds, lit candle, births, gifts, weddings
Feminine	• in life and pathworking, this energy creates relationships, flow, beauty, birth, receptivity and acceptance • symbols include vessel, cave, womb, queen, doorway, priestess, wells, moon, veil, scabbard ...
Masculine	• in life, it deals with fathering, making, directing, organizing, building, active and assertive, penetrating; it initiates • symbols include kings, unicorns, phallus, sun, sceptre, sword, tools ...
Heroic	• deals with facing difficulties and the insurmountable, conquers, heals, etc. • symbols include battles, struggles, teachers and new knowledge, youth, shields, healing balms ...
Adversary	• "All is Change," the agent of change, destroys or wounds what is, brings unexpected, tearing down of old, uses anger, morose ... • symbols include monsters, tyrants, beasts, demons, suffering, walls and the abyss ...
Death/ Rebirth (Transition)	• deals with the end of one and beginning of another, crisis, change bringing sacrifice and new life ... • symbols: Solstice and Equinoxes, rite of initiation, altar, clock, dance, prayers ...
Journey	• deals with movement forward, development, aging, building on previous, new directions • symbols include Tree of Life, winding roads, ascent upward, mountains, staff, guides, rivers, streams, vacations, pilgrimages ...

but with most symbols each individual will place his or her own particular twist on its use and interpretation. Each individual has his or her own unique energy field, and thus the symbol must be utilized in a somewhat unique manner for it to be truly effective, especially when beginning to use it. As we learn to work with them we draw closer to their more pure form, and there occurs a growing realization that the particular twist we each applied will ultimately result in a more universal and united application. Thus a wide variety of images and symbols will lead back to a particular archetypal energy that had been reflected within them all. For example, a doorway, a womb, the Moon, a scabbard are all different symbols but reflect the energies of the same *archetype*—the feminine energy of the universe. (Refer to the chart on page 86 for a list of basic archetypes.)

The symbols and images touch both the objective and subjective realities of the individual. They are a way in which the subconscious can objectively bring forth information to the rational mind that might otherwise not discern it. They are also a way the rational mind can communicate with the subjective world of the subconscious. In other words, the symbol and image is an attempt by the subconscious to convey information and directions to our conscious mind and a way for our conscious mind to convey directions to the subconscious.

Sometimes as we go through life, we tend to form our own realities and we allow our energies to adjust and to become complacent. This complacency, which often manifests through our convictions and opinions, keeps us from thinking and developing fully. We can use symbols of intensity to shake this complacency. This is why symbols change as we grow. We need stronger symbols to shake deeply ingrained forms of complacency and non-movement within our lives. As a child, a snake may signify something to be afraid of, but as we evolve and expand our awareness, we can understand that it is a powerful universal symbol of knowledge and higher initiation.

Symbols span the world of thought and the world of being—the mental and physical bodies. Symbols form the bridge between them. They provide the means of communicating with the true world of hidden realities within us. Symbols express what we have no words for. By being willing to work over them and with them, we utilize both sides of the brain and more fully tap our subconscious, which opens all of the doorways to our intuitive self.

Dreams, scriptures, and myths all contain common meanings based upon their symbols, but there are also other places and forms of symbology. Numerology, astrology, graphics, color geometry, and letters all contain symbology of higher inner energies and truths. By looking beyond the obvious and learning to consciously work with set symbols, we open our mind and the doors to other levels of consciousness. Symbols are the keys to the doors of the temples within the Tree of Life. They are the lamps which shine upon the paths between the inner temples. All we need do is learn to use them, and the universe becomes our own!

Inner Temples of the Tree	Colors of the Temples
Temple of Malkuth	Citrine, Olive, Russet & Black
Temple of Yesod	Purple
Temple of Hod	Orange
Temple of Netzach	Green
Temple of Tiphareth	Yellow/Gold
Temple of Geburah	Red
Temple of Chesed	Blue
Temple of Binah	Black
Temple of Chokmah	Gray
Temple of Kether	White

In working with the Tree of Life, we are consciously learning how to use specific symbols and how to tap the energies represented and reflected through the symbol. Each of the sephiroth—each level of consciousness—is a temple in which specific energies and potentials are available to us. Those energies are translated into our consciousness through symbols. They are reflected through the color vibration, names, letters, tarot associations, and astrological relationships—all of which helps us to understand the energy and to focus and direct it more consciously. We are taking an "intangible" expression of energy within us and giving it a tangible representation through the symbol and its reflections (correspondences), so we can focus and utilize it more effectively.

The symbols for the paths that connect the different levels of our consciousness activate the energy to clear the debris from the path. This increases the flow between and the interaction of the various levels of our consciousness. It is not enough to just activate energies at the various levels of our consciousness. We have to link them all, get them so they are working together. To do this, we must keep in mind that although we initially treat them as separate, distinct levels of

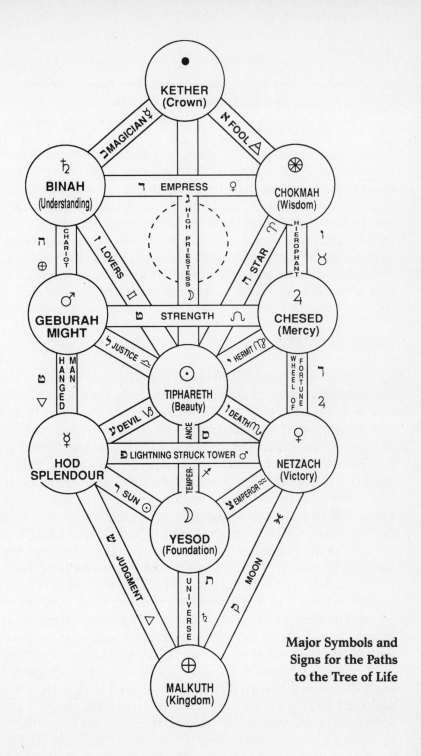

Major Symbols and
Signs for the Paths
to the Tree of Life

consciousness, they are simply different functions or expressions of the same energy and consciousness.

The symbols are reflections of more archetypal energies, and thus they serve to stir up our energies and set them in motion so that we can learn to use them all. Along this same line we can look at the sephiroth as the storehouses of our potentials, and the paths as the generators for setting that energy in motion and into expression. As one continues to work with the exercises within this book, that energy is set in motion to clean out the channels between the various levels, point out where the bridges need to be repaired, and manifest in a myriad of ways according to how we utilize the symbols. The symbols in essence are the tools that we use to build irrigation channels to fertilize and water all aspects of our consciousness.

IMAGICK TECHNIQUE: Opening the Doors

This exercise sets the energy so that when we involve the more intricate techniques of an entire pathworking (as described in the next two chapters), they will be more easily accomplished. This exercise helps in the visualization and creative imagination to activate the energies of the symbols associated with paths to the Tree of Life.

All of the paths connect two levels of consciousness. Thus there must be a door exiting one level and opening into the next, from bottom to top or top to bottom. Eventually we have to be able to walk the paths—to activate the energies in both directions. This exercise enables one to use the symbols to create "astral doorways," to open the doors and to close the doors behind us. In the following chapters we will learn specific techniques for exploring the paths and activating the energies between the two levels of consciousness. This is also a good technique to begin to learn about the basic symbols themselves. The more we know about the symbols and what energies they reflect, the more they can work for us. The diagram on the previous page shows the basic symbols for the paths and doorways from one level of consciousness to the next. On the next three pages are the energies and symbols traditionally associated with each of the 22 paths connecting the sephiroth. We will use these symbols and associations to open the entire Tree of Life to us in the rest of the book. Familiarizing oneself with these before the actual pathworking will enable you to achieve better results. It is for this reason that basic

PATHWORKING ENERGIES AND SYMBOLS

Path	Sephiroth Linked	Virtues & Vices of the Linked Sephiroth	Energy as a Color	Hebrew Letter	Astrology	Tarot Card	Magickal Tool of The Path
32	Malkuth to Yesod	Discrimination & Independence/ Avarice & Idleness	Indigo/ Black	ת TAU the cross	♄ Saturn	The World	The T-cross, a cauldron, a girdle.
31	Malkuth to Hod	Discrimination & Truth/ Avarice & Dishonesty	Orange Scarlet	ש SHIN tooth	△ Primal Fire	Judgement	Flint and steel.
30	Yesod to Hod	Independence & Truth/ Idleness & Dishonesty	Orange	ר RESH head	☉ Sun	The Sun	All solar symbols; lion; sparrowhawk.
29	Malkuth to Netzach	Discrimination & Unselfishness/ Avarice & Lust, Impurity	Crimson	ק QOPH back of head	♓ Pisces	The Moon	The scarab or the beetle; dolphin.
28	Yesod to Netzach	Independence & Unselfishness/ Idleness & Lust/Impurity	Violet	צ TZADDI fishhook	♒ Aquarius	The Emperor or Star	Cup; grail; a star; the apple; the eagle.
27	Hod to Netzach	Truth & Unselfishness/ Dishonesty & Lust, Impure	Scarlet	פ PEH mouth	♂ Mars	The Tower	Lightning; wolf; bear; rubies.
26	Hod to Tiphareth	Truth & Devotion to the Great Work/ Dishonesty & False Pride	Indigo	ע AYIN eye	♑ Capricorn	The Devil	Yoni and lingam; goat and the ass.
25	Yesod to Tiphareth	Independence & Devotion to the Great Work/ Idleness & False Pride	Blue	ס SAMECH prop	♐ Sagittarius	Temperance	Rainbow; bridge; bow and arrow; the centaur.

PATHWORKING ENERGIES AND SYMBOLS

Path	Sephiroth Linked	Virtues & Vices of the Linked Sephiroth	Energy as a Color	Hebrew Letter	Astrology	Tarot Card	Magickal Tools of The Path
24	Netzach to Tiphareth	Unselfishness & Devotion to Great Work/ Lust, Impurity & False Pride	Green/ Blue	נ NUN fish	♏ Scorpio	Death	Scarab; death boats; stinging insects & plants to soaring eagles.
23	Hod to Geburah	Truth & Energy & Courage/ Dishonesty & Cruelty	Deep Blue	מ MEM water	▽ Primal Water	The Hanged Man	Cup & sacramental wine; clay pot; asbestos.
22	Tiphareth to Geburah	Devotion to Great Work & Energy & Courage/ False Pride & Cruelty	Emerald Green	ל LAMED ox goad	♎ Libra	Justice	Scales; single feather; spider & elephant.
21	Netzach to Chesed	Unselfishness & Obedience/ Lust & Impurity & Pride and Hypocrisy	Violet	כ KAPH palm of hand	♃ Jupiter	Wheel of Fortune	The open hand; Grail; the Fleece; all quests.
20	Tiphareth to Chesed	Devotion to Great Work & Obedience/ False Pride & Hypocrisy	Yellow	י YOD hand	♍ Virgo	The Hermit	Wand; Lamp; Eucharistic host;
19	Geburah to Chesed	Energy & Courage & Obedience/Cruelty & Pride & Hypocrisy	Greenish Yellow	ט TETH serpent	♌ Leo	Strength	Lion and serpent; vinegar wine; cup of bitters.
18	Geburah to Binah	Energy & Courage & Silence/ Cruelty & Avarice	Amber	ח CHETH fence	♋ Cancer	Chariot	Silver star; the sphinx; chariots;
17	Tiphareth to Binah	Devotion to Great Work & Silence/ False Pride & Avarice	Orange	ז ZAIN sword	♊ Gemini	Lovers	Doubled-edged sword; woman crowned with stars; whale; girdle.

PATHWORKING ENERGIES AND SYMBOLS

Path	Sephiroth Linked	Virtues & Vices of the Linked Sephiroth	Energy as a Color	Hebrew Letter	Astrology	Tarot Card	Magickal Tools of The Path
16	Chesed to Chokmah	Obedience & Devotion/ Pride and Hypocrisy	Red Orange	VAU nail	♉ Taurus	Hiero-phant	Wand; phallus; dove; weddings; bull.
15	Tiphareth to Chokmah	Devotion to Great Work & Pure Devotion/ False Pride	Scarlet	HEH window	♈ Aries	The Star or the Emperor	The spear; solar symbols; stars; chalice; hawk.
14	Binah to Chokmah	Silence & Devotion/ Avarice	Emerald Green	DALETH door	♀ Venus	Empress	Girdle; full moon; equal-armed cross; egg; dove
13	Tiphareth to Kether	Devotion to Great Work & Completion of Great Work/ False Pride	Blue	GIMEL camel	☽ Moon	High Priest	The moon; bow and arrow; silver; the dog.
12	Binah to Kether	Silence & Completion of the Great Work/ Avarice	Yellow	BETH house	☿ Mercury	The Magician	Caduceus; Ibis; all-seeing eye; sword, cup, wand & pentacle.
11	Chokmah to Kether	Devotion & Completion of the Great Work/ (No vices)	Bright Pale Yellow	ALEPH ox	△ Primal Air	The Fool	The fan; hat with one feather; staff and a rose; nakedness.

knowledge of the Hebrew alphabet (the letters and their meaning), astrology and the tarot will help. Every student of the Qabala should become familiar with the tarot cards, if only as an aid to meditation and as a tool for releasing energies from the Tree of Life. These basic symbols are what will become the astral doorways to exploring the Tree of Life and making it active within your own life.

PRELIMINARIES:
1. Find a comfortable place where you will be undisturbed.
2. Choose the two sephiroth (the two levels of consciousness) that you wish to bridge. Initially, it is recommended that you work from the bottom up, following the order given on pages 91 to 93. Once the entire Tree has been worked and you are familiar with the process and its effects, then you can "mix and match" according to your own desires.
3. Familiarize yourself with the colors of the Temples of Consciousness that you will be bridging. Use the chart on page 88.
4. Using the charts on pages 91 to 93, familiarize yourself with the Virtues and Vices and the symbols associated with the path that links the two levels of consciousness.
5. Light a candle the color of each of the two sephiroth. Light the incense from one or both of the sephiroth as well. Use the chart on page 95 as a guide. The candles and the incense will set up a vibration in the area that will facilitate a triggering of the energies from the two levels of consciousness. This will make it easier to bridge them.

    Some fragrances won't seem to blend well together. This varies from individual to individual and from time to time. When they do not, it is significant. They are simply telling you that some levels of your consciousness are more difficult to bring into harmony than others. As we work more and more with them, the mixed vibrations of the different levels will become less discordant.
6. Close your eyes to eliminate visual distractions.
7. Make sure the phone is off the hook and eliminate any auditory disturbances or distractions.
8. Do a progressive relaxation. Focus on each part of your body from head to toe and back again, feeling and imagining warm, relaxing feelings filling that part.

9. Take time to develop the visualizations of this exercise so that the astral doorways can be effectively used throughout the rest of this work and your life. Visualize, imagine, taste, touch, smell, hear and feel everything! Focus only upon the images or ideas within the exercise. These are the warm-ups. They loosen the "spiritual" muscles for the great work to come.

    The exercise for the astral doorways should not take longer than 20 to 30 minutes. Do not get upset if the mind wanders. Just bring your attention back to the image you are supposed to be focusing upon. Remember that we are training the subconscious to work for us and to focus its energies upon what we want. You may have to repeat this, but each time, you train the subconscious to follow your directions and your will even more fully. This will develop the ability to form, empower and then dissolve images and the energies of the archetype to which they are linked.

10. The following exercise and those that follow within this book work with any two sephiroth, although the sample is ostensibly for Malkuth and Yesod. We will start in Malkuth, learn to open the astral door to Yesod, but we must also learn to start in Yesod and open the door as it leads to

Candle and Fragrance Stimulants

Sephira	Candle	Fragrances
Kether	White	Frankincense, Ambergris
Chokmah	Gray	Eucalyptus, Musk, Geranium
Binah	Black	Myrrh, Chamomile
Chesed	Blue	Bayberry, Cedar, Nutmeg
Geburah	Red	Cypress, Pine, Tobacco, Gardenia
Tiphareth	Yellow	Rose, Jasmine, Lily
Netzach	Green	Rose, Patchouli, Bayberry
Hod	Orange	Rosemary, Frangipani, Wisteria
Yesod	Violet	Lavender, Myrtle, Honeysuckle
Malkuth	Citrine, Olive, Russet, Black	Sandalwood, Lemon, Carnation

A greater elaboration of how these work and how they can be used to more fully activate the energies within these levels of our consciousness can be found in Simplified Magic: The Beginner's Guide to the New Age Qabala.

Malkuth. Energy ascends and descends and we must learn to work with it in both of its manifestations. Everything on the astral is polarized. We must also learn to start in Malkuth, go to Yesod and then return to Malkuth. Each way opens the flow of energy into manifestation with its own intensity. This is why it is important to learn to use the symbols as astral doorways!

Creating the Astral Doorways

We begin as always outside the Tree of Life. The guardian raises up to block the entrance and demands to know what you seek. Although you expect this, the energy and the power of the beast still intimidates. In spite of what you feel, you show no fear, and you speak the words that permit entrance.

You step through the small opening and into the darkness of the Tree. The feelings are warm and familiar. This is your Tree. There is nothing within it that can harm you as long as you do not give in to your own doubts and fears. Your eyes adjust, and the room lightens.

In the center is the stone altar sitting between the two stone pillars. Upon the altar sits the familiar bowl of water, the plate of salt, the flint and the fan. On the floor are the baskets, overflowing as before. Burned into the altar are the words that burned into your heart. You know you are in the temple of Malkuth. You know you are home.

Suddenly, the sound of stone grinding against stone fills the temple. It penetrates you like fingernails across a blackboard. You turn to see the entrance closing behind you, sealing you into the Temple. For a moment you panic, frightened, but then you remember that this temple is yours. If it opened once, it can open again. You relax yourself and then you intone, slowly—reverently:

"ADONAI HA-ARETZ!"

The Temple turns black. You intone the name again, "ADONAI HA-ARETZ!"

The color shifts from black to an olive green. You intone the name a third time, and the temple color shifts for the third time. The room is filled with a golden citrine light.

You intone the name one more time, and the citrine shifts, melting into a beautiful shade of russet. From behind the altar steps a young woman, crowned as if stepping down from a throne. About her is the fragrance of new-mown hay, of summer innocence. There is an air of confidence, as if the entire world belongs to her. The world and all its treasures are her inheritance.

She smiles and says, "All that you need to move anywhere within the Tree has been given to you. Knowing and doing are separate; they must be brought together if understanding is to come forth."

She steps back from the altar and fades from sight as if melting through the walls. It is then that you remember the symbols that open the paths, leading to the other levels within the Tree. Yesod is closest to Malkuth. It runs straight up the Middle Pillar of the Tree from Malkuth. You pause, bringing to mind the symbols governing that path. You draw to mind the Hebrew letter Tau. You visualize it, projecting its image against the back wall. You see the energy flowing; it is like heat rising off the street on a hot summer day.

It stops.

You must concentrate harder. Again you visualize it, as if it is carved into the wall itself. It begins to take form. It grows in clarity, and as it stands out upon the wall, a door forms around it! As you hold the focus upon that newly formed door and the symbol which created it, it swings open. Through the open doorway, you see the path that will lead to the Temple of Yesod. It is a crystalline indigo shade. You smile, thrilled by the accomplishment.

Mentally, you close the door and allow it and the Hebrew letter to fade, until the wall again is visible.

Next, you visualize the astrological sign for Saturn. You project it onto the wall, focusing until it stands out in perfect clarity. When fully formed, the door manifests around it and swings open to reveal that same crystalline indigo path leading to Yesod. You close the door and dissolve the image.

This time you visualize the tarot card associated with the path. You begin to visualize it as a life-sized painting upon the wall. It is the World card. As you focus, it shimmers, melting into the wall itself. It takes on three-dimensional proportions. You could step up to it and just walk into the scenery of the card itself.

You know you have found the doorway to the path leading from Malkuth to Yesod. You dissolve the picture mentally, knowing now that you can recreate it at any time. You now understand the way to open the doorways to all of the paths and the temples. You understand the words of the young woman now. You understand that with practice it will become even easier to use any and all of the symbols.

You look around the Temple of Malkuth, and you see that there is still no doorway out of the Tree. It is still sealed. You are puzzled. You know the symbols and images that will open the doors to the other levels of consciousness within the Tree, and which you can use to exit the Tree to return to your normal state of consciousness. Maybe the God-name again?

You step up to the altar. You pause, take a deep breath and intone the God-name once more. The bowl of water begins to bubble. You look down into it; it is like looking into a deep well. The water settles, and an image takes form at the bottom. It is simple. It is personal. For some it is a color, for others a flower or even a geometric shape. It can be a design of anything. And as you look upon this image, you begin to understand why you have been drawn to it throughout your entire life.

The image fades, and you turn to face the wall where the entrance in the Tree used to be. You visualize this symbol against that wall. As it takes shape, becoming more distinct, the wall opens up, allowing you to exit the Tree of Life. You step outside, amazed. The guardian rests peacefully. You turn to face the Tree. You see your personal symbol upon the doorway to the Tree.

This is your image, your personal symbol of power for the astral plane. It is what will provide protection. If ever lost or confused while doing any work within the Tree this symbol will create a doorway that will allow you to exit safely. It will allow you to return to your normal state of consciousness. It is a private symbol of power for you and you alone. The more you learn about it and use it, the more it will do for you. As you understand this, you close the door and dissolve the image. You draw that symbol back inside of you, into your heart, and you return to your normal state of consciousness.

This technique of learning to create the astral doorways should be practiced for each level and each path. It can even be done as a prelude to the actual pathworkings described later. It will help empower them and manifest even stronger effects. We should enter into the Tree—into *each* individual sephira—and practice forming *all* doors that lead to the other sephiroth from it. This practice serves a two-fold purpose:

1. It demonstrates that we can, through the symbols, open the doors that lead to every other level of consciousness. We have the capability of opening and closing the astral door-

ways in a controlled and concentrated manner.

2. It manifests our own individual and creative power symbol for protection and balance. It becomes our personal totem to serve us while working with the energies of the Tree, especially on the astral level. As we grow and expand our consciousness, this symbol may change from time to time. Usually this happens when it is time to work with the energies of the Tree on a much higher level than we have done previously.

Empowering the Magickal Body

One of the greatest benefits in working with the Tree of Life is the manifestation of the "magickal body." This "magickal body" is the new, more conscious you that is created through the work. When we work with the Tree of Life, we are bringing to life the energies inherent and yet unexpressed within us. We use the Tree to awaken into expression our higher, more powerful selves.

Each sephira reflects specific energies that can become a manifest part of our reality and essence on any plane of existence, physical or otherwise. When we work with the sephiroth, we awaken the innate energies of ourselves and begin to manifest them within our life. For some, the release of such internal abilities and capacities is very subtle, but for others it is quite apparent. If we are to more effectively empower our essence, we need to become more cognizant of this process. Again, the Law of Correspondence is reflected within this. If we do anything on one level it will affect us on others. What we are trying to do with the techniques within this book is more consciously bring to life those aspects of ourselves that we wish, dream, hope and *can* manifest.

The magickal body is the ideal you, with the capability of manifesting and appearing in the manner that to you is the most powerful and effective for your life. We assume the manners and powers that are necessary for whatever the task may be. But in order to do so we must first have energies, abilities and powers to assume. We are *creating* a new *you*—we are *not* changing the old. This must be kept in mind at all times. We need to turn our focus to the image of the ideal within you—physically, mentally, spiritually. We want this image to be strong and vital.

The formation of the magickal body begins with the formation of the imagickal body. What is the highest, brightest, most creative image of yourself that you can create? What characteristics could you have? What abilities and energies would you be able to express? How would you ideally like others to see you? How would being that way change your life at home and at work? If you could manifest those abilities now, what are some ways that you could use them so that no one would ever know? How would you be able to help others without them ever knowing? Imagine it, envision it, know that it can be real. *Remember that if we can imagine it, it can be! When you change your imaginings, you change your world!*

All energy follows thought. This occult axiom is very important to the formation of the magickal body. Form follows idea. Thus, thought and images create the energy matrix or blueprint by which the form will manifest within your life:

1. Visualize exactly what it is you wish to be, with all of its variations and in as much detail as possible and *as if you are already it.* Do this especially at the end of each imagickal pathworking and exercise.
2. Do whatever is necessary in the physical to help it along. Act according to the way you have imagined. The key to magick is being who you truly are. Our magickal essence is a reflection of our higher, truer essence.
3. Stay relaxed during the visualization.
4. *Use the sacred power in your name to accelerate the manifestation!* Our individual names contain much power, and if we come to know and use them properly, we can discover much about our soul's purposes and how to release our spiritual energies more strongly into our physical lives. One of the great mystical secrets of the essence of man lies hidden within his or her name. The meaning, the sounds, the rhythms, the nature of the letters and their combinations all hold secrets about an individual's essence—past/present and spiritual/physical. Our potential creativity is reflected within the name we have chosen for this lifetime.

   Our Christian name (first name) is the most powerful. It gives the identifying, creative essence of the soul. The family name or surname indicates energies inherited from our ancestors. Together they reflect the motives, knowledge, creativity and potentials we have come to awaken and use to walk this life's path.

One powerful technique using one's name to amplify the energies of the magickal body is combining the name, its meaning, and a God-name from the Tree of Life in an affirmation:

a. Take your first name and look up its meaning. (Example: Lisa = "consecrated one.")

b. Attach an "I AM" phrase to the name and its meaning: "I AM LISA. I AM THE CONSECRATED ONE OF GOD." The first name reflects your basic energy pattern (your most creative aspect). The "I AM" phrase is related to the highest divine aspect within ourselves and within the Tree of Life. The God-name for Kether at the top of the Tree is EHEIEH, which translates to "I AM THAT I AM." When we use our name and its meaning with this, we are aligning our essence with that aspect of the Divine which operates at that level. Using one's name and its meaning in an "I AM" affirmation is strengthening, energizing and protective, and it releases inherent creativity and power into one's life. It balances and heals. It re-establishes the link between the you in your physical life and the divine part of you that is a part of all energies and light within the universe.

When we add this affirmation to the visualization for the magickal body, we release tremendous power for manifesting it more strongly. Our name becomes part of what can be called "words of power." The ancients understood that to "know the name of anything was to have power over it," but this meant knowing all aspects of that name. Working with our name in this manner—especially in conjunction with the creation of the magickal body—will release that sacred power inherent within our essence. It will release the unseen spiritual force within.

When we use visualization, imagination and words of power, we take advantage of the creative energies of all realms of the universe. We use the mental realm, and we ground it into the physical through the vocalizations. This enables us to ground the ethereal energies much more fully into our physical life. We are learning to work between the visible and the invisible, the spiritual and the physical.

We utilize both; we use creative imagination and sound to draw forth and focus energy from the invisible realm to manifest within the visible one. We are in essence learning to work between all worlds so that we can live more fully in this one.

The amount of energy available to each of us is limited by our capacity for realization. If we increase our awareness, at the same time removing our inhibitions and limitations, we increase our intake and access of cosmic energy. Whatever we are or are becoming is intensified. *Every aspect of our nature is intensified!*

We are physical beings. This means our primary focus should be within the physical world, but we can use other dimensions and levels of consciousness to create more productivity within our physical lives. If we are to use other levels of consciousness for our betterment, then we need to learn to transform the energy of the inner realms to the outer. It is the magickal body that can assist us in this. With each touching of the sephiroth, we release energy that assists in the molding and creating of your ideal self—the true magickal you. This magickal body is a reflection of the divine god or goddess that is inherent within you.

Associated with the sephiroth and with each level of consciousness is a magickal image. This magickal image is a tremendously powerful thought form that has been created through constant work on the Tree of Life. Learning methods of tapping these thought forms will assist us in creating our own variations of energy that are reflected within these magickal images. We can in essence learn to assimilate these energies into ourselves and enable ourselves to more fully tap and utilize the energies of the sephiroth on spiritual and physical levels. These magickal images reflect on a much more "tangible" level the abstract energies that we access at each level of consciousness. They reflect how we an utilize them in our own life to create not just an ethereal "magickal body" but a very real "magickal being"!

One very simple technique for utilizing the magickal images in the creation of your own magickal body is through each individual sephirah. Using the methods previously discussed, enter into the Tree of Life and into the sphere within the Tree that you have chosen. As the inner temple becomes alive, allow the magickal image to step from behind the altar to speak to you. Allow the image to speak of what it reflects about the energies at that level of the Tree and at that level within your own consciousness. Let it explain how you can manifest the same energies in your own unique manner. Let the image teach

TABLE OF MAGICKAL IMAGES IN THE TREE OF LIFE

Sephira	Magickal Image	Magickal Gift
KETHER	Ancient, bearded king, seen only in profile	Spinning Top
CHOKMAH	Bearded male figure	Sceptre of Power
BINAH	Mature woman; matron	Cloak of Concealment
CHESED	Mighty, crowned and throned king	King's Cup
GEBURAH	Mighty warrior in his chariot	Sword
TIPHARETH	Majestic king; sacrificed god; a child	Crown that is too large
NETZACH	Beautiful, naked woman	A Rose
HOD	Hermaphrodite	Caduceus pendant
YESOD	Beautiful naked man, very strong	Silver slippers and a mirror
MALKUTH	Young woman, crowned and throned	Corn

you how it has operated and been used by you—positively and negatively—in the past, consciously and unconsciously. Let this wonderfully powerful form show you how to use its energies to amplify your own, so that you can create your own magickal body. Remember that we use specific images to trigger levels of consciousness, but only so we can awaken our own highest essence—initially to create a magickal body, but ultimately to create the magickal being!

After the teaching has occurred, allow the image to step forward. Feel it melt over you and into you. Feel yourself becoming one with the image, inseparable. You become the image. It becomes strengthened in you and by you, for you. It infuses you, adding to your repertoire of magickal energy. In essence it is simply another reflection of yourself that you are merely leaving to reintegrate back into your life. Then as you leave the sephirothic temple and the Tree, know that you carry this image and all of its powers and energies permanently with you. You can awaken it at any time, simply by relaxing and seeing your outer self melt away and the inner magickal self manifesting to the outer world.

You are learning to become the Alchemist—the master shape-shifter! If the need arrives to use the energies associated with this image and the level of your consciousness that it reflects, all one need do is relax and visualize that image coming to life, melting over into the physical. This technique is especially effective when applied to the dances for the Tree of Life as described in chapter 6 of this work. It will enhance the power of the movement, giving it greater life, energy and magic, bringing their energies into manifestation within the physical realm much more quickly and powerfully. We all adapt ourselves, according to situations and people, every day of our lives; but with the magickal image we are learning to shape-shift more consciously, more powerfully and so much more effectively than we could ever do otherwise. Since all life situations can fall under the "rule" of one or more of the sephiroth, we can learn to transmute all situations, by controlling our own energies in relation to them. We need only practice assuming and shifting our shapes—calling forth our magickal essence into play in an otherwise seemingly magickal world. And that is when we truly become alive!

IMAGICKAL TECHNIQUE: Empowering the Magickal Essence

As always, we must face the guardian before we can enter the Tree. Today it is different. The door is no longer opened for you. You must use your own personal symbol to open the door for yourself. This is a positive sign. It is your signal that you are becoming stronger and more responsible for your own growth. All are invited to enter the Mysteries at some point within their lives. All invitations include an open door. Those who have chosen to explore further the inner

Mysteries and who have earned their acceptance and entrance are no longer guests. They are workers within the Mystery system.

You are now a worker within the Mysteries. You must now open and close your own doors. It is part of the training. It is part of the responsibility.

You focus your personal symbol upon the trunk of the Tree, and the door forms around it. You enter, closing the door behind you. You smile, exhilarated. You have been accepted. You are no longer a mere guest or visitor. You are a full student of the inner Mysteries!

You step into the inner room, and the light comes up. The temple is familiar now, and you smile. No longer is there the fear you first experienced. We have not come as far as we often believe. Humanity still fears most what it cannot see.

The temple is as it was. The altar, the pillars, the baskets stand before you. Today the scent of sandalwood is strong within the temple. You breathe deeply, inhaling its fragrance. You close your eyes and you slowly intone the God-name ADONAI HA-ARETZ. Slowly, reverently, you repeat it three more times. You open your eyes; the temple is bright and warm. The statues surrounding the outer edges of the temple are much more distinct than when you first saw them. They are ten in all, nine of which have doors behind them. These are the doors to the other nine temples within the Tree of Life.

You stand before the altar and look upon the figure of that which stands directly behind. It is the statue of the young woman who assisted you in opening the astral doorways. As you look upon it, it shimmers into life and steps forward to you. It is a young woman, crowned and appearing as if she has just stepped off the royal throne. She smiles warmly and takes your hand in hers. She places a piece of bread within it and speaks.

"Eat of this bread. As in all foods, it will nourish you for the journeys ahead. As you eat, know that all you ever need to nourish your life is upon the Earth for you. Humanity is not meant to suffer and be without. Just as a prince or princess knows that he or she will inherit the kingdom, so too must you realize. To produce food, one must work, but there is always a harvest. It is not the finishing but the doing that leads to the harvest that holds the treasures of the kingdom to come."

As you place the bread within your mouth, her image shimmers, and as you swallow, she is drawn into you. You are filled with simple confidence, and her sense of royalty comes alive within you. You know that you will never be without again.

You close your eyes and mentally give thanks. As you open your eyes, you find standing before you a beautiful, naked man, strong and vibrant. He smiles with confidence at you. He kneels before you, and raising each of your feet in turn, he places silver sandals upon them. As he stands, he hands you a silver mirror, framed with intricate carvings of all the phases of the Moon.

"These sandals are so you can walk in all worlds and in all dimensions. They will keep your steps firm and steady, light and quick. They give you agility in all areas of your life. You will move with greater ease, greater transition and greater strength. The mirror is to see how all things reflect the energies of your life. There are no accidental stumblings. Everything has its cause and effects. All people, all situations reflect you and your energy in some way. Use the mirror of others to help you to know yourself. Use your world to understand and walk with confidence in all worlds!"

You test the sandals, raising up on your toes. You feel light, unbound. It is as if there is no gravity, and yet you are very much aware of the Earth beneath you. You thank the young man for the gifts, and he shimmers, melting into you. You glance into the mirror, and you see the image of this young man within you. You feel strong, independent, assured. As you continue to gaze into the mirror you see the young woman. It is then you understand that they are reflections of you. All will be reflected within you. You set the mirror upon the altar for those times when you need to see more clearly.

As you step back from the altar the third statue shimmers into life and steps forward. At first, it appears more masculine, but as it draws your eyes, you cannot be sure. Its cloak disguises its sex. Upon its forearms are copper bracelets of two intertwining snakes. Upon its orange cloak at the shoulders are embroidered wings. Its features are soft, its hair long and flowing, but its eyes speak of intelligence far beyond anything humanity has yet experienced. Before you stands one of the many forms of the hermaphrodite.

The figure smiles at your confusion. It takes your right hand with a quick movement of its own. It removes one bracelet of intertwining snakes and fits it securely about your forearm. Your forearm tingles. The metal feels alive—as if the snakes are alive.

"I am knowledge as you "know" it and as you do not "know" it. Knowledge is universal. It is neither male nor female. Nor is it for one or the other. Knowledge and truth is for all. Especially is it for you! No one has the right to deny you the truth. Truth is available to all who would seek it. Knowledge and knowing how to use it are two different things. Do not confuse them. One must understand how to use knowledge, when to use it, where to use it and to what degree. To ask the question is the first step to receiving the answer—the first step to awakening the magic of your true essence."

With a quick movement, he melts into you before you can even assimilate what was said.

Before you now stands a beautiful naked woman—bright, warm and fertile. Her eyes melt your heart and stir you. It is obvious that she is in love. She radiates it, and it warms your heart and amuses as love truly should, whether it is our own or others'. As she looks upon you, you feel newly born and beautiful. Her eyes see all beauty in all things. She extends a rose, and you take it with your left hand.

"The rose lives forever within the heart of every man and woman. It is the rose of beauty. Beauty lies within all life, animate and inanimate. We must all learn to look upon the rose within those that we encounter rather than at the covering that may hide the rose itself. There is nothing but beauty in life. What we do with life can mar or enhance that beauty. We are all meant to love and be loved. As you discover your own rose, it will be as a magnet. As we learn to love ourselves, so will others. As we learn to see the rose in ourselves, others will see it in themselves. It is only when we deny our own innate beauty and demonstrate a lack of non-love for ourselves that we deny ourselves the beauty and wonder of the universe."

Then with a soft embrace that melts all doubts, she melts into you. For the first time in ages, you feel alive and beautiful and as striking as the rose. You begin to realize that you can never truly be alone nor be lonely, for there is life on all planes and dimensions filled with love and willing to love you just as you are. It is O.K. to be human. It does not make you any less lovable!

(For some, it may be easier to stop at this point and go to the end, where you exit from the Tree. This concludes the bottom four sephiroth, those that deal with the energies of the lesser mysteries. These four stimulate energy for that part of our magickal body that unfolds the personality, etc. If you are having no trouble concentrating, then continue through the rest.)

Before you now stands a young child. He has a playful look upon his face—innocent and puckish. He motions you to lean down, and as you do, he places a crown upon your head. It is too large, and it sits a little lopsided upon the head. You are afraid of moving too suddenly in case it would fall. The child grins.

"All the masters taught that it is necessary to become again as little children if we are to touch the heavens. To be a child is to be open enough to hear the elves whispering in your ear, and it is to know that nothing is impossible. It is having the confidence to say to the world: 'It will all be O.K.!' "

"We are all children of God, growing and learning so that we can inherit the kingdom that will be ours."

The image changes from that of a little child to that of a god hanging upon the cross of sacrifice. Only the eyes of the child remain with the image.

"We can sacrifice the child so that we can learn to live the life of a god; but only by obeying the spiritual over the physical can we do so. This alone will retain the purity of heart to see the force of the Creator within our lives and the lives of those we touch."

Again the image shifts. Before you now is a majestic king, standing upon the globe of the Earth.

"This crown is to remind you of what you will inherit upon the mystic path. For now it is too large for the child within you. As you grow, as you learn, as you sacrifice the lesser for the higher and the material for the spiritual, you will grow into it. As you do, the world becomes your own."

The image shimmers and melts over and into you. You feel like a child—so much to do, so much to explore. You understand that it is time to put some aspects of your life away, for you are destined to inherit and rule. The world truly is yours.

"Sometimes the world must be won!"

The words snap you from your reverie. You find standing before you a mighty warrior with sword drawn.

"A sword is an instrument that can kill or defend. It can protect or it can attack. There is no right or wrong. The sword is double-edged. Choices and decisions are always double-edged. They have consequences, but one must be strong enough to make the choices and be willing to take the consequences of such choices for good or bad. That alone builds responsibility. Before the new can be built, the old must be torn down. That demands strength and courage. If one is to grow and evolve, one must become a spiritual warrior. This means one must carry the Flaming Sword of Truth. One must wear it within the scabbard, but be able to draw it and use it when necessary. Remember: what you wound, you must heal. What you kill, you must bring back to life. What you tear down, you must build up. What you protect, you must strengthen!"

With that, the warrior salutes, takes the scabbard from his waist, places it about your own and inserts the sword. He nods and melts into you. In that instance, you know what it is to be a true warrior. You know what it is to fight unnecessarily. You know what it is to defend yourself. You know that all the strength you ever need will be there. You will never face anything that you do not have the strength to deal with.

Before you now stands a mighty crowned king, dressed in royal blue robes trimmed in gold. He holds within his hand a chalice of gold. His eyes are warm and merciful. You know that this man is kindly and gracious to all within his kingdom.

"A king has many things. He has great wealth—a never-ending supply. He has people who love to do his bidding. He can get anything made, anything done, anything he wishes—when he wishes. He rules all of the kingdom. He may divide the work, but he reaps all the rewards. It is his God-given right as king. All within the kingdom is his to claim as his own. All of the Earth is yours to claim. Allow your kingdom to provide for you. Be willing to accept what it gives. Abuse is not only taking too much without giving back to the kingdom, but it is also not taking when it is offered.

"Kings have responsibilities. We must do our part if we are to receive from those within our kingdom. By requesting treasures from your kingdom, you provide opportunities for others to fulfill their lives by delivering your rewards. Each is a king or queen, but we all must claim our kingdoms. We must not give up our rights to our kingdoms out of fear or self-effacement. A king provides for his subjects, and they in turn reward his favors. A king helps his subjects discover their own kingdoms.

"If we are to receive all that we can from our kingdoms, we must realize that they are ours by divine right. We need only claim them. We must express appreciation for what we already have, and give up what we do not use or need, and pass it on to others. Drink from this cup and know that it is ever full. It is the Grail of Life and all the treasures within it. To drink from it is to claim all that is your divine right to claim!"

You drink from the cup; its nectar is sweet upon the tongue. You stand taller, and you begin to understand that the world is yours to claim as the figure melts into you!

(You can stop here or go on. This ends the sephiroth of the greater mysteries and the energies that can augment the magickal essence for more fully enhancing your life.)

"If you wish to claim the kingdom, it must be done in silence." You stare as a matronly woman with a black robe steps forward to greet you. Her eyes are warm, nurturing and mothering, and there is a strength that is only developed through time. She will nurture, but she will also be stern when necessary, for the protection of her children.

"On the path there is a need to understand how to express one's energy in the most creative manner. Plans should be nurtured and held close to one's heart until truly safe to be brought out. A true king must keep his own confidence. He or she must know when to speak and when to keep silent. He or she must know how to create in all ways. Giving birth is both pleasure and pain, and that which is created must always be watched over. To give birth to the higher requires great care. Too many are still unenlightened and would seek to stop or hinder you in your plans. They do not understand and so have chosen to be effects and not causes. You have chosen to be the cause, so great care must be taken."

She removes the black robe from her own shoulders and places it over you.

"This is the Robe of Concealment. Within it is hidden the light to be revealed when you decide. There are many things that men and women conceal from the outer world, but can never be concealed from themselves. From the darkness of the womb we give birth to new life; from the darkness of that which you conceal, you can find new light! This robe is for your protection and your care. Do not use it to hide yourself, rather use it to reveal your light!"

She steps forward and places your head upon her chest. She kisses you lovingly upon the top of the head. It is so comforting; and then she melts quickly into you.

Before you now stands a tall, bearded figure. If ever an image looked like the ancient master Abraham or Melchisedek, this one does. The power is strong, and you feel the need to back away. There is a hint of amusement from his face.

"All you need do for yourself is to simply do it. Make your plans and act upon them. All that you need to fulfill your dreams is already there for you. Initiating the action is often the most difficult part. Once it is set in motion, it all moves of its own accord. If you wish to change your life, set it in motion. Give it a push, until it is capable of moving on its own.

"To you I give this sceptre of power. It strengthens and initiates the energy. It enables you to prime the pumps of life, arouses the creative forces so that you can impregnate your life. Your thoughts, your feelings and your actions are all expressions of the creative force. You give birth through all of them. Like all mature men, the ability to impregnate is inherent. It is the responsibility of such that is often neglected. Use this sceptre to awaken the wisdom to know how and when to act upon these energies so that you initiate only that which will be of benefit to you and all of mankind."

He hands you the sceptre and melts into you. You feel old. You have done so much, and yet there is still much to do. You begin to understand.

The last of the statues does not step before you. It comes to life behind the altar: an ancient bearded king, seen only in profile. One side of its face is hidden. You know that while in the physical, there will always be an aspect of the divine hidden from you.

The image shimmers and then swirls, spinning in vibrant, crystalline light. It forms a spinning whirlwind that shoots out toward you. You raise your hands in defense, and you feel it rest lightly within them as a small ball of light energy. Its swirling takes upon itself the appearance of the atom and spins like a top in the palm of your hand. It pulses and hums. And then it speaks—inside your head only.

"Nothing is ever the same. All is moving; all is change. All we need do is learn to focus the energy so that it spins and flows with us and for us. This is the cycle of all. We live that we may die, only so we can live and grow even more."

The spinning energy rises from the palm of the hand and enters into you through the crown of your head. For an instant you see yourself as a baby, born again.

You look about you, the room is empty, and yet you are energized. You never knew you had so much within you. You now have the keys to empowering your life. You offer a silent prayer to the universe and bow to the altar. You turn to exit. Using your symbol, you open the door to the outer world. You exit, bringing with you an empowered and magickal essence to incorporate into your physical life!

This exercise can be taken even further, with the individual going to each sephira and working with each magickal image and its gifts. This will enable you to use them more fully in your life. It is empowering and energizing on all levels.

The idea of taking on the attitudes and energies of associated sephirotic images is very ancient. We have always been told to live according to the examples of others, i. e., the saints, Jesus, etc. With these images, we are linking their energies to specific areas of our life to which they can be applied. It must be remembered that all gods are aspects of the One God. We are simply distinguishing, so we can learn to more fully incorporate the associated energy into our lives.

These images are reflections of archetypal energies. We work with them in order to go beyond them to their archetypal source. They are tools to help us build until we can create. They reflect divine aspects that we are trying to incorporate into our lives. Magickal images are used through an identification process. The qualities symbolized by the images are recognized and then experienced. As our own knowledge and experience grows, so will the power and the effect of the images as we synthesize them into our essence and being. Ultimately, the energies associated with them and reflected by them become an innate, active expression of our own energies. It is then that we have created the magickal existence and can begin to dance the Tree of Life upon all planes.

chapter four

The Power of Pathworking

The voice sounded a bit like mine so I was inclined to trust it. The voice told me some things about myself that needed changing for my own good. I knew these things; I had just never done anything about them. The voice told me it was now time to stop procrastinating. It reminded me that if I continued to wait for tomorrow to make needed changes in my life, tomorrow would never come. Tomorrow is only a convenient scapegoat for refusing to face reality today.

That little voice was very convincing. It promised me if I would heed its advice, something very good would come of it. I listened, I heeded and something unusually good came of it.

—JOSEPH WHITFIELD
The Eternal Quest

There is a great mystique associated with the "occult" practice of pathworking. It is seen as the be-all and end-all of metaphysical skills. In essence, it clears the bridges from one level of our consciousness to the next, so that we have a steady flow of energy from all levels into our normal waking consciousness. Our own fears, doubts, self-created limitations and perspectives—along with those imposed upon us by society—create barriers to accessing and utilizing in a fluid manner the energies and capacities that exist within these various levels of consciousness. Pathworking serves to show us what these hindrances are, and where they are; and it brings them out so that we must do something with them. We open the channels that create transition in cleaning out the debris we have accumulated.

Pathworking is often viewed as a means of opening up wonderful gifts. It is viewed as the epitome of spiritual unfoldment. It is the "pot of gold" at the end of the rainbow, but this conception is somewhat misleading. It is instead the *pathway* to the pot of gold, and that

113

pathway must be walked. Pathworking is only a method of undertaking the great Quest.

It is very easy to think that we know all about the world and its various realms. After all, explorers have touched the four corners of the Earth. We have ventured into space. Others have passed on their own explorations of the more subtle realms, realms that constitute much of our ancient myths and legends. These are the realms that more people are rediscovering today.

Reading about them and experiencing them are two entirely different things. You cannot truly know something until you have experienced it. Theory without application is only words. Our legends and myths and tales are only words, but there is a means to discovering the truth upon which they are based. It is why they still intrigue and fascinate us today.

As we move toward the New Age, we are all becoming aware that life and energy exist on all levels and on all planes, not just on the physical plane. We are learning that our physical plane interpenetrates more ethereal realms. We know from the various tales and writings of their various names and "localities," and of the portals to these kingdoms. Whether we call them planes, dimensions, levels of existence, Eden, Hesperides, Elysium or Avalon, the existence of other realms side by side with our own physical realm is an established belief on its way to becoming an established fact.

Almost every myth or heroic tale starts with a younger son or daughter leaving home to seek a fortune. Esoteric lore and hero tales in particular are giving us pictures of the journey we all must take toward initiation into higher mysteries and energies. These tales often have older male/female characters who, when met along the road, offer advice. These elders represent those who work with the physical in conjunction with the more spiritual plane, and who become available to us as we begin to expand our awarenesses. It is how the advice is then acted upon that decides the future of the young hero and what progress is made.

The call of the Quest in tales and legends is a call to adventure and excitement, but it is not always seen for what it really is: a *time of growth and emergence into responsibility and maturity!* One of the goals of the Quest is entering into the service of a mighty king, symbolic of a greater force or even of our own higher self.

It is a time of transition, and a time of dynamic growth, growth that can entail some very strong emotional highs and some very intense emotional lows. It is a time in which you are forced to make a serious self-assessment and self-evaluation. You are forced to take a look at the circumstances, the people, the situations and the beliefs of your life. You are forced to examine them to find out what has been lost, stolen, broken and no longer necessary, so that you can clean it out to make room for that which will be more beneficial to you in the future. It is an "attic-cleaning" time.

Many enter into metaphysical and occult practices as a means of escaping their physical lives. They look for these to solve their problems. They view their spiritual studies as though leading up into a blinding Light, in which all of their troubles and problems will be dissolved. If a person cannot handle the situations of his or her physical life, invoking spiritual energies will not make things easier. The energies of other realms will only serve to intensify physical circumstances.

This will continue until you have no choice but to deal with the situations. At that point the spiritual helps by forcing a reckoning that ultimately makes one more responsible and stronger. This is how pathworking operates. It brings the energies that block the flow of higher levels of consciousness to the surface, so that they must be dealt with. For this reason, every student of the metaphysical and spiritual realms needs to know that *within every problem and difficulty is hidden a gift; but the only way to get to that gift is to deal with the difficulty.*

Initially, everything may be "goodness and light," which is wonderful and as it should be. Many times this is a strengthening process, a building-up of energies before the greater tasks and mysteries are undertaken.

When we use pathworking, we are saying to the universe, "I am ready to take on greater work and responsibility, and I am taking it on in full awareness." We are working to trigger and set loose the debris we have accumulated in this lifetime as well as in those of the past. We are forcing, in a sense, greater tasks, tests, responsibilities and initiations upon ourselves. We are attempting to accelerate our growth.

This accelerates the meeting of karma, but it also accelerates the release of our higher gifts, which we can then manifest on our physical plane. Instead of seeking some light to shine down upon us, we develop our own light to shine out from us. We are clearing the bridges—the paths—that link our normal, waking consciousness with all those other levels of consciousness within us.

The paths are bridges that link the various sephiroth of the Tree of Life. These bridges can become congested with outworn ideas, attitudes and perceptions. They become clogged with our fears, our doubts, and the multitude of hindrance that we accumulate throughout life. Pathworking is a means of clearing the bridges. It is comparable to clearing the water lines, so that the water runs free and strong throughout the house we live in.

This is why "continual watchfulness" in the form of self-assessment and self-examination is so important. The Qabala stirs up great energies, and we need to be able to put it into its proper perspective, and begin to recognize exactly what stirs up what within our learning and growing process. With pathworking, we are stirring and bridging our energies in a controlled manner. This is all comparable to what is often termed a "healing crisis," in the holistic health field. A healing crisis occurs as a way for the body to cleanse itself and make itself stronger. This often occurs when a person resolves to improve their health. He or she may start eating correctly, watching the diet, exercising, reducing the bad habits. After a week or two this can trigger an illness—cold or flu-like symptoms. Usually the individual wonders what is going on. He or she doesn't understand how they can be getting sick when they had been doing so well in improving their health habits.

They may have a runny nose, watery eyes, or a wide variety of symptoms. Unfortunately, the individual usually takes a medicine that dries up the runny nose, or stops the irritation. This is the wrong thing to do. What has occurred is the triggering of a healing crisis. Our bad habits accumulate within the physical body as various forms of toxins. Our physical body has a high tolerance and thus can become acclimated with them to a degree. When we improve the health, these toxins get stirred up, so that you can become aware of them and clean them out. It is like the silt that settles at the bottom of a river. When we go to clean it up, it gets stirred up, mucking up the water. It comes to the surface so that we can skim it off and rid ourselves of it. Unfortunately, we may use medicines, etc. that stop the runny nose, not realizing that a runny nose is the way the body cleanses itself of toxins. When we take an antihistamine to stop it, we are putting a stop to the entire cleansing process. *The symptoms, although irritating, are signals that your efforts are being rewarded.* There will be some discomfort for a while, but this will pass!

Pathworking triggers a healing crisis within our spiritual life. It brings to the surface those things that need to be cleaned out if we are to manifest capacities that will give us greater control and energy within our lives. Pathworking provides greater illumination, an illumination according to the levels of consciousness or sephiroth with which you are working. Illumination is a higher form of consciousness which changes the mind and its perceptions. The mind expands upon the past while staying linked to it, but going forth in what is for the individual a creative manner.

When we tap specific sephiroth of the Tree of Life, stimulating them into greater activity, the result is *illumination*. When we bridge them together for forced growth through pathworking, we institute the *initiation* process. We open ourselves to the Mysteries—Lesser, Greater and Supreme.

When we begin the process of forced initiation, we must use the illumination we receive from the levels of our consciousness to climb the Tree of Life ever higher. Through applying energy to our physical, emotional and mental essence, we are attempting to awaken a revelation of the higher spiritual and religious truths—of ourselves and the universe.

The mysteries and their lessons are enacted through the normal circumstances of our lives, not through some artificially contrived experience. Through the work with the Qabala we set energy in motion so that it plays upon us through our physical lives and circumstances, and through the people and situations we meet daily. Again it is important to take time to evaluate, daily, weekly or on some regular basis, what has occurred in our lives. We must recognize that nothing is insignificant and that all circumstances have import. Everything gives clues as to the spiritual truths and mysteries we are involved in and have set in motion through our studies and through contact with the sephiroth of our essence. There is an underlying lesson in all these things.

The *Lesser Mysteries* are those of the bottom four sephiroth in the Tree of Life. They are for the unfoldment and the development of the personality. They involve the search of and awakening to the need to have more than a physical existence. It is the looking-beyond of the seeker. The tests in these paths as they are awakened involve the development of good character, which forms the foundation for higher development. This involves learning to open the subconscious and its levels.

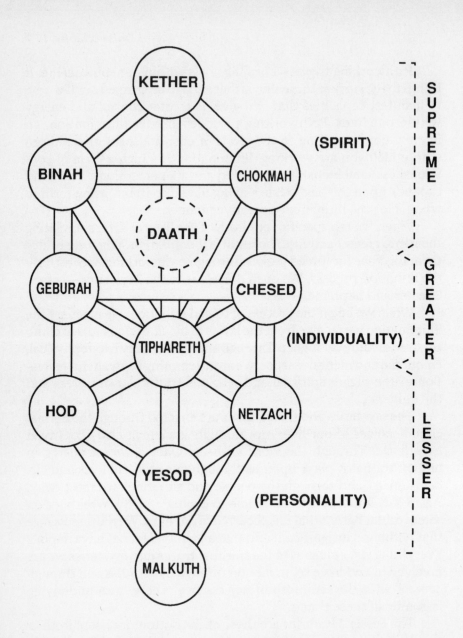

The Mysteries upon the Tree of Life

118

Everything in the Lesser Mysteries involves other people and our relationships to them. Our greatest learning comes through the groups that we encounter, formally and otherwise. It involves maintaining a sound mind and body and controlling the instincts and passions, and the strengthening of the mind. All of this involves the lower four sephiroth—Hod, Netzach, Yesod and Malkuth—and their corresponding paths.

The Greater Mysteries involve the middle three sephiroth upon the Tree of Life—Tiphareth, Geburah and Chesed. These involve the awakening and development of the individuality—our own uniquely creative energies that last for more than a single lifetime. These are the qualities that we strengthen and manifest more with each lifetime. Within these Mysteries is the lesson of true faith, which opens the veils to true spiritual insight. The lessons change our focus from the outer world to the inner world. Here, the inner principles are focused and dedicated to higher service.

These Mysteries always involve probationary periods in which the individual's dedication to the higher is tested. It is here also that one meets what is referred to by many occultists as the *inner plane adept*, who guides the individual in greater teachings and in the development of dedication.

Dedication, however, does not imply neglect of the physical for the spiritual, because it is only by our work in the physical that we learn to apply our teachings. Dedication also involves recognizing that some very important duties in the physical will have precedence over the work in the Mysteries if there is a conflict. It is the fulfillment of our obligations to ourselves and to others that demonstrates our dedication to the higher; and these obligations may actually be part of your probationary testing!

The individual must learn to act upon his/her own resources, without reliance upon others. The personality is sacrificed for the spiritual. This involves facing karma and duty in this lifetime, and learning to take responsibility for our thoughts, feelings and actions to more consciously work out the individual destiny. It is recognizing that one can be alone without being lonely, and that one has to deal with the concept from many levels as old conceptions are dissolved and stripped bare.

The Supreme Mysteries are those that deal more specifically with teaching us the path of our true spiritual essence, its effects upon our physical life, and how the spiritual life and energy is structured.

These involve the energies associated with Binah, Chokmah and Kether. All the Mysteries—Supreme, Greater or Lesser—are of equal importance within our evolution, as all of the sephiroth are of equal importance. They simply serve different functions; they are different expressions of energy to help us in our growth.

The Supreme Mysteries many times involve great leaps of faith. It is here that we begin to understand how everything works together, and we begin to know how to set it all in motion for the benefit of all. We begin to recognize that there are universal rhythms, and we begin to align ourselves with them more fully.

We work on all of these levels simultaneously, and most of the time we are not even cognizant that the experiences within our physical life are reflecting teachings from some level within these Mysteries. When we work with the Qabala and pathworking we are attempting to become more cognizant of this process and to more consciously control and direct it. We set it in motion, accelerating our teaching and learning. Because we are focused within the physical, it is absolutely necessary that we pay heed to our outer circumstances in order to know what we have set in motion, and so that we can control them without being overcome by them.

PATHWORKING

There are only twenty-two paths that link the levels of our consciousness and can be termed true paths. The other ten of the "Thirty-two Paths of Wisdom" within the Tree of Life are the sephiroth themselves. They provide the illumination as they collect and hold traces of energies from all the paths that enter or leave. Thus, every level of our consciousness—every sephira—contains not only influences from all of the other levels but also from the connecting paths between them.

The paths are keys for astral travel and can be used for the more occult techniques of "skrying in the spirit," and for others. They traverse the mind, the various bodies of man and all the planes of existence. By travelling and working the paths, one can open and awaken resources of the mind—ideas, skills, creativity, and other abilities and attributes that lie beneath the surface.

Although the pathworkings may seem like a fantasy of the mind or even a daydream, it is dangerous to assume they have as little effect upon our lives. We are working with powerful symbols which generate energy connected to the archetypal energies of the universe. They contain symbols that will act upon the subconscious mind and awaken what lies hidden there. Because the situations, experiences and workings are symbolic, they will also strongly affect the physical world.

It must be remembered that whatever we do on other levels of our consciousness will seep down and create similar situations within the physical or more mundane level. We are using symbols to activate energies and form a matrix for a particular experiencing of them within the physical life. This occurs through our normal, day-to-day circumstances. Those who doubt that such relationships exist, or have only intellectualized about it to this point, will come face-to-face with the interpenetrating and interrelating of all levels and planes.

The Qabala is a system of evolvement, and through the pathworkings we instigate specific energies that in turn manifest as experiences and situations that hasten our growth. It makes us face what we have not faced, to search out our hidden fears, overcome them and then open ourselves to yet higher and stronger knowledge and experience. Through the pathworkings we become the catalysts for our own lives. By working the paths, we begin the process of consciously seeing the dross of our lives and then stripping it away to reveal the light within. It brings upon us those situations and activates those stresses that must be dealt with in order for change to occur. We are in essence "killing ourselves" through the paths, so that we may be reborn.

The Qabala acts as a conscious agent for transformation between the upper and lower and the inner and the outer worlds, and for the bridging of all levels of our consciousness. The raising of matter, energy and awareness from an ordinary level to a higher state, and then the bringing down and transmission of energy and consciousness into our physical lives, is part of the work of the Qabalist. It is the work of the Seeker.

Without the pathworkings, the task becomes difficult. The seeking is random and often atavistic. It is the conscious work of the paths that provides a system that can adapt itself to each individual and his or her own present state of awareness. It must be stressed though that one needs some preparation. One needs to be at least somewhat familiar with the energies that exist at the levels of our consciousness before starting to link them. One needs to have experienced them and activated them singly before inducing double and even greater effects. *More is not always better!*

When one begins to bridge the levels of consciousness, he or she is opening up to a whole series of tests and initiations. These manifest through the normal experiences within a day-to-day life. They begin and end there. Experience with the good and bad is to be expected. Greater power will be given, to see how it is handled. Temptation in many forms will occur. Tests of character and stress will be encountered. The Seeker's values will be challenged both inwardly and outwardly through external situations within his or her life. By working the paths and bridging the levels, we are inviting the tests so that we can attain the rewards!

Pathworking shows us both common and uncommon relationships within our lives. In order to recognize them for what they are, and to assist ourselves in expanding our awareness through them, a watchfulness is absolutely necessary. The symbols reflect specific energies of the universe. When we consciously use them, we are bringing those energies into expression somewhere within our lives. It follows the universal law of energy: *all energy follows thought!*

It triggers an awareness of synchronicity within our lives. "Synchronicity, as described by Jung, is when events coincide relatively within the same period and cluster around a central dynamic or value which gives meaning to the whole. It is not quite simply events occurring at the same time that creates synchronicity, but rather events occurring in simultaneous relation to each other to produce meaning. It is present when extraordinary coincidence is experienced within a larger context of meaning—both in terms of a person's own life journey and in terms of universal principles." (P. 268, *Jungian-Senoi Dreamwork Manual* by Strephon Kaplan-Williams; Journey Press, Cal. 1985.)

BENEFITS OF PATHWORKING:
1. Enjoyment (giving the conscious mind an opportunity to relax).
2. Enhance concentration.
3. Stretch and improve the imagination.
4. Develop the ability to work with symbols.
5. Increase and enhance ability to visualize.
6. Stimulate awareness of the significance and continuity of all life circumstances and events.
7. Awaken hidden skills, ideas and inspirations.
8. Invoke a testing that can lead to higher perceptions and realms.
9. Intensify the communication between levels of our consciousness.
10. Integrate the more subtle levels of consciousness with the normal waking consciousness.
11. Stimulate greater self-control.
12. Manifest a facing of ourselves on ALL levels.

PRECAUTIONS:
1. The invoking of energies may be too intense for those who have difficulty handling the energies of physical life. The energies awakened intensify the physical life experiences, so that the individual has no choice but to transmute them.
2. The subjective world may grow too real for those who cannot cope with the physical world. Pathworking is not an escape. Those who use it as such will find themselves lost in all areas of their lives.
3. A pathworking is a powerful tool of invocation. The symbols serve to activate and manifest the play of universal energies upon the physical world more strongly. It is easy to underestimate its ability to affect the physical world and your own physical life. Its effects can be felt for long periods of time. It is also easy to become "fairy charmed" and disappear into the world of uncontrolled fancy within the mind. Other realms are there for us to explore and to learn and grow from, but only so they can enhance our physical world. They are not escapes from reality on any level.
4. The energies invoked and stimulated, and their corresponding physical life experiences, must be synthesized. Discrimination and discernment is ever important. Failure to do so at all times can lead one astray. Everything that occurs in your life will take on greater significance.
5. Some individuals may not like having to face and experience the aspects and situations that are stimulated into play by these techniques. It must be remembered that the Qabala shows us our greatest fears and weaknesses, but only so that we can develop our greatest strengths.

PRELIMINARY CONSIDERATIONS:

1. In the beginning, do no more than one per week. It is sometimes effective to repeat the same path within that week. This
will intensify the experience. Make sure you are familiar with
the sephiroth and their corresponding energies prior to performing a pathworking. Do not work two paths together! You
need time to synthesize and discern how the energies are playing upon your life. Working two paths will complicate that
process of realization.

2. As mentioned earlier in the text, we are initially working with
the creative astral plane, although in essence we are touching
the paths at different levels based upon previous growth and
development. The more you use them and their symbolic keys,
the easier it will be to bridge to other levels. The more you use
them, the stronger the effect they will have upon your physical
life. Remember: *The astral world is a world where things
change and dissolve as soon as the mind is taken off of them.*
This is why specific symbols are utilized and it is why focus
and concentration are developed while working with them.

3. Other people will be using these symbols and these paths.
Sometimes people and images appear that are out of context or
with which you have no familiarity. Leave them alone until
you can test them and find what relates to you and what does
not. *Test all things!*

4. All pathworkings have a guardian aspect for your safety,
security and balance. These are the God-names associated
with the sephiroth that you are bridging, as well as the archangelic energies associated with them. When working the
paths, it is good to always visualize yourself in the company of
the archangel of the temple you begin in. (See "Temple-to-
Temple Visitation" later within this chapter.)

5. All meditations, journeys and imagickal pathworkings have a
beginning, middle and end. Most will begin inside the Tree,
where the Temple of Malkuth is found most easily (refer to
earlier description of it). Malkuth is one step removed from the
physical. You can travel to other places and temples of consciousness within the Tree from that point. If your work or

exercise is interrupted, simply visualize the Temple of Malkuth, step out of the Tree, and you will be brought back to your normal state of consciousness—*safely!*

6. There should be no interruption. Make sure the phone is off the hook and that you will not be disturbed. This is a form of deep meditation, and all altered states of consciousness induce a state of hyperaesthetics in an individual, making one hypersensitive. Sounds are more shattering, lights more penetrating, etc. Any interruption will be disruptive to the nervous system.

7. Use the incense, candles and music to set the tone and energy of the area in which you will be working. Guidelines for their proper use are given in the text. The atmosphere in which you operate is extremely important to a successful performing of the imagickal pathworking ritual.

8. Familiarize and review the basic symbology of the sephiroth with which you will be working. Review the information given concerning the energies and symbols of the path itself. You do not have to keep the symbology and its significance in mind constantly throughout the pathworking, but reviewing it beforehand allows the symbols to strike a responsive chord. The symbols are linked to archetypal energies. Whether you are aware of their significances or not, if you use them, they will trigger a release of energy into some area of your life.

9. Every path contains definite milestones or markers to identify the right path once you have started your imagickal working. This is why previewing the symbols helps. If you do not see them in any form along the path, or if the path changes color, it indicates that you have wandered off track. Returning your focus by visualizing the path in the appropriate color, or by visualizing it into existence as you learned to do in "Creating Astral Doorways" in the previous chapter, will keep you on track. If that becomes difficult, focus on the Temple of Malkuth and return.

It is good to plan on seeing these symbols somewhere along the path, and it is easy to do, especially if you utilize the methods of creating the pathworking scenarios yourself (described later in this chapter). The symbols are the keys to a successful pathworking. They relate to the energies and lessons of the path itself and serve as a catalyst to the archetypal energies they reflect. They keep us connected to the spiritually subtle energies of the bridges linking our levels of consciousness.

10. There may arise a point along some path where you feel you cannot go on with the working. You may be uncomfortable with the energies, too fearful, too doubtful, etc. *Do not be upset at this!* Ultimately, you know what you can handle and at what rate. Simply visualize the Temple of Malkuth, allow yourself to return to it, and then exit the Tree. Work on other paths below it until you feel capable of working the one that caused the distress. Emotional upset can occur, but this is more often an indication of success than of failure.

11. Some workings will have immediate effects upon your life. Others may take weeks or even months before their manifestation is recognized. *Be assured that they will affect you and your life on all levels and will continue to do so until you learn the lessons.* Initiation involves change and growth. By pathworking, we hasten that process. The phrase "Be careful what you ask for because you may receive it!" is quite appropriate. When you work with the Qabala and imagickal pathworking, you are asking for a complete awakening—not just enough to satisfy curiosity or a need for psychic thrills. The energy released and its effects can be stronger than you ever imagined.

12. Some of the more abstract paths and levels can be the most powerful and the most effective.

13. Not everyone will be affected in the same way. We each are progressing and developing in our own unique manner. The energy released will play within our lives in a unique manner.

14. Every word, phrase and picture can trigger chain reactions which rise to the surface. There is freedom within the paths and the visual images created through the workings. This is why the most powerful and effective pathworkings are those in which you create the scenario in accordance with the energies inherent to the path itself. This technique is described elsewhere in this work. The archetypal energies we are trying to access and bridge into our lives will play upon each of us in

a unique manner. This is what makes it such an individual and yet vital growth process. It amplifies the effects.

15. *Do not make the mistake of thinking that these techniques are an excuse for daydreaming and psychic thrill-seeking! They are so much more than mere fantasy, and such assumptions could be devastated by the realizations being driven home.*

GROUP AND CEREMONIAL WORK:

1. Should be kept simple and of no great length.

2. Group energy is mixed and thus will be increased. It will only be as effective as that which the weakest member of the group can handle.

3. Requires preparation of the place to perform the working.

4. Requires proper preparation by the individuals of the process and familiarity with the symbology.

5. Includes the lighting of candles and incense, if used.

6. Official banishing and purifying of the atmosphere. (Refer to chapter 7 for the "Banishing Ritual of the Pentagram.")

7. General invocation and opening. This can simply be a review of the purpose and symbology.

8. The imagickal pathworking itself.

9. Closing and grounding of the energies, i.e., discussion, writing, acknowledgment in some physical manner of the experience.

10. Banishing and cleansing. This is for protection and to make sure the astral doors that were opened by the exercise are closed and sealed tightly. This is particularly important when group work is involved.

All energy is neutral. When it is released through such techniques as pathworking, it may manifest in positive or negative experiences. If it manifests positively, it is so you can utilize the energies even more fully and productively. When it manifests in a "negative" expression in your physical life, it is so you can confront it and transmute it, releasing the positive, creative energy that lies behind and has been blocked.

32nd PATH

SEPHIROTH: Malkuth/Yesod
SPIRITUAL EXPERIENCE: Vision of the Holy Guardian Angel and Machinery of the Universe.
VIRTUES: Discrimination and Independence
VICES: Avarice and Idleness
COLOR: Indigo and Black
ASTROLOGICAL INFLUENCE: Saturn
TAROT DESIGNATION: The World
TALES AND MYTHS: All descent myths: Orpheus and Eurydice; Persephone and Pluto; Alice and the Looking Glass; Madagascar tale of Sand Children.

HEBREW LETTER ת / PSALM

Let my cry come before you, O Lord; in keeping with your word, give me discernment.
Let my supplication reach you; rescue me according to your promise.
My lips pour forth your praise, because you teach me your statutes.
May my tongue sing of your promise, for all your commands are just.
Let your hand be ready to help me, for I have chosen your precepts.
I long for your salvation, O Lord, and your law is my delight.
Let my soul live to praise you, and may your judgments help me.
I have gone astray like a lost sheep; seek your servant because your commands I do not forget.

This is a path that takes the seeker from the material to the astral plane. Here begins the evolution toward spirit. It is the path that reveals the light within illumination. This is the path of descent into the subconscious, with its hidden fears, and the ascent to the higher self—with the promise of new life. On this path the symbols awaken the fears that burden the imagination and block the flow of energies. This path clears and liberates us from the weight of physical existence. It can be used in pathworking scenarios for releasing energy to overcome depression, to develop greater intuition and to strengthen the light bodies This is the path of wisdom gained only through the passage of time. It is a path whose symbols release energies that bring on experiences of self-discipline (or the need for it), which can lead to the liberation of the soul. This path can show us through our life experiences the limitations of life, so that we can have the proper foundation. It forces confrontations with subconscious fears which will play themselves out or reveal themselves within our physical lives.

This is also a path whose symbology releases energy into expression that brings upon us helpful limitations, greater self-discipline, common sense and an understanding of the need for structure in our lives. It may also manifest as conditions that show us where we have needless restraints within our lives, or too much calculation and a lack of human feelings. It is through the energies of this path that we begin the process of dying to the physical focus of life, expanding our awareness of what lies hidden behind it. It triggers energies that show us that there is life beyond the physical.

31st PATH

SEPHIROTH: Malkuth/Hod
SPIRITUAL EXPERIENCE: Vision of the Holy Guardian Angel and Vision of Splendor.
VIRTUES: Discrimination and Truth
VICES: Avarice and Dishonesty
COLOR: Orange and Scarlet
ASTROLOGICAL INFLUENCE: Fire
TAROT DESIGNATION: Judgment
TALES AND MYTHS: Prometheus and the Stealing of Fire; The Necklace of Brising; The Tinder Box; West African tale of Fire Children.

HEBREW LETTER ש / PSALM

Princes persecute me without cause but my heart stands in awe of your word.
I rejoice at your promise, as one who has found rich spoil.
Falsehood I hate and abhor; your law I love.
Seven times a day do I praise you for your righteous judgment.
Those who love your law have great peace, and for them there is no stumbling block.
I wait for your salvation, O Lord, and your commands I fulfill.
I keep your decrees and love them deeply.
I keep your precepts and your decrees, for all my ways are before you.

This is a path of relationships. It is a path whose symbols release energies so that you can truly discover your relationships to others in your physical life and what they can teach you about yourself. It provides and releases energies for visions of what needs transformation and renewal, and can release energy that increases the will to endure.

It is a path that releases into our physical lives the trial by fire that we all must undergo in the quest for the higher. It can be used to strengthen fortitude, arouse the kundalini, and to free ourselves from emotional problems. Remember, we are creating scenarios to release the energies associated with the symbols associated with the path. We can learn to utilize and manipulate those symbols so that the energies play in our physical lives in the desired manner.

It is through our experiences with others that we grow. Cloistering is escapism. This path releases energy so that we begin to see our relationships for what they truly are—not for how we wish they were.

This path and its symbols can stimulate situations where expressions of greater strength, courage and self-assertiveness arise. It can release a sense of idealism into your life and activate the life force more strongly. You may experience or see within your life ruthlessness and self-imposition, and your disruption of the lives of others. You may see where you are self-indulgent and loud, and you may as a result of confronting such attributes become ardent, strong, helpful and kind. This path can bring the opportunities that will stimulate great inspiration, initiative, courage and creativity. Behind every difficulty or negative expression is an opportunity to discover a hidden gift and blessing.

30th PATH

SEPHIROTH: Yesod/Hod
SPIRITUAL EXPERIENCE: Vision of the Machinery of Universe and Vision of Splendor.
VIRTUES: Independence and Truth
VICES: Idleness and Dishonesty
COLOR: Orange
ASTROLOGICAL INFLUENCE: Sun
TAROT DESIGNATION: The Sun
TALES AND MYTHS: Tales of Phoebus Apollo; Grimm's Rumpelstiltskin; Snow White and Rose Red.

HEBREW LETTER ר / PSALM

Behold my afflictions, and rescue me, for I have not forgotten your law.
Plead my cause and redeem me; deliver me according to thy word.
Far from sinners is salvation; for they seek not your statutes.
Your compassion is great, O Lord; according to your word, give me life.
Though my persecutors and foes are many, I turn not away from your decrees.
I beheld the transgressors and I knew they had not kept your word.
See how I love your precepts, O Lord; in your loving kindness give me life.
The foundation of thy word is truth, and each of your judgments is everlasting.

This is a path whose symbols release energy to shed light into the dark corners of our consciousness. It is the path of an enlightenment, comparable to opening the windows and shutters to admit the Sun. It is the path of science and occult astrology. It releases energies that uncover hidden parts of us that need to see the sun, including our half-formed ideas. It balances the rational and intuitive minds. It awakens powers of alchemy and can stimulate greater power in healing (of ourselves or others). Its energies can stimulate the development of diligence or show us where it is needed or lacking in our life. It releases energy that enables our visualizations to become more fruitful. It also releases artistic inspiration and can open one to prophetic insight.

Within the physical life, the workings of this path may result in circumstances that release greater courage, bountiful energy and pride. Situations may arise to test our stamina and show us where we lack it. We will see situations that display our lack of self-confidence, and we may begin to see where and to what degree we may be overly egocentric. This path releases energy into our physical life that animates all aspects, so that we develop greater individuality and learn to utilize our vitality productively. The symbols trigger an energy release that manifests situations that bring on the opportunity for self-mastery.

29th PATH

SEPHIROTH: Malkuth/Netzach

SPIRITUAL EXPERIENCE: Vision of the Holy Guardian Angel and Vision of Beauty Triumphant

VIRTUES: Discrimination and Unselfishness

VICES: Avarice and Lust / Dishonesty

COLOR: Crimson

ASTROLOGICAL INFLUENCE: Pisces

TAROT DESIGNATION: The Moon

TALES AND MYTHS: Eros and Psyche; Romeo and Juliet; Artemis and Endymion; Navajo tale of Coyote the Trickster; Tale of Tontlewald; Rescue of Aphrodite and Eros from Typhon.

HEBREW LETTER ק / PSALM

I call out with all my heart; answer me, O Lord; I will observe your statutes.

I call upon you, save me, and I will keep your decrees.

Before dawn I come and cry out; I hope in your words.

My eyes greet the night watches in meditation on your promise.

Hear my voice according to your kindness, O Lord; according to your laws give me life.

They draw near who follow after mischief who are far from your laws.

You, O Lord, are near, and all your commands are permanent.

Of old, I know from your decrees, that you have established them forever.

This is the path of sexuality and its symbols activate such energies and their play upon us from all levels. It is also the path of creativity and physical evolution. It is the path of spiritual progress shared in fellowship with students from all eras. It releases energy that teaches us about the life that exists in all things—not just human life. It releases energies into situations that teach us to see only what is, without the additions of the ungoverned imagination. It helps us to recognize that we are a part of all living things and thus require only a simple life. Its symbols have the capability of releasing energies that help instigate the resolving of family disputes and the spreading of harmony. It releases energy for working with animals, and can be used to assist oneself in scrying, mirror and crystal "magic." It can stimulate energies that will assist one in working with all of nature and in being able to link with those energies of the natural world. It can be used to manifest opportunities to increase prosperity or for stirring up those aspects of ourselves that prevent us from having what we need or desire. It is a path that governs our attitudes toward others (including the physical aspects of sex), and it will stimulate our personal relationships.

It stimulates an increase in imagination, and it can manifest situations that place you in a position to be more unselfish and innovative. You may find yourself immersed in situations where you or others seek to control through giving. Our potential can become so locked within that there is a tendency at times to withdraw. This path can release energy that can be expressed as a sensuality in everything. The idea of separateness within your own life will emerge in some form.

28th PATH

SEPHIROTH: Yesod/Netzach

SPIRITUAL EXPERIENCE: Vision of the Machinery of the Universe and Vision of Beauty Triumphant

VIRTUES: Independence and Unselfishness

VICES: Idleness and Lust, Impurity

COLOR: Violet

ASTROLOGICAL INFLUENCE: Aquarius

TAROT DESIGNATION: The Emperor

TALES AND MYTHS: Zeus and Deucalion and the Deluge; Zeus and Ganymede; The Elves and the Shoemaker; Rip Van Winkle.

HEBREW LETTER צ / PSALM

You are just, O Lord, and your ordinance is right.

You have pronounced your decrees in justice and in perfect faithfulness.

My zeal consumes me because my foes forget your words.

Your promise is very pure and your servant loves it.

I am small and despised, yet I do not forget thy commandments.

Your justice is everlasting justice and your law is permanent.

Though distress and anguish have come upon me, your commands are my delight.

Your decrees are forever just; give me understanding and discernment and I shall live.

This is a path that releases energies, forcing us to deal with and manifest the higher, perfected aspects of sex. It is a path whose symbology releases tremendous creative power, imbuing our hopes, wishes and dreams with life force. It brings tests upon us in relation to mankind's dreams throughout the ages—youth, beauty and wealth. We find ourselves in situations where we have to assess and choose according to our highest aspirations. It is a path that releases energy of tremendous inspiration, but we must face the dangers of following our dreams, which often confront us face-to-face. Are we giving up our security for a pipedream, etc.? Our doubts surface, but so will our inspiration and hope.

The energies that manifest from this working can create situations that construct new attitudes in your affairs. They can be used to assist in gaining new insight into astrology, particularly in relation to planning careers. They promote peace at any level and help us find suitable work and educational opportunities. A willingness and opportunity to experiment arises. New ideas, inventions and social activities increase. You may find yourself more social and outgoing. The intuition will be sharper, and you may find yourself becoming loyal to some new cause. The energies may manifest as an over-talkativeness and a flightiness of behavior. You may find yourself or those around you demonstrating more "fanatical" ideas. There may be a tendency within you and your environment toward the imposition of ideas on others. The energies activated may manifest zany schemes, or impracticality—all so you can learn to handle such creative energies and make them productive within your life.

27th PATH

SEPHIROTH: Hod/Netzach

SPIRITUAL EXPERIENCE: Vision of Splendor and Vision of Beauty Triumphant

VIRTUES: Truth and Unselfishness

VICES: Dishonesty and Lust, Impurity

COLOR: Scarlet

ASTROLOGICAL INFLUENCE: Mars

TAROT DESIGNATION: The Tower

TALES AND MYTHS: Greek Tales of Ares; David and Goliath; Jack the Giant Killer; Noah's Ark; The Garden of Eden; Chinese tale of Tseng and the Holy Man; Tale of Snowdrop.

HEBREW LETTER פ / PSALM

Wonderful are your decrees; therefore I observe them.
The revelation of your words sheds light, giving understanding to the simple.
I gasp with open mouth in my yearning for your commands.
Look upon me and be merciful to me because I love your name.
Steady my footsteps according to your promise and let no iniquity rule over me.
Let thy countenance shine upon your servant and teach me your statutes.
My eyes shed streams of tears because they keep not thy laws.

This path releases the energies used to tear down the old within our lives. Its symbology activates energies in all areas of our life which relate to conflicts and their resolution. It brings on the trials of endurance and of courage and faith. It unites us with emotional forces, so that we have no choice but to deal with them. It brings circumstances that offer the chance to survey our entire personality. It creates situations that force us to see what can be salvaged. It stirs up situations so that we see what needs to be thrown away or torn down, and what is still in good condition. It provides the opportunity to recreate ourselves.

It is a path that can be used "magickally" for any kind of balancing or banishing within our spiritual and psychic natures. It releases energy that can assist us in debates of any nature, and it creates situations that make us look at ourselves from all aspects. It is the first of three paths that cross the Tree, so its energies are stronger and play more fully within the physical. Its effects are more discernible within the physical life.

In the area of personality, it manifests situations that force us to see where we are fooling ourselves and others, giving the opportunity to correct it or continue it. We are forced to confront our weaker aspects and to build upon the stronger. It releases the force of the ego and reveals it within every aspect of our life. It can stimulate the desire to succeed, a fighting spirit. It plays in our lives dually—as a creative force and as a destructive force. It will manifest situations that reveal the degree of our animal nature we have yet to change, and provides the opportunities and the energy for such changes.

26th PATH

SEPHIROTH: Hod/Tiphareth

SPIRITUAL EXPERIENCE: Vision of Splendor and Vision of Harmony

VIRTUES: Truth and Devotion to the Great Work

VICES: Dishonesty and False Pride

COLOR: Indigo

ASTROLOGICAL INFLUENCE: Capricorn

TAROT DESIGNATION: The Devil

TALES AND MYTHS: Pan and the War between the Titans and the Gods of Olympus; Aladdin and His Lamp; Amalthea and Zeus (The Horn of Plenty); Ahriman; Krishna and Serpent; Garden of Eden.

HEBREW LETTER ע / PSALM

I have fulfilled just ordinances; leave me not to my oppressors.

Be surety for the welfare of your servant; let not the proud oppress me.

My eyes strain after your salvation and your just promise.

Deal with your servant according to your kindness, and teach me your statutes.

I am your servant, give me discernment that I may know your decrees.

It is time to serve the Lord, for they have nullified your law.

For I love your command more than gold, however fine.

For in all your precepts I go forward; every false way I hate.

This path releases energies for the spiritual experience known as the Dark Night of the Soul. It is a path that releases energy to assist us in linking our personality with our individuality. It throws us back upon ourselves to the well of truth that lies within each one of us. All of our wrong ideas are exposed to the Sun. Our illusions and beliefs are challenged. It is a way of darkness, where situations arise that teach us to live upon our faith in our ideals. Our ideals challenged, we are put in a position of having to face what must be faced, so that we can be rid of it. This path can change our ideas of spiritual levels and consciousness.

The energies released by the symbols of this path can serve as a form of exorcism. They can be activated to provide protective energies for the home. It can help us in overcoming domineering aspects and assist us in overcoming selfishness and conceit. It stimulates the need for tolerance.

This path releases those universal energies that will manifest in situations that force pragmatism. You may find yourself needing to become more prudent and self-sacrificing in your life. Your trust and loyalty will be tested, as will the trust and loyalty you place in others. Organizational abilities will increase, if only out of necessity. There will be an increased awareness of others' needs. You may find yourself exhibiting a miserly or demanding tendency, and you may become secretive, dictatorial or ambitious. (You may also see this manifesting in others.) These energies may also manifest opportunistic tendencies that will have to be dealt with.

25th PATH

SEPHIROTH: Yesod/Tiphareth
SPIRITUAL EXPERIENCE: Vision of the Machinery of the Universe and Vision of Harmony
VIRTUES: Independence and Devotion to the Great Work
VICES: Idleness and False Pride
COLOR: Blue
ASTROLOGICAL INFLUENCE: Sagittarius
TAROT DESIGNATION: Temperance
TALES AND MYTHS: Biblical story of Joseph; Chiron and the Centaurs; Chinese tale of Tseng and the Holy Men; David and Goliath; The Little Mermaid; Rapunzel.

HEBREW LETTER ם / PSALM
I hate men of divided heart, but I love your law.
You are my refuge and my shield; In your word I hope.
Depart from me you wrongdoers that I may keep the commands of my God.
Uphold me according to thy word, and I shall live; and let me not be ashamed of my hope.
Help me that I may be safe and ever delight in your statutes.
Thou has rejected all of them that stray from thee, for their deceitfulness is in vain.
Sustain me and I shall be safe, and I will always meditate upon thy commandments.
My flesh shudders for fear of thee, and I am afraid of thy judgments.

This is a path that releases energies of the temptations of the physical world so that we face them. It is here that choice becomes agonizing. Because of this, we are experiencing a rebirth of a major change in consciousness. The energies activated create situations that change our ideas of self-sufficiency and demonstrate to us within the physical world the need for faith in the deepest sense. It is a path that brings the opportunity to develop new spiritual self-responsibility, self-confidence and progress.

It is also a path that can release energies assisting us in the development of astral projection, higher forms of psychism, and protection while traveling or on the move.

It manifests in situations in the physical life that present you with the desires and choices to improve and perfect understanding. It activates situations that bring you face-to-face with the beast within. This may occur personally or in a reflected manner through those you associate with. It activates your vital energy into mobility—positive or negative. It manifests opportunities to expand and inspire the mind. It creates situations where it becomes necessary to see the larger issues at hand. It awakens the energy of boldness and straightforwardness. It can also manifest as an inability or fear to regulate or balance the mind with matter. There can arise tendencies to false exaggeration, to gluttony or to coarseness. However it manifests, it creates energy upon the physical that leads one to self-discovery, and provides training for participation within the universal scope of life.

24th PATH

SEPHIROTH: Netzach/Tiphareth

SPIRITUAL EXPERIENCE: Vision of
Beauty Triumphant and
Vision of Harmony

VIRTUES: Unselfishness and
Devotion to the Great Work

VICES: Lust/Impurity and
False Pride

COLOR: Green Blue

ASTROLOGICAL INFLUENCE:
Scorpio

TAROT DESIGNATION: Death

TALES AND MYTHS: Adam and
Eve; Apollo and Phaeton; Orion;
Dickens' A Christmas Carol;
Chinese tale of Tseng and Holy
Man; Sumerian tale of Gilgamesh,
Utnapishtim and the Flood; Story
of the death of Siegfried.

HEBREW LETTER נ / PSALM

A lamp to my feet is your word,
a light to my path.
I resolve and swear to keep your
just ordinance.
I am very much afflicted; O Lord,
give me life according to your
word.
With the words of my mouth be
pleased, O Lord; and teach me
thy judgments.
My soul is continually in thy
hands; I do not forget thy law.
The wicked have laid a snare for
me, but from your precepts
I have not strayed.
Your decrees are my inheritance
forever; the joy of my heart
they are.
I intend in my heart to fulfill
your statutes truly, even to
the end.

This path and its symbols activate the archetypal energies for the transmutation of the personality. It initiates a facing of our fears of change in all respects. It is a path that shows us death (in whatever form) as being nothing more than part of the evolutionary process. This is the path of death and rebirth, where we learn in the physical to transmute our fears of change into acceptance of what is and what will be.

This is a path that stimulates circumstances that can be used to assimilate and deal with grief and to enable us to see death as a rebirth. It can be used to awaken energy that enables us to understand adolescents (and the changes they go through) and those with emotional problems.

This path manifests energy, so we can recognize the subtle shifting and merging of life-forces and energies. If experienced properly, both can give rise to a new form of divine expression.

It is an activation of the urges of the life force. It may manifest with creativity, such as through building or opportunities to build within your life. Healing may be stimulated more strongly. Friendships will have the opportunity to strengthen and deepen. It inspires faith and creates circumstances that instill a desire to merge the physical with the spiritual.

It can manifest destructively, though, unless controlled. It can seduce, as when friends are used for personal gain and self-satisfaction. Psychic vampirism can also result, with expressions of strong egotism. This path releases the energy that gives us a choice of rising high into the light or falling into darkness.

23rd PATH

SEPHIROTH: Hod/Geburah

SPIRITUAL EXPERIENCE: Vision of Splendor and Vision of Power

VIRTUES: Truth and Energy and Courage

VICES: Dishonesty and Cruelty

COLOR: Deep Blue

ASTROLOGICAL INFLUENCE: Water

TAROT DESIGNATION: The Hanged Man

TALES AND MYTHS: Noah's Ark; David and Goliath; Hansel and Gretel; Story of Siegfried; Australian tale of The Rainbow Snake.

HEBREW LETTER מ / PSALM

How I love your law, O Lord! It is my meditation all the day.

Your command has made me wiser than my enemies, for it is ever with me.

I have more understanding than all my teachers when your decrees are my meditations.

I have more discernment than the elders because I observe your precepts.

From every evil way I withhold my feet, that I may keep your words.

From your ordinances I turn not away, for you have instructed me.

How sweet to my palate are your promises, sweeter than honey to my mouth!

Through your precepts I gain discernment; therefore I hate every false way.

This is the beginning of the more abstract paths and their energies. This is a path of the breaking down of outworn forms. It creates situations that show us those aspects of ourselves that are no longer viable or usable. It creates situations that reveal the attitudes and activities that are no longer necessary. It gives us the ability to take a new perspective on the world—our world—and everyone and everything within it. It gives us the ability to see everything reversed. Opportunities arise to exchange our views for different and more exact ones, in which spirituality plays a more dominant role.

This path creates circumstances that show us what needs to be dissolved within your life. You may see a breaking down of various aspects. Water washes away the old, keeping life moving. Although on the surface some situations may seem calm, we may need to trust our instincts, which tell us there are strong currents in motion. Initially, the effects may not be tangibly visible, but they will manifest.

This path and its symbols manifest conditions in the physical that place you in a position to be put upon by others. You may become prone to daydreaming unproductively. You may see yourself or others becoming self-indulgent and exaggerating feelings out of proportion. It will stimulate greater psychic energy and thus make one more sensitive to everything, and more impressionable. It may manifest in a desire to be of greater service to others, enabling you to develop greater compassion and understanding. This path creates conditions and situations where we learn our emotional limitations.

22nd PATH

SEPHIROTH: Tiphareth/Geburah
SPIRITUAL EXPERIENCE: Vision of Harmony and Vision of Power
VIRTUES: Devotion to the Great Work and Courage
VICES: False Pride and Cruelty
COLOR: Emerald Green
ASTROLOGICAL INFLUENCE: Libra
TAROT DESIGNATION: Justice
TALES AND MYTHS: Tales of Pluto and Hades; Ali Baba; Elijah and the Prophets of Baal; Sleeping Beauty or Tale of Briar Rose; Judgment of Themis.

HEBREW LETTER ל / PSALM

Your word endures forever, O Lord; It is firm as the heavens.
Through all generations your truth endures; you have established the Earth and it stands firm.
According to your ordinances they still stand firm; all things serve you.
Had not your law been my delight, I should have perished in my affliction.
Never will I forget your precepts, for through them you give me life.
I am yours; save me, for I have sought your precepts.
Sinners wait to destroy me, but I pay heed to your decrees.
I see that all fulfillment has its limits; broad indeed is your command.

This is the path that releases energy for justice and karmic adjustment. The energies that are triggered and set in motion from its symbols manifest conditions and the opportunity that enables one to balance what needs to be balanced. It frees you through the balancing to then pursue the course which will be the most beneficial. This path releases energy that will reveal the duality of our nature—the good and the bad. With all circumstances that arise, you must learn to face them and forgive yourself for them (recognizing that we are human and make mistakes when we are growing and learning). Then we must learn to love ourselves in spite of our mistakes.

This path creates crossroads within our lives. Major decisions about whether to continue with actions in different areas of our lives or to alter them manifest strongly, with the facing of the consequences either way.

The energy may manifest in conditions of limbo, in which you seem incapable of making decisions. This is a sign that it is important to do so, while recognizing that either way you choose or decide, you will encounter those situations that will help you to grow and learn. It may manifest in revealing manipulation of others or by others, and it may show where there is superficiality or deceitfulness. It stimulates the need for impartiality.

This path also activates energies of an artistic nature. It can make one more sociable and inspiring of the talents of others. It manifests conditions that give the opportunity to balance your nature and the expression of your male and female energies, both of which exist in each of us.

21st PATH

SEPHIROTH: Netzach/Chesed

SPIRITUAL EXPERIENCE: Vision of Beauty Triumphant and Vision of Love

VIRTUES: Unselfishness and Obedience

VICES: Lust, Impurity and Pride; Hypocrisy

COLOR: Violet

ASTROLOGICAL INFLUENCE: Jupiter

TAROT DESIGNATION: Wheel of Fortune

TALES AND MYTHS: All Quests; Grail Quests of the Knights of Round Table; Jason and the Argonauts and the Quest for the Golden Fleece; Moses and the Burning Bush.

HEBREW LETTER ⸵ / PSALM

My soul hath longed for thy salvation, and I hope in thy word.

Mine eyes wait for thy word, when Thou wilt comfort me.

For I have shriveled like a leather flask in the smoke, I do not forget thy statutes.

How many are the days of thy servant? When wilt thou execute judgment on them that persecute me?

The wicked have digged a pit for me, which is not in accord with thy law.

All thy commandments are trustworthy; yet the wicked persecute me.

They had almost destroyed me upon Earth; but I forsook not thy commandments.

Qucken me after thy loving kindness; so shall I keep the testimony of thy mouth.

This is a path that manifests in our life as ups and downs. It releases energy so that the call to the Quest can be heard. The choice to hear and respond always remains with us; we can close our ears and ignore it. This path creates circumstances that offer a way to the Grail—our spiritual essence and how to manifest it within our life. It opens the door within the physical, but insures that it is not too easy to follow. It opens the opportunity for maturity and growth. It gives us the opportunity to commit to the more eternal. It may bring you in contact with a group or a person who can guide you in your spiritual aspects of life. It may manifest as a departure from a job or city, or it may manifest as an offer that has always been a dream. It opens the doors to opportunity, but you must recognize the opportunity and walk through the doors.

This path and its symbols release energy into the physical, so that you can begin to recognize that Divine Law operates upon Earth. It can open up the gift of prophecy or the opportunity to awaken it. It creates situations in which you begin to understand that universal laws govern man. It opens the doors to expand in many areas of life. You begin to recognize that there is justice in all aspects of the world, especially within the physical, where we often feel it is lacking the most. It opens the doors to revealing greater philosophy, theology, religion and ritual as an integral and workable part of life.

20th PATH

SEPHIROTH: Tiphareth/Chesed

SPIRITUAL EXPERIENCE: Vision of Harmony and Vision of Love

VIRTUES: Devotion to the Great Work and Obedience

VICES: False Pride and Hypocrisy

COLOR: Yellowish Green

ASTROLOGICAL INFLUENCE: Virgo

TAROT DESIGNATION: The Hermit

TALES AND MYTHS: Ruth of Biblical Old Testament; Ceres and Demeter; Virgin Mary; Erigone and Dionysus; Snow White and the Seven Dwarfs; Demeter, Persephone and the Eating of Six Seeds; The Night Journey of Muhammed.

HEBREW LETTER ' / PSALM

Thy hands have made me and fashioned me; teach me thy law.

So that those who revere thee may see and rejoice, because I have hoped in thy word.

I know, O Lord, that thy judgments are right and that thou in thy faithfulness has humbled me.

Let, I pray thee, thy merciful kindness be for my comfort, according to thy word to thy servant.

Let thy tender mercies come to me that I may live; for I have been taught thy law.

Let the wicked be ashamed, for they have humbled me unjustly; but I have meditated in thy precepts.

Let those who reverence thee turn unto me, and those who have known thy testimonies.

Let my heart meditate in thy statutes that I be not ashamed.

This is the path of the Hermit, the Wayshower, the Adept. Here we can release energy that creates opportunities to explore the teachings of all those who brought knowledge to mankind. We have placed before us the opportunity to become a *new person*. On a spiritual level this path stimulates a commitment to the spiritual life, and an opportunity to do so. You are setting energy in motion that is saying to the universe, "I am ready to accept change in my life."

It often manifests conditions where review of past situations, feelings and attitudes occur. This assists us in throwing light on the soul to lead us to higher goals. It creates energy and situations where we must choose. We cannot linger or deliberate any longer.

In the physical this energy can manifest opportunities to learn and explore techniques that will make the most of inherent talents. It creates opportunities to become more helpful. It will show us where we are helpful and unassuming, dependable and unselfish, calm and self-reliant. It will also open the doors of research into new areas in which there has been a desire to explore. It creates situations that will show where one has been manipulative or underhanded. It sets energy into play that reveals faultfinding, superficiality and indecisiveness. It releases the energy that enables us to become the selfless servants of others somewhere within our lives, doing so in complete understanding.

19th PATH

SEPHIROTH: Geburah/Chesed
SPIRITUAL EXPERIENCE: Vision of
  Power and Vision of Love
VIRTUES: Energy, Courage
  and Obedience
VICES: Cruelty and Hypo-
  crisy, Pride
COLOR: Greenish Yellow
ASTROLOGICAL INFLUENCE:
  Leo
TAROT DESIGNATION: Strength
TALES AND MYTHS: Theseus and
  Minotaur; Beauty and the Beast;
  Hercules and Nemean Lion;
  Richard the Lionhearted.

HEBREW LETTER ט / PSALM
Thou has dealt well with thy
  servant, O Lord, according
  to thy word.
Teach me good judgment, grace,
  and knowledge; for I have
  believed thy commandments.
Even before I was humbled, I
  believed, and I kept thy word.
Thou art good, O Lord, and doest
  good; teach me thy statutes.
The injustice of the proud has
  multiplied, but I keep the commandments with my whole heart.
Their hearts are stubborn, but
  I keep thy law.
It is good for me that I have been
  humbled, that I might learn thy
  statutes.
The law of thy mouth is better to
  me than thousands of things of
  gold and silver.

This is the path of fire, releasing such into our lives so that we have no choice but to burn out the dross that has been accumulating. It creates situations that strip away our illusions and the outer faces that we present to the world. It manifests situations that place us in the position of being only ourselves—the place where we find our only true strength. This is a path that manifests in situations that reveal the height and depth of ourselves, opening our eyes to who we really are. It creates the opportunity to face the darker twin within us. It manifests physical life circumstances in which self-pride will trip us up. Our personal myths are destroyed. Energy gets set in motion in a way that demands we put our destiny into operation. The effects of this path are long lasting, and can take a while to fully play out through physical life circumstances. This is the path of the Cup of Sorrows that must be drunk by everyone upon the spiritual path. It is through such trials that we derive strength.

This path and its symbols awaken the creative urge in man, one that manifests in our life environment as a reflection of our own being. It forces a look at what we may not wish to see. It can manifest situations that can make us self-assured, protective, warm and sincere—inspired by universal love. It can create situations in our life that will reveal vanity, self-seeking, dictatorship and egotism in ourselves or in others. It is only by facing those aspects we have hidden that we can learn to love ourselves and transmute the lead into gold. We experience the bite of the Serpent of Self-Knowledge!

18th PATH

SEPHIROTH: Geburah/Binah

SPIRITUAL EXPERIENCE: Vision of Power and Vision of Sorrow

VIRTUES: Energy, Courage and Silence

VICES: Cruelty and Avarice

COLOR: Amber

ASTROLOGICAL INFLUENCE: Cancer

TAROT DESIGNATION: The Chariot

TALES AND MYTHS: Hercules and the Lerneaen Hyra; The Elves and the Shoemaker; St. George and the Dragon; Moses and Parting of Red Sea; Grimm's The Seven Ravens; Grimm's tale of The Fisherman and his Wife.

HEBREW LETTER ח */ PSALM*

On the Lord's business have I meditated, that I may keep thy commandments.

I entreated thy favor with my whole heart; save me according to thy word.

I thought on my ways and turned my feet to thy paths.

I prepared myself and delayed not to keep thy commandments.

The bands of the wicked have beset me; but I have not strayed from thy law.

At midnight I rise to give thanks to thee, and of them that keep thy commandments.

The earth, O Lord, is full of thy mercy; teach me thy statutes.

This is a path whose symbols release energies into our life so as to regain balance and a feeling of stability. It opens up those energies that provide feelings of protection and renews our will to carry on after our trials. It creates situations that let us know that everything will be okay. It enhances our concentration—that which was distracting will settle down or become less so within our life. This is also a path whose symbols release hidden knowledge that can be found by "climbing the fence" (the Hebrew letter and symbol Cheth).

This path releases energies that let us know through the outer circumstances in our life that discipline, determination, and the hard work we have expended in other areas of our life is rewarding. It does not mean the work is over, but you will begin to recognize your progress. You will also be able to use your energies even more productively.

This path releases energies that will enable you to focus individual attention to the present. It will strengthen psychic energy, and it will manifest situations that will bind the family together. You may find yourself caring for other's needs and wants, and being able to do so! It can create situations that place you in a position to overcome any tendency to hysterics and irritability. It can force a reckoning with selfishness—in yourself or around you. It manifests situations where the direction of thought, feelings and action must be focused on the present, and this serves to relieve worry and pressure.

17th PATH

SEPHIROTH: Tiphareth/Binah

SPIRITUAL EXPERIENCE: Vision of Harmony and Vision of Sorrow

VIRTUES: Devotion to Great Work and Silence

VICES: False Pride and Avarice

COLOR: Orange

ASTROLOGICAL INFLUENCE: Gemini

TAROT DESIGNATION: Lovers

TALES AND MYTHS: Castor and Pollux; Romulus and Remus; Prince and the Pauper; Beauty and the Beast; Grimm's tale of The Old Woman in the Forest.

HEBREW LETTER ‫ז‬ / PSALM

Remember your word to your servant since you have given me hope.

My comfort in my affliction is that your promise gives me life.

Though the proud scoff bitterly at me, I turn not away from your law.

I remember your ordinances of old, O Lord, and I am instructed.

Indignation seizes me because of the wicked who forsake your law.

Your statutes are the theme of my song in the place of my exile.

By night I remember your name, O Lord, and I will keep your law.

I have been comforted because I kept your precepts.

This is a path that often releases energy into our physical life that is difficult to understand. It brings together the twin aspects of ourselves, the male and the female. We are all a combination of both aspects, and we utilize the masculine and feminine energies in many ways. This path's symbols release energy so that within the physical we begin to realize there is another side to ourselves. We are all dual. If we are more predominantly one, then situations will manifest to where we see that other side. If we are more assertive and masculine in our expression of energy, then we may be shown our softer, more feminine side. If we are more feminine, then the assertive, masculine may emerge through the life circumstances. It creates situations where we must try to unite and integrate more fully that opposite aspect we may have been ignoring or giving little credit to.

This path manifests situations that show we must love ourselves to be able to fully love another. It releases energy into our life that reminds us that the outer world *always* reflects aspects of our inner selves. Paying close attention to the actions and attitudes of people you are around after this pathworking will reveal much about your own inner self—both good and bad.

It is with the energies of this path that we learn to be more selective of those we choose to associate with in this life. It demonstrates that we all have a variety of aspects that must be integrated. This path manifests situations that show us our intelligence, our versatility, and our sensitivity to others (or lack of it). It will manifest situations that will clearly reveal where we dissipate our energies and are aloof and indiscriminate. This is a path that can show us within our physical lives how to utilize all of the instruments of our personality for the greatest expression of our individuality.

16th PATH

SEPHIROTH: Chesed/Chokmah

SPIRITUAL EXPERIENCE: Vision of Love and Vision of God Face to Face

VIRTUES: Obedience and Devotion

VICES: False Pride and Hypocrisy

COLOR: Red Orange

ASTROLOGICAL INFLUENCE: Taurus

TAROT DESIGNATION: Hierophant

TALES AND MYTHS: Minotaur; Tale of King Minos; Hercules and the Cretan Bull; Tale of Europa; Grimm's tales of Water of Life and The Three Languages.

HEBREW LETTER ‎ו‎ / PSALM

Let your kindness come to me, O Lord, your salvation according to your promise.

So shall I have an answer for those who reproach me, for I trust in your words.

Take not the word of truth from my mouth, for in your ordinances is my hope.

I will keep your law continually, forever and ever.

And I will walk at liberty, because I seek your precepts.

I will speak of your decrees before kinds without being ashamed.

And I will delight in your commands which I love.

And I will lift up my hands to your commands and meditate upon your statutes.

This is a path whose symbols open the energy that triggers a probing of the mysteries of how you came to be where you are. It creates a need and desire for serious introspection. Situations arise that bring about such deep considerations. It manifests situations that drive home the need to place Divine Will first. It manifests in circumstances that make one aware that there must be a reason for where you are and who you are—even if it does not reveal the reason. Only time and meditation will reveal this. This path shows the potential of the marriage of the higher and lower selves. It provides a glimpse of the higher levels your life has been leading to up to this point, whether you were cognizant of it at this point or not.

This path often manifests energy in the physical that reveals the creative talent that lies within. It reveals only that there is creative talent; such talents must be dug out and given more light once revealed. It may create situations that test loyalty and understanding (of yourself and others). It may also test an individual's fertility in life and productivity. It will reveal stubbornness, rigidity and overindulgence that must be overcome before the seeds of creativity can truly take root and sprout.

15th PATH

SEPHIROTH: Tiphareth/Chokmah
SPIRITUAL EXPERIENCE: Vision of Harmony and Vision of God Face to Face
VIRTUES: Devotion to the Great Work and Vision of God Face to Face
VICES: False Pride
COLOR: Scarlet
ASTROLOGICAL INFLUENCE: Aries
TAROT DESIGNATION: The Star
TALES AND MYTHS: Jason and The Golden Fleece; Chinese tale of One Honest Man; Grimm's Tale of Boy Who Went Forth to Learn What Fear Was; Cinderella; Snow White.

HEBREW LETTER ה / PSALM

Teach me, O Lord, the way of thy commandments, and I shall keep them unto the end.

Give me understanding and I shall keep thy law; yea, I shall observe it with my whole heart.

Make me to go in the path of thy commandments, for therein do I delight.

Incline my heart unto thy testimonies, and not to fables.

Turn away mine eyes that they may not behold falsehood; and quicken thou me in thy way.

Strengthen thy word unto thy servant, who is devoted to thee.

Turn away my reproach, because thy judgments are good.

Behold, I have delighted in thy precepts, quicken me in thy righteousness.

This is a path whose symbols release and free energies for incoming life upon all levels. It is a path that opens the energies to the Vision of God (face to face), but it must be remembered that a vision is not the same as seeing first-hand. The energies operative at this level of our consciousness are subtle, and the symbols are abstract in the manner in which they reflect and manifest as energies within our lives. They are no less intense, though, and they actually may be more so. This helps us to connect our own existence with that of all creation; the whole of our universe surfaces within our life, revealing to us just what is capable. It manifests situations that show us that we are connected to all times and all people, making us confront that aspect. Past-life information and connections reveal themselves.

This path releases energy that shows us our life-potential; thus our awareness of ourselves and all humanity grows. We begin to realize that we are both creator and created in our physical life circumstances, and thus we must take responsibility for them.

Opportunities manifest to increase our courage and our ability to inspire and bring new life to others. Our intuition increases, and we have the opportunity to take the initiative within our life circumstances. We may also see the effects of past foolhardy actions and egotism. Acting without proper forethought, without subtlety or in an opinionated manner will create strong learning situations for us and for those around us. We become involved in situations that make us very much aware of ourselves and how we are affecting the growth of others, positively or negatively.

14th PATH

SEPHIROTH: Binah/Chokmah

SPIRITUAL EXPERIENCE: Vision of Sorrow and Vision of God Face to Face

VIRTUES: Silence and Devotion

VICES: Avarice

COLOR: Emerald Green

ASTROLOGICAL INFLUENCE: Venus

TAROT DESIGNATION: The Empress

TALES AND MYTHS: All goddess tales, i.e., The Birth of Aphrodite; All tales of birth; Tale of Tontlawald; The Tinder Box; Rumpelstiltskin; Cinderella

HEBREW LETTER ר / PSALM

I lie prostrate in the dust; give me life according to your word.

I declared my ways and you answered me; teach me your statutes.

Make me understand the way of your precepts, and I will meditate on your wondrous deeds.

My soul weeps for sorrow; strengthen me according to your words.

Remove from me the way of falsehood and favor me with your law.

The way of truth I have chosen; I have set your ordinances before me.

I cling to your decrees, O Lord, let me not be put to shame.

I will run the way of your commands because thou has made me of joyful heart.

This is a path that releases great power; it is often hard to interpret how it manifests within the physical life of the individual once it is set free. It is at the level of the supernal sephiroth, and it crosses the width of the Tree, activating opposite poles of energy in one's life. It is here that we begin to activate more fully the archetypal energies that play upon us in various forms. It is here that we activate those energies involved in the principles of life and life-force at its most intimate level. It initiates new birth, bringing together the male and female. It initiates the ability to believe the impossible. It opens doors and opportunities that we have not even seen or considered, and thus we find ourselves looking upon the world with new eyes once its effects are fully grounded into the physical life. It joins the archetypal male energies within us with those of the archetypal female—and the union of the two on any level always gives birth to a third.

This path is called the "Illuminating Intelligence"—it reveals the hidden talents and potentials we can give birth to. It shows our divine potential. It can manifest opportunities to prosper in new ways in the physical. We find opportunities to merge the imagination with reality and produce something expressive within our life. It can stimulate attractiveness to the opposite sex, and it can awaken new sentiments of love and sharing. There occurs a polarization; positive energy meets with negative energy to produce a new creation in your life!

13th PATH

SEPHIROTH: Tiphareth/Kether
SPIRITUAL EXPERIENCE: Vision of
Harmony and Union with God
VIRTUES: Devotion to the
Great Work and Completion
of Great Work
VICES: False Pride
COLOR: Blue
ASTROLOGICAL INFLUENCE:
Moon
TAROT DESIGNATION: High
Priestess
TALES AND MYTHS: Isis and
other goddess tales; Ceres;
Ceridwen; Diana; Demeter;
Rapunzel; Artemis and
Endymion.

HEBREW LETTER ג / PSALM
Answer thy servant that I may
live and keep thy words.
Open mine eyes that I may behold
wondrous things out of thy law.
I am a sojourner with thee; hid
not thy commandments from me.
My soul is pleased and desires thy
judgment at all times.
You rebuke the proud and all who
turn away from your commands.
Remove from me reproach and
contempt, for I have kept
your testimonies.
The ungodly sat and plotted against
me, I meditated on your statutes.
Your decrees are my delight;
they are my counselors.

This is a path that opens the energies of the Abyss and crosses through the hidden sphere of Daath. On a physical level, it is the path of the flow of energy from the feet, through the spine and all the chakras of the human Middle Pillar, to the crown at the top of the head. This path and its symbols release energy in unusual ways into one's life, making it difficult to comprehend at times, even though the effects are obviously felt. *No one remains untouched by this path!*

This is the path of the final dark night of the soul journey. It manifests energy to where you are left to your own resources in order to achieve success in whatever endeavors you are focused in, physical or spiritual. You must draw upon all your resources and all of your past learnings. At some point, even they may be stripped away, leaving you only with your desire to experience the Crown (Kether). This desire is what must move you and help you to bear the burden of this energy within your physical life. It brings upon one a tremendous test of faith!

One will find that in different aspects of his or her life there will occur a confronting of being alone with only faith in the Higher. With this path, we find that what used to bring light and benefit to ourselves is taken, hindered or hidden. We learn the powerful lesson of giving birth to the light within ourselves, and that what we used to rely on was only the light reflected from our own inner light. We incur circumstances that force us to draw upon the well of truth and light that lies innate within each of us! It is here that we have the opportunity to awaken our strongest intuition and to awaken the urge to impregnate ourselves with the light and life of the divine! It is a path that teaches us to pay attention to the subtleties of life.

12th PATH

SEPHIROTH: Binah/Kether

SPIRITUAL EXPERIENCE: Vision of Sorrow and Union with God

VIRTUES: Silence and Completion of the Great Work

VICES: Avarice

COLOR: Yellow

ASTROLOGICAL INFLUENCE: Mercury

TAROT DESIGNATION: The Magician

TALES AND MYTHS: Tales of Thoth, Odin and Mercury; Rumpelstiltskin; Grimm's tale of The Riddle.

HEBREW LETTER ב / PSALM

How shall a young man be faultless in his way? By keeping your words.

With all my heart I seek you; let me not stray from your ways.

Within my heart I treasure your promise, that I may not sin against you.

Blessed are you, O Lord; teach me your statutes.

With my lips I declare all the ordinances of your mouth.

In the way of your decrees, I rejoice, as much as in all riches.

I will meditate on your precepts and consider your ways.

In your statutes I will delight; I will not forget your words.

This path's symbols and workings release energies to fulfill the realization of our abilities—physical, emotional, mental or spiritual. It does not confirm through any life situations that the abilities and potentials are fully trained, but we become very much aware that they are there and can be finely developed. This path releases energies that manifest opportunities to develop seership in any area to which we may have a propensity: business, spirituality, education, etc. It opens the energies, but to make it more than mundane divination demands dedication and work. This is a path of vision; situations manifest so that we realize we can attain any of our hopes, wishes and dreams. We begin to see that we are capable of becoming anything we desire, and thus it is called the path that opens the energies for the making of the *true magician* or *alchemist*!

This is a path that will manifest separating of physical activity from the spiritual. We begin to see definite distinctions, even in those areas we thought were "spiritual." We also see ways of integrating and making both work for us. It activates situations so we can expand our intelligence and our studies, manifesting educational opportunities, formal and informal. Communication increases—with others and with our own Higher Self. It stimulates a restlessness within the physical life that can only be resolved by balancing the spiritual with the pragmatic. It opens strong emotional sensitivites, exposing them so they can be expressed by the mind in various forms of artistic and creative endeavors.

11th PATH

SEPHIROTH: Chokmah/Kether

SPIRITUAL EXPERIENCE: Vision of God Face to Face and Union with God

VIRTUES: Devotion and Completion of the Great Work

VICES: None

COLOR: Bright Pale Yellow

ASTROLOGICAL INFLUENCE: Air

TAROT DESIGNATION: The Fool

TALES AND MYTHS: All tales of rebirth; Grimm's tale of the Devil with the Three Golden Hairs; Grimm's tale of the Foundling and Thumbling.

HEBREW LETTER א / PSALM

Blessed are they whose way is blameless, who walk in the way of the Lord.

Blessed are they who observe His decrees, who seek him with all their heart.

And do no wrong but walk in His way.

You have commanded that your precepts be diligently kept.

Oh, that I might be firm in the ways of keeping your statutes.

Then should I not be ashamed when I behold all your commands.

I will give you praise with an upright heart, when I have learned your just ordinances.

I will keep your statutes, do not utterly forsake me.

This is the last of the actual paths, the last of the linking of the various sephiroth. It is a path of simplicity, and its symbols activate and play upon us in that powerfully simple manner. It brings upon us situations where we can become again "as a little child." Here is the energy of all manifestation. It is the path taken by Enoch, the prophet who walked with God and was no more. One is often left to find his or her own meanings and correspondences.

On a mundane level, it will manifest in experiences that are as variant as the individual's upon this planet. It may create a "fog-like" status of the individual, walking and acting as if not knowing what to do next; or it may make the mind clear as can be in how to initiate new work or to continue with the old.

For some it will stimulate a gregariousness and a cooperative attitude within his or her life. You may find yourself more inventive and inspired, full of workable ideas. On the other hand, it may manifest a predisposition to repetition, hyperactivity and coldness, which must be balanced for productivity on a new level to occur. At its best expression, it creates situations that stimulate the intellect, the intuitive faculties and the artistic mind.

CREATING THE PATHWORKING JOURNAL:

This is a manual to assist us in the assimilation and synthesis of the energies we are setting in motion within our physical lives. It also familiarizes us with the Tree of Life and the symbology we are using as our "magickal tools."

1. Before each pathworking, review the symbology and the energies associated with the path and with the two levels of consciousness we are trying to bridge. This creates the proper mindset, which facilitates the meditational and pathworking efforts, and stimulates the energies reflected through the symbols.
2. In the journal, write down the path, the sephiroth, and the vices and virtues. Draw the Tree of Life, coloring in the path you will be working. This physical activity sets the tone for bridging the outer and inner realms.
3. It is good to write down what you hope to achieve with this imagickal pathworking. What energies of the path and the sephiroth are you hoping to set in motion within your physical life? *This is important! If the purpose is not suitable for the path you have chosen, your teachers upon the path itself (archangels and magickal images) will let you know.*
4. Writing your hopes for the path and the review of the symbols will activate the energies more fully and in the appropriate manner. They will manifest more dynamically and more tangibly within the physical life. With pathworking, we are trying to bridge and ground the more subtle archetypal energies into the physical life. Doing something with our physical consciousness that relates to this spiritual process intensifies the stimulation of these energies, enabling you to experience them more fully. The journal and the dance postures and movements described in chapter 6 enable you to access them more effectively.
5. Take time afterward to write down the experience, your impressions, your imaginings, anything that comes to your mind. Take ten minutes to write down a stream-of-consciousness flow from your mind—anything and everything. Every pathworking releases energies that need to be grounded into the physical life. This *initiates* that process!

6. *Leave a space for assessment.* At the end of a week, go back and review what you wrote. Look back upon the week's events in your life. Meditate upon the correlation. There will definitely be ties!

7. This whole process strengthens your knowledge and awareness of the energies you have set in motion within your life. It assists you in recognizing these archetypal energies as they affect you individually and uniquely. You will begin to recognize how they play within your life, and you will thus be able to synthesize them more fully into all aspects of your life.

8. Write a dedication of your journal to the spiritual value of it in understanding your life and more consciously controlling it. Take time to re-read what you have experienced and assessed. Soon you will recognize the creative aspect of your work and life, and you will recognize the correspondences and ties between all aspects of your life!

IMAGICKAL TECHNIQUE: Temple-to-Temple Visitation

Each sephira or level of our consciousness is actually a temple of consciousness, in which more universal capacities and energies are inherent. In this imagickal pathworking, one uses these temples as starting points *and* destinations, thereby bridging the energies of two levels of our consciousness more strongly. In the past, we have learned to activate the different levels of consciousness, stimulating their energies to provide greater *illumination*. We are now linking the levels in order to set specific energies into play within our lives. This will bring conditions for *initiation*, and learning to apply that illumination more fully.

We always start by entering the Tree of Life, as within the imagickal workings described earlier. Once inside the Tree, we follow a passage into the temple of the sephira from which we will be starting. At the back of the temple, a doorway should be created using either the Hebrew letters or the astrological symbols described earlier. (All techniques within this book build upon each other. If we have consciously been exercising this creative ability, there should be no difficulty at all.)

Through the doorway we walk onto a path of the appropriate

color leading to the second temple. As you step onto the path, you are met by the archangels of the two sephiroth, or the magickal images. They are your escorts. As you walk, you discuss the purpose and function of this path and how its energies will come to play within your physical life. Along the way, various things may be encountered. These vary from individual to individual. With all paths, though, there will be appropriate markers to let the individual know that he or she has not wandered off the path. This is important; in some paths there are no companions to walk with. The individual must walk and experience and synthesize the energies alone. The archangelic influence may decide not to appear until the destination is reached.

Plan to experience these markers upon the path. If not seen, then it is important—as in the method of "Creating the Astral Doorways"—that you visualize them into being:

1. The color of the path that links the two sephiroth. No matter how long the "journey" may seem, as long as you stay upon a road of the appropriate color, you will ultimately reach your destination.
2. Plan to encounter a roadmark of some sort approximately halfway through the working. This roadmark should have the appropriate Hebrew letter for the path or the appropriate astrological symbol. This helps activate the energies that will bridge the two levels of consciousness.
3. Individuals other than the guide may appear upon the path. The more you learn about the path and its energies, the more significant they will become. There are many symbols that reflect similar energies or forces of the path. With time and practice, these become more evident. Those individuals that are a part of the path's experiences will have insignias upon them that serve to inform you that they are of the path. Usually it is the Hebrew letter or the astrological symbol. It may appear as an insignia upon the individual's attire or even upon the body itself.

Specific Instructions for Temple-to-Temple Visitation:

1. Fill in the journal for the path you will be working, and review the basic symbology associated with it. Make sure you review the energies associated with each of the two temples.
2. Set the atmosphere. Choose appropriately colored candles and the fragrances associated with both temples. Use the fragrances and candles simultaneously. Remember that pathworking is a linking of the energies of different levels of our consciousness. One can use a candle for each of the sephiroth and a candle the color of the path as a symbolic link between the other two. If the appropriate color for the path cannot be found, use a simple white candle. Light it and place it between the candles to link the two sephiroth.

   The burning of the incenses (or the mixing of the fragrant oils) and the burning of the candles sets up an energy vibration around you that will resonate with the appropriate level of your consciousness. This facilitates tapping and releasing the energies within. If the fragrances do not seem to blend well, it may tell you of the effort needed to blend and bridge the energies of the two levels of your consciousness. Nothing is insignificant. As you work with the energies, the blending of the fragrances will be less and less discordant.

   Having a place that you can use as an altar upon which to set the candles side by side is very effective. Encircle them in some manner, such as with a rope, to symbolize the tying together of these levels of your consciousness. This adds to the room's vibration. The more significance you can create in associating and binding the two levels, the greater the effect the pathworking will have upon your physical life.
3. One can also use the energies inherent within stones, gems and crystals to assist in the meditational procedures. On the following page is a list of stone and crystal correspondences to the various levels of consciousness depicted with the Tree of Life.

   Holding the stone of one sephira in one hand, and the stone of the second sephira in the other, will help stimulate the appropriate energies. If a sephira with which you will be working is located on the right-hand Pillar of the Tree of Life,

Meditation Stones for the Tree of Life

KETHER
- **Double-terminated quartz.** Kether leads to the Malkuth of the next level of consciousness or the next Tree.

CHOKMAH
- **Opaque fluorite** activates high energies and wisdom; the opaque corresponding with the clouds to be cleared away to reveal the light within.

BINAH
- **Obsidian** awakens the darker self within so we can transmute it into the higher. It is a powerful stone that can be used to give birth to the new, to bring the light from the womb. Most people have difficulty with its energies.
- **Black tourmaline**, the highest of the black stones; protective and nurturing and, like the obsidian, it can teach us how to bring more light into the darkened world. Black tourmaline is a devoted servant to the light and helps one to radiate a spiritual consciousness in all situations.

CHESED
- **Lapis lazuli.** The gold within the blue of this stone is power and royalty. With it one can learn to become a representative of the gods and empower one's life.

GEBURAH
- **Garnet**. Once known for their powerfully protective energies, garnets provide strength and courage. They balance and uplift. The Hebrews called the garnet "barak," which means lightning. Garnet is often associated with Kamael and his assistance in our lives.

TIPHARETH
- **Rose quartz**, for the heart chakra and the heart of the Tree of Life; it awakens self-fulfillment, healing and inner peace. It is gentle like a child, loving like the Christ and strong like a king.

NETZACH
- **Malachite** helps one who is dedicated in the grounding of higher healing energies into the planet and all growing life. It is a good friend which brings one into line with nature and all its forces.

HOD
- **Citrine** awakens the brain to higher knowledge, and its yellow-orange ray can shine like a sun into our lives. Excellent for applying spiritual energies to accomplish earthly matters.

YESOD
- **Amethyst**. An excellent meditation stone, as it facilitates the change of consciousness from our normal waking state into the more ethereal levels of consciousness. Yesod is the gateway to the deeper levels of the Tree.

MALKUTH
- **Smokey quartz**, grounding to our energies, also helps to lift our energies and consciousness away from the physical. It helps the mixing of the energies of the earth with those of the spirit so we have our feet upon the ground and our heads within the heavens.

154

hold the appropriate stone in the right hand. If it is located on the left, hold the stone in the left hand. Use the other hand for the other stone and its sephira. One may also cup the hands within the lap, holding the two stones together. There are many ways of working the stones and crystals into corresponding with the Tree of Life. These are only examples, and you should not limit yourself to them exclusively. Different stones can be used for releasing different energies from the sephiroth into your life. This serves to assist in the releasing and tapping of more archetypal energies.

4. Help create the proper mindset by using the dance movements and postures described in chapter 6. These movements stimulate electrical responses within the brain that correspond to the levels of consciousness associated with the sephiroth on the Tree of Life. Begin with the movements of the first sephira of the path you will be working, and make a transition to the movements of the second sephira by utilizing the "Tibetan Walk to Knowhere" (as described in chapter 6). These physically stimulate the levels of consciousness; if you are one of many individuals that often have difficulty with visualizations, the energies of the Tree can thus be stimulated into activity. These movements can be done as a prelude to the actual meditation, or as a conclusion to help bring the energies out and ground them into your physical life. You can also begin with the movements of the second sephira of the path and move to the movements of the first.

5. As in the previous imagickal workings, enter into the Tree of Life, creating a doorway into the astral by using your personal power symbol. As always, the guardian must first be met and encountered in the appropriate manner.

6. Once inside the darkness of the Tree, use the god-name of the first sephira of the path to bring the temple into light, and to focus within your mind's eye and within your life.

7. All temples should be built up in the mind with the basic accoutrements:
   a. An altar standing between two pillars.
   b. An ever-burning lamp upon the altar, burning in either a white light or a light of the color for the sephira.
   c. The magickal image somewhere within the temple. This

       may be a statue, a painting, engraved upon the wall, etc.

   d. The symbols of the magickal gifts of that level of consciousness, to remind you what you have access to.

   e. All other aspects of the temple will vary and one should learn to create his or her own unique temples and temple images—always in relation to the energies associated with them.

8. See yourself standing within the temple and, using the appropriate Hebrew letter or astrological symbol for the path, create an "astral doorway" as described earlier. As the doorway opens, see the path (in its appropriate color) leading to the second temple.

9. Step out onto the path. As you step through the doorway, pause to allow the archangels of the two temples to step forward to greet you. Never step out onto the path until the archangels have greeted you. They are the guardians of the seekers, and even if it is a path that you must walk alone, they will always greet you first. (You may also want to use the magickal images for this.)

     As they step up, use the God-names and the archangelic names to test them. If they are not truly the guardians for this working of yours, they will dissolve from view when the God-name of the temple is intoned. The archangels expect this testing, so you will not offend. Remember that other beings exist on this plane—some of whom can be quite mischievous.

     Having tested, begin to walk with the archangels along the path leading to the second temple. As you journey, allow them to speak to you of your life as it has related to this path in the past. Allow them to tell you how the energies of this path will play out in your physical life. As they walk and talk with you, make sure you pay attention to the appropriate road-markers. You can even have the archangels tell you the significance of the Hebrew letter and astrological symbol.

     Imagine them asking you questions as to why you wish to travel from one sphere to the next. Converse about why you wish to connect the two levels of consciousness involved. Allow the teachers of this path—be it the archangels or the magickal images—to inform you about what you can expect by joining and activating these two levels of consciousness. Allow them to lead you to the second temple— your destination.

10. Initially, do the paths in their proper order, climbing the Tree from path **32** to path **31**, etc. Once you are more familiar with the paths and their play upon your life, you can be more selective. Also, allow the experiences to unfold along the path. These steps are guidelines, and there will be great individual variations in what is actually experienced.

11. When you arrive at the second temple, allow the archangels to present you with a gift that symbolizes the energy of the path that is now more active within your life. This is a gift that you will carry out of the spiritual Tree of Life into your physical Tree of Life.

12. Acknowledge the symbolism of the second temple (the proper accoutrements and colors, etc.). Thank the teachers. Ask permission to return. Courtesy operates on all planes and dimensions! Turn to the back of the temple and, using your personal symbol of power, create an exit doorway from the Tree itself. Leave the Tree, taking your gift with you. Close the door behind you, acknowledge the guardian of the Tree and allow yourself to return to your normal state of consciousness.

13. At this point, you can do the dance movements in reverse of how you did them in the beginning. Perform the "balancing postures" to ground the energies stimulated by the working and to rid yourself of the "spacey" afterglow that often occurs with altered states.

14. Extinguish the candles. If the incense is still burning, allow it to burn itself out. As it does, it carries your wishes for the path energy to the heavens to work more fully for you.

15. At this point, you can also perform a "banishing" as is described in the last chapter. This prevents any astral energy other than that which was specifically related to the path itself from entering into your life.

Hints:

At your destination temple, pay attention to how the archangels and the magickal images relate to each other and to you. It is also good to take a few minutes at the end to contemplate and reflect upon what you have experienced. This helps put it into perspective. Using the journal to write these reflections helps bridge the energies of the inner realm to the outer world. It also elicits greater insight.

IMAGICKAL TECHNIQUE: Tales and Legends

As you become familiar with the various energies and associations of the paths that link our levels of consciousness, you will also begin to realize that there are certain myths, legends and tales that also strongly correspond to and can reflect those same energies. Many of the ancient myths and legends hold within them the keys to understanding the mysteries of the universe. These mysteries were veiled in tales to provide, for those willing to explore them, the opportunity to discover them. The images and characters—and the actions— within the tales often reflect archetypal energies and lessons. An effective technique of imagick involves using these myths and tales in specified "semi-ritualistic" manners to release the archetypal energies into the physical realm. Combining the tales with Qabalistic pathworking is a powerful means of doing so.

The individual simply places himself or herself within the role of the protagonist of the myth or tale. You hold to the basic structure as previously outlined, i.e., entering the Tree and the initial temple, and then opening the door onto the path leading to the second temple. As you step through the door, you enter into the tale itself. Corresponding tales and myths have been listed in the previous pages. Remember that these tales have a tremendous thoughtform energy attached to them, as do the paths themselves. Used together, the effects are amplified.

Many wonder how to do this, but explicit directions cannot be given. Each must adjust the tale to him- or herself. This allows for our own creative input, and it allows you to awaken the energies in your own unique manner upon the paths. There is no right or wrong adjustment, as long as we keep to the basic tenets and as long as we keep the symbols of the path somewhere within the tale's structure. For example, one can have all the characters of the tale in dress that has the symbolic insignia upon it somewhere. The basic symbols keep us in the proper place within this astral dimension and enable the power of the tale to work more fully for our benefit. In this way, the entire tale becomes a symbol of the archetypal energy that lies at the core of the pathworking.

We begin this process by entering into the Tree in the usual manner. We then enter into the beginning temple, visualizing it and crystallizing it with the God-names. We then create an "astral doorway" that opens onto a path that leads to the destination temple. As we step through the doorway, we enter into the scenario of the myth or tale. At the end of the myth, we enter into the destination temple, there to be greeted by the two appropriate archangels. They will provide commentary and further instruction about the experience.

We leave the Tree in the manner previously described and ground the energies into the physical through the dance or through the journal. This may seem like some kind of fanciful daydreaming, but when applied in this manner it becomes a powerful force, and daydreams are much more important in our lives than is often believed.

Dreams, whether of the night or of the day, are much more than just a stress-release mechanism. Dreams put us in touch with other realities and planes of life that we do not consciously acknowledge on a day-to-day basis. Our dreams, though, must be translated through the reality of the flesh, which is what we are attempting to do.

We are using these "mythical dreams" as an arena for developing a greater relationship between our physical self and that divine consciousness operating in the universe and through us on other levels. They are ways to foster practical connections between inner and outer awarenesses, between symbolic processes and our daily choices. They are a way of fostering a relation to our soul/higher self and to God.

They are very powerful, which is why this technique and the next imagickal pathworking technique will stimulate greater activity of nighttime dreams as well. Paying closer attention to them will reveal how the pathworking is playing upon your own consciousness. We must remember, though, that dreams do not always provide answers. They can often be viewed as a *question*, an invitation to explore relations. They are callings to the spiritual journey to greater consciousness.

They point out personality issues being activated. They lead to sources of anxiety, and they fill us with creative ideas and potential that had been lying dormant. They inspire and they entertain. They offer new ways of being. They mirror the soul and they offer ways of harmonizing the inner and the outer worlds. They provide opportunities for growth and for manifestation of higher capacities. Dreams and these imagickal techniques work upon the same principles.

With dreams, we are the receiver in the communication process in which our higher self speaks to us. Through the techniques we learn to speak back. We can access the potentials of the higher self at any time, rather than waiting for it to communicate to us at night. We are learning to actualize our hopes and wishes and dreams; we are learning to actualize our lives!

IMAGICKAL TECHNIQUE: Creating the Life Adventure

When we use the technique of "Creating the Life Adventure," we are in essence setting in motion very powerful, ritualistic energy. It is similar to the mythwork previously described, but we are setting the scene and building the entire adventure of the path, complete with the basic symbolism.

When using this method, take time to contemplate what you wish to set in motion by this pathworking. In your journal, give this working a title, just as if you were titling a short story. In essence, we are translating our purpose into dramatic form, empowering it with the appropriate symbols and then setting it in motion by playing it out in the mind in the appropriate altered state of consciousness.

Putting your purpose into dramatic form, as if to act it out, is extremely powerful. It gives your purpose structure and animation through symbology. The ancients used such ceremonies, mystery plays and rituals to stimulate energies and to effect the resolution of problems. Theater was part of the ancient mystery school temples. The symbolic enactments of specific universal energies brought about the release of such energies more effectively within the physical plane. This has also been a form of sympathetic magic throughout the ages.

1. Choose the problem or area of your life that you wish to resolve or enhance with more energy.
2. Choose the path that has the energy that is most in line with your own unique purpose.
3. Play through the scene in the mind in the ideal manner that you would like to see it play itself out in real life. If it is a problem you are trying to resolve, visualize yourself meeting it, facing it and then resolving it.

When we use these techniques, we are trying to release energy into our life that has been blocked or hindered, so that we will have full access to our resources at any time. This activation always intensifies life situations, often to the point where they can no longer be ignored. We are forcing resolutions, so that we are free to expend our energies on more creative endeavors. The resolving energy may not initially bring happiness, but rather a stronger confrontation with reality so that happiness comes out as a secondary benefit. The *gift* is always hidden within the problem. We are setting in motion powerful healing energies for our life!

4. Place within the scenario the basic symbols of the path—the appropriate colors, letters, astrological symbols, etc. These may be a part of the scenery or even the dress of the individuals within the scene. You decide. Part of what you are learning to do is utilize your own creative input in order to manifest the conditions that will enhance your life. This means taking greater responsibility and action in the process.

5. Set the atmosphere for the working with candles, incense, dance movements, journals, etc.

6. Enter into the Tree of Life in the usual manner. Use the God-name to bring the temple into focus.

7. Offer up the problem at the altar of the temple in which you will begin this pathworking. Again, invoke energy of the temple by using the God-name and the archangelic name. It is this temple which will initiate the release of energy for the resolution of the life situation you are concerned about.

8. Using the appropriate symbol(s), create an astral doorway that opens onto the path that leads to the temple where the situation will be resolved.

9. Enter onto the path itself, and allow the drama to unfold just as you had rehearsed it earlier in your mind. Let it play itself out while on the path, replete with all of the appropriate symbols. The symbols then trigger a release of the archetypal energies that play out in your life according to the manner of the script you have created.

10. As your drama concludes (just as you would have it do in real life), leave the path to enter into the second temple. Invoke the God-name and the archangelic name appropriate for the temple. Give thanks to those beings that operate through

that level for assisting you in the resolution of it in your real life. You are thanking them in advance for what you know they will help manifest.

This method triggers a confrontation within your life with the problem or purpose, providing the opportunity to clear it up. You are creating a flow out of transforming a particular set of symbols into new materials. You have chosen the scenario for the pathworking according to your own unique purpose. Visualizing it being enacted is the same as daydreaming. The only difference is that now we are empowering those energies with specific symbols, and then we are grounding those creative energies. We chose images and clusters of images, which evoke strong feelings, and linked them to universal concepts. The images and symbols together trigger a release of corresponding energy into manifestation within your life.

Trust your own intuition in creating the scenario, but you *must* employ the basic symbology of the path. The symbols serve as catalysts to the levels of our consciousness. Remember: consciousness is awareness joined with appropriate creative action.

With this kind of pathworking we are recommitting to our spiritual goals in order to become more than what we are now. This implies that we must transmute what we are now to something greater. Change brings growth. Resolution of present situations brings change. If conflicts and imbalances arise or intensify in relation to the situation, it is only so that we will be forced to look at new possibilities. We are resolving our life experiences by consciously working from the outer to the inner and back to the outer again. We are bridging and expanding our resources. We are weaving together the elements of physical life and the elements of spiritual life. Rather than remaining passive creatures, we are becoming conscious *creators* of our life experiences.

chapter five

Experiencing
the Archetypes

Believe nothing on the faith of traditions, even though they have
been held in honor for many generations and in divers places. Do not
believe a thing because many people speak of it. Do not believe on
the faith of the sages of the past. Do not believe what you yourself
have imagined, persuading yourself that a God inspires you. Believe
nothing on the sole authority of your masters and priests. After examination, believe what you yourself have tested and found to be
reasonable, and conform your conduct thereto.
                                        —GAUTAMA BUDDHA

Imagickal techniques, as are often found in many forms of
meditation, produce altered states of consciousness. If concentrated
upon and focused through the proper directed use of symbols and
images, they can connect our energies with the *archetypal* energies of
the universe. The archetypal energies, and their corresponding images
and symbols, are shared by all people, and affect all people at some
level in basically the same manner. They form part of what Carl Jung
called the Collective Unconscious. They are the original energies
from which all others that manifest within the physical worlds came
forth. They are the matrix, the blueprints. They reflect the primary
energies of the universe as they were in the beginning. They are the
primordial source of energies.

As they manifest upon the physical and throughout all of the
planes of existence, they take various forms that reflect the play of
those energies in the world. These reflections become the tools—in
the form of specific images and symbols—of the spiritual student
and disciple.

Guided imagery and symbols are derived from the archetypes,
and thus at some point our development must lead back to them.

They are the manifesting energies, the points where the abstract divine begins to take upon itself the concrete form or image. If we do not attempt to reach the archetypes, and clear the debris from our lives that prevents the free flow and play of them within our lives, we will not progress beyond a certain point. The symbols and images assist us in merging our finite minds with the infinite mind of the universe.

Symbology and imagery are a part of our essence and have tremendous spiritual import to us. They are accumulators of energy, which if utilized in the proper manner can release this energy to play within our lives. The techniques of this book are designed for the spiritual student to learn how to release and control them for greater, more conscious growth. When they are set in motion, they can then play within our lives on many levels, enabling us to change the world around us.

There are many archetypal energies within the universe. With the Qabala we attempt to consciously experience and release them in a controlled manner. Through the pathworking symbology and imagery, we activate the energies so that they play out more noticeably in the physical life. This expands awareness and assists the individual in discerning how to activate and use those energies to their greatest benefit.

Again, there is a need to be ever discerning and discriminating (Malkuthian energies) in order to more fully perceive the play of archetypal and universal energies. We must become cognizant of all that we are setting in motion, and recognize that everything within our lives has significance for us. Continual self-assessment and life-experience assessment is essential. Because we are attempting to consciously manifest archetypal energies, we must also reflect on the situations of our life in relation to what we are setting in motion. We are setting up correspondences so that we can become more active and more controlled.

The ancients recognized this and modern humanity is beginning to as well. Imagickal techniques are being redeveloped and designed specifically to elicit effects so that we can more fully comprehend and experience the play of energies in and around us at all times. The symbols and images resonate with the archetypal energies, serving to activate them more strongly within our life so that we can recognize their play.

Most pathworking techniques are used in meditations of a journey.

The journey reflects the archetypal energies of growth stimulation within our lives. The purpose of the meditational journey and its symbols will determine what actual manifestations of the archetypal energies will be released.

The use of magickal and mythical journeys in our meditational processes enables us to take a more active role in our growth and unfoldment. It enables us to learn how to align ourselves with the forces of the universe, rather than being at odds with it. It enables us to work with that Law of Correspondence.

When we create a magickal journey, we create a series of images and actions—empowered with specific symbols—that we play out within our minds in a relaxed (altered) state of consciousness. The relaxed state enables us to activate greater inner energies, which are empowered by the symbols, which then trigger the release of the archetypal energies. This is reflected in the normal everyday experiences and incidents of the physical life; it does not occur in an artificially contrived situation.

We set the archetypal energies in motion to manifest specific conditions. We utilize the power of our imagination—controlled, directed and enhanced through the use of specific symbols—to elicit specific responses. The journey then becomes a symbolic representation of that which you are wishing to manifest, overcome or grow through in day-to-day life. This can include greater clairvoyance, higher tests and initiation, prosperity, love, encounters with those of like mind, overcoming obstacles, etc.

Imagination is one of our greatest assets, but we must use it in a consciously controlled manner or it becomes little more than uncontrolled fancy. It is a human quality that can be developed to enhance and augment our lives. It is not an escape tool, but an unfoldment tool. It is the means to directing specific images in a controlled manner in order to manifest what we need.

With the imagickal journey, we build a story much like the normal daydream. The difference is that you will be part of it and follow a set pattern, using specific symbols as was outlined in the previous chapter. One can construct his/her own, or one can use traditional myths and tales as mentioned and described in the previous chapter. Many times the archetypal energies impress themselves upon and within the myths and tales so as to elicit higher learning and consciousness. The ancient figures, images and actions within them are steeped in this energy. They have a powerful thoughtform connected to them, so when we utilize them, we tune in with that energy. This in turn triggers a greater release of the archetype within our own lives.

Utilizing the legends and tales of the past is often easier than constructing one's own symbolic journey, at least initially. Most of the ancient scriptures and stories contained esoteric teachings and energies that could be accessed by those willing to put forth the effort. Familiarizing oneself with the legends and myths and their esoteric meanings will assist in experiencing the archetypal energies more consciously through these imagickal techniques. If there is a particular culture that you feel an affinity to, go to the stories and legends within it. You may be feeling drawn to them because they may be where you first opened up to esoteric teachings and to a heightened consciousness, which has been waiting to be reawakened.

Find the tradition(s) that seem to best reflect what you are going through or wanting to accomplish in this current life. You do not have to stick with that particular tradition, but it will give you a starting point. Remember that many of the ancient traditions used their folklore and myths to mask deeper teachings and energies. By working with those that seem to coincide with your own particular purpose, you amplify their effect, because these actions will stimulate your emotional and mental self more strongly.

One can take the myths and tales of the Greek gods, goddesses and heros and easily apply them to the pathworking techniques. The tales of these heroes become the basis for our own Qabalistic imagickal journey. If we have reached a point in our development where we wish to take upon ourselves greater initiations, we can use the tales of Hercules and his Twelve Labors. We could just as easily use the tale of Odysseus or the travels of Jason and the Argonauts as the basis for our empowered imaginings. We simply substitute ourselves for Hercules or Jason or any other character that we may wish to relate to.

We enter into the Tree, then the appropriate temple and next the path between the temples, on which we play out in the mind the events of the tale. The only difference is that now we are activating the thoughtform of the tale through the imposition of specific images and symbols into the imaginings.

Even when using the ancient tales and myths, remember to utilize your own imagination and construction. You do not have to hold to the letter of the tale. Adapt it, construct it according to the individual purpose and the energy that can be released from the individual path itself. A degree of spontaneity is vital if it is to work and release energies. Those who think this process nothing more than mere fantasy need only attempt it for one month in order to discern the effects it creates.

Because we are trying to release the archetypal energies in a specific manner, before you place yourself in a meditative condition or an altered state of any kind, you should know exactly, step by step, what you wish to happen within this journey. Construct it and adapt it so that the outcome meets your own unique purposes. Then choose the path whose energies most reflect your personal purposes. These have been described elsewhere. Employ within its constructs those symbols which will activate the energies of your purpose. Then stick to it. If you have never done anything like this, you may wish to repeat it several times (three is usually all it takes). This insures that the effects are created. It is the number that symbolizes the giving of birth to the new. It is also the number for Binah, the archetypal Mother, the silence of the womb from which all things are born. Meditation on this aspect alone will yield much illumination.

As with all things, practice will result in more effectiveness. You will gain experience in this process, and the images that could distract you or lead you astray from your original imagickal journey will dissipate. Spontaneity is vital, but *control* is even more vital! Make sure you reach your destination before you end the meditation.

Learning as much as possible about symbology, especially archetypal symbols, will help you to utilize your own symbols and empower the meditational process. Do not perform the technique more than once a day, and take time each day to evaluate the day's events in relation to what you are attempting to set in motion. This will enable you to recognize when the process has started for you, and it will help you to understand how intensely it is working. Depending upon your own concentration, the symbology, the time and effort you place into this, and the time needed for it to begin to manifest in your life will vary. Using the techniques of candles and fragrance, and the techniques of "Dancing the Trees," as described in the next chapter, will accelerate the manifestation process.

You can also use music to assist this process. Archetypal energies are reflected through all things: color, sound, fragrance, number, form, etc. Sound and music amplify and accelerate the imagickal process. They are a powerful means of stimulating the unconscious energies to which we have access. When used with the imagickal pathworking techniques, they stimulate deeper feelings and emotions, and greater associations on all levels of our consciousness. The rhythms, sounds and musical patterns can be added to enhance the altered state of consciousness, even to induce trance-like conditions.

There are two kinds of trance. The first is the mediumistic trance, in which the individual ego leaves the physical vehicle, turning it over to a spirit guide or teacher to communicate through. The second type is often considered "shamanic trance." It is the basis of the *vision quest*. In this technique the ego leaves the physical vehicle, exploring other dimensions, setting energy in motion, communicating directly with the guides and entities and then returning with the information. It is this second form that we are developing through the imagickal techniques. *We must have control!* We are developing the ability to maintain *conscious* union with the supersensible world. If we are to consciously direct our unfoldment, we must be able to control all of our energies at all times. If we give our vehicle to another entity, we give up our control, which can lead to problems.

Guided imagery and creative imagination do produce altered states of consciousness in which archetypal energies can emerge more easily. The music should accentuate and facilitate this process, but we must *always* maintain the option to proceed further into the imagickal journey or to end it at any time we desire. Control at all times enables us to proceed further into the sacred areas of our being, which will facilitate the flow of transformational energies into our life. It is our own *personal inner reality* which is of significance within this process. If we are to experience our innermost reality in a creative and healthful manner, we must maintain control.

COMPANIONS UPON THE PATH

There are forces in the universe that we barely understand or even recognize. Because we do not understand, we are afraid or hesitant to work with them. Given the correct information, and by approaching these forces with openness, we can begin to see that the physical world in which we are so strongly focused is just a minuscule part of all the worlds that exist. Few of us realize, until we consciously step out onto the path of evolvement, that many of these other worlds interpenetrate our own at all times.

This is why the Qabala teaches how to connect with beings who are companions in our journeys. These beings are the archangels and angels, as well as the archetypal thoughtforms manifesting in specific "magickal images and forms." There are many who fear contact with any being outside the physical. Usually, these people also fear contact with anyone outside their own neighborhood, ethnic background, religion, etc. We each have the capacity to set limits on what we will tolerate and what we won't in all of our relationships, physical and spiritual.

Yes, there are negative and ignorant energies in the so-called spirit realm and in the ethereal dimensions that we are trying to access. They also exist within the physical world as well. This does not preclude trying to develop relationships with those who can benefit us. We do not hide in our homes, afraid to make contact with other humans, because we have heard there are bad people walking around the streets. We alone decide who we allow into our lives, in the physical and the spiritual worlds.

Most of the guides and beings that we meet in the processes of this book are simply disseminators of information. They help illuminate us about ourselves. Most are protective helpers and companions. With the Qabala, there is a built-in safety check to insure that those we encounter are there to help and assist. This is why the God-names of the sephiroth are so very important. We can intone the name around or at those we encounter. If they are not of benefit to us, they will dissolve, for the God-name represents the highest, most spiritually powerful force at that level of our consciousness. It rules above all else.

The name of the archangels also serves to protect and can be used in a like manner. One should use the God-name or archangelic name(s) of the individual sephiroth that are linked by the path you are using. In this way, something from outside the path cannot intrude into your own working. *Test all things! Do not assume the image you are seeing is appropriate. Test it with the use of the God-name(s). If it stands firm, then you know it is appropriate.*

TO INSURE THE BEST WORK WITH THEM:

1. Clean and balance the chakras first.
2. Clean the area in which you will be performing the meditation. Use a "banishing ritual," described in the last chapter.
3. Thoroughly ground yourself.
4. Allow them to behave as individuals.
5. Do not impose your own expectations. It is a blessing to have an archangel or angelic being work with you. Let them decide how best it should be done. Even the lowliest of angels is more highly evolved than mankind.
6. For the time being, accept non-judgmentally the reality of the situation. This will help prevent self-delusion, positive or negative.
7. They will appear distinctly male or female, although they are truly neither. They often appear in the gender you will accept most easily.
8. If they display a quality or temperament that you do not like, dismiss them strongly. The astral plane is full of beings—good and bad—that can take on any appearance they desire. Use the God-names. If it is an imposter, or one that is not for your highest good, they will dissolve. At that point, it is best to return to your normal state of consciousness, perform the banishing ritual and try another day.
9. These wondrous beings are bound by universal laws. They can only help as much as they are allowed. The symbols and imagery used in the pathworkings send the message out, inviting their assistance and guidance in your growth process.

MEETING THE ARCHETYPES OF THE TAROT

This book is about working with images and learning to enter into them in a sympathetic manner. One must be able to loosen the restriction of the mind in order to do so. Any creative person, artist or inventor, has already learned to do so. We are learning to use the imagination in a productive manner. As with all things, persistence will pay its rewards. Do not be discouraged if there are no immediately recognizable results. Energies play subtly upon us, through normal life circumstances. We are developing the ability to see the significance and interrelatedness of all things. This takes time and practice, but the rewards, once accomplished, grant one power, strength and control over one's life and destiny.

The images upon the tarot cards are reflective of certain archetypal energies. That and the thoughtform energy that has developed around them through centuries of use enable one to use it as a bridge to the universal energies. The twenty-two cards of the major arcana reflect the energies that are inherent within the paths of the Tree of Life. They reflect the combined energies of the sephiroth they link.

PATHWORKING WITH THE TAROT:

1. Choose the starting temple as previously described.
2. Set the tone for the energy of the path to be awakened with candles, fragrances, dance movements (chapter 6), etc.
3. Familiarize yourself with the tarot card reflecting the energy of the path. Read about it, its basic meaning, etc. Record this in your pathworking journal.
4. There is a difference in the temple with this technique. In place of a door behind the altar leading to the second sephira of the path, there is a life-sized depiction of the tarot card hanging upon the wall behind the altar.
5. As you stand before the picture, with the archangel of the temple beside you, call the picture into life with the God-name of the temples of both sephiroth of the path. The picture takes on three-dimensional form, and you enter into the scenery of the tarot trump.
6. The figure in the picture walks the path (in the appropriate color) with you. He or she teaches you how these energies will play upon you and your life circumstances. The images of the trump, and the thoughtform energies built around them, become teachers to awaken your awareness.
7. Impose the astrological symbol, the Hebrew letter and any personal symbols into the scenery in any way you desire.
8. As you approach the second temple (the end of the path), visualize the tarot card forming a doorway into it. Superimpose the astrological symbol or Hebrew letter over the tarot card to open the door. Enter a second temple, to be greeted by the archangel of it.

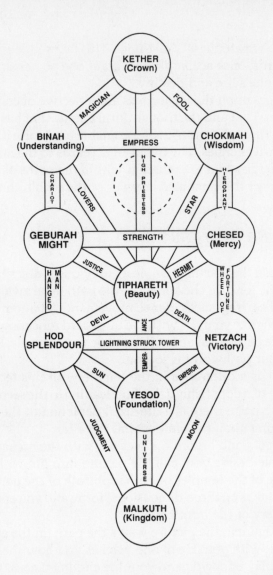

Tarot Within the Tree of Life

* The Star and The Emperor are often interchanged upon the Tree. All tarot assignments are flexible. The path of Netzach to Yesod is one of hope and creative power; thus the Star can provide an excellent symbol for this, as can the Emperor, the card of poets and dreamers. Likewise on the path from Tiphareth to Chokmah. The Star links the sphere of the Sun, our own star, to the Wisdom of Chokmah. Since it links the higher light with our own internal light, the Emperor can also provide an excellent door.

You create the images within the picture and within the meditation. Magickal use of the imagination to bridge the levels of consciousness involves a skilled blend of deliberate and concentrated visualization, with spontaneous allowance of images to arise in association with it. It takes time and practice.

Images grow and change in meaning and in depth, and in their effects upon us as we grow and change. Sometimes too much intellectualizing about them can hinder the process. Converse with the characters in the cards. You may hear other voices as well. File them away for future meditations. You may also discover that the scenery in the picture is different, while you are in it, from how you first perceive it as a card. This is a common occurrence. Archetypal energies play upon us and within our lives differently. It is what makes each of us uniquely creative. If the color of the path is correct, and if other symbols of the path are visible, do not be concerned. If there are no indications that you are where you are supposed to be, just visualize yourself back into the Temple.

Archetypal Energies of the Tarot

THE FOOL—Path 11 *(Chokmah to Kether)*

This is the path of complete trust. For those whose life path it may be, it stimulates the development of poise in the universe. It manifests and reflects renewed innocence. It is the energy of childlike wisdom in response to the world. It involves learning to keep this wisdom alive in the physical, while at the same time infusing the physical with the spirituality of higher consciousness. Each day must be seen as new and approached without fear. It is the path for those who will be or are becoming the true teachers of wisdom, often merely through example. It is the path of the High Temples, retreats and monasteries, filled with scrolls of ancient wisdom and teachings to be passed on.

THE MAGICIAN—Path 12 *(Kether to Binah)*

This path presents the individual with all the tools necessary for growth and higher consciousness. Opportunities become plentiful when its energies are activated, but they can go unrecognized because they are often in a primitive state. This is the path that awakens the realization that we have all we need to achieve success, but must learn to use all of our spiritual and physical tools as well. The use of divine power is available to us on this path. It is a path that awakens energy to teach wisdom, truth and dexterity. It is the path to recognize that which hasn't been nourished. It is the energy of mother figures and womblike settings; it is the feminine energies we use to give birth.

HIGH PRIESTESS—Path 13 *(Tiphareth to Kether)*

This is the path to learning of our self-made obstacles. It is a path whose energies work to remove the barriers between the inner and the outer worlds. It is a path that teaches us to face all that opposes us in realizing our higher self. It is a path that is referred to as the "Gateway to Knowledge," because when we can balance the emotions, we can hear our own inner voice. It is a life path that enables us to begin to overcome the obstacles we have created in this life or in past lives. Part of what is experienced is termed the "Dark Night of the Soul" that ultimately brings the hidden mysteries to the surface. It manifests experiences that help us to recognize that there is a constant flow of positive and negative energies, both of which serve a purpose in our lives. This is the path of masters coming and going. It is a bittersweet path which can open a wealth of higher intuition.

THE EMPRESS—Path 14 *(Binah to Chokmah)*

This is a path of energy and blessings. It awakens opportunities for us to learn to acknowledge and give thanks. It is a path of status in the physical world, as physical actions determine the growth of the soul. It is a path of birth and changes that can fulfill every person's dreams. It involves lessons in understanding the feminine principle of evolution and birth. It is through the feminine (illumined soul) that the Christ is born within. It is a path to recognizing the feminine energy in everyone, the power to create and give birth. It is a path of joy and love through understanding the universal process of reproduction, physical and spiritual. It unites the male and female to create new life. It brings an appreciation of the splendor that exists in every growing thing.

THE EMPEROR—Path 15 or Path 28 *(Tiphareth to Chokmah /*
Yesod to Netzach)

The Emperor is linked to those archetypal energies that assist us in recognizing the laws of God and man. When used with the paths, it releases energies that lead to respect for other authorities. It releases energy that teaches us to strive for higher, more spiritual laws within our lives. It manifests in life experiences which teach us that our balance is only disturbed when we are not in tune with the necessary order of things. The individual upon this path in life must learn to attune to the necessary order, even if it means facing bitterness. At such time, pathworking with the Emperor will be of assistance. It opens the doors to the laws of the higher planes and disciplines. When used with the 15th Path, it is known as the "Angelic Gateway" across the Abyss because it fills our lives with guiding spirits to teach us the laws and how to work with them. It is a path that manifests guardian angels and friends—calming hands within our lives. It brings clarity of soul.

THE HIEROPHANT— Path 16 *(Chesed to Chokmah)*

This is a path for the upliftment of the soul. It is tied to those archetypal energies that contribute to the spirit of God on Earth in any number of ways. Conditions manifest that help us to learn to defend our beliefs and to live by the truth. Upon this path we learn to face all false sense of security, as well as our ancestral fears. It is a path of freedom only when released from everything that is not of your own belief. This path links the archetypal rulers of wisdom and mercy, the kindly and the compassionate. It is the path of the Round Table and leads across the Abyss through the "Gateway of Royalty." The Hierophant opens the gate for you to "know thyself."

THE LOVERS—Path 17 *(Tiphareth to Binah)*

This is the path of choice, discrimination and communication. It teaches us to listen to our own inner voice. It manifests circumstances to teach us that we hold our destiny within our own hands. It releases the karmic desires of the higher self. Upon this path in life we learn that we cut ourselves off from the blessings and guidance by using only our conscious intellect. This path holds the promise of the Almighty to mankind. It is known as the "Gate of Fate" across the Abyss. It implies that we are fated from prebirth by what we have already set in motion. It is a path whose energies include both the serious and the funny, and its energies can help us find our own true path within this incarnation. These energies become most active when the advancement of humanity is upheld. It contains the gold that is encased in lead. It is the path of alchemy.

THE CHARIOT—Path 18 *(Geburah to Binah)*

This is a path whose energies contain opportunity for self-discipline and control. It is a path that teaches that we are first a soul, and thus we have responsibilities as such. Its archetypal energies stimulate a merging of the divine with the soul, which can create a new consciousness. By controlling and understanding the God-power within us all, we can realize all we need. It is our divine right to explore and to realize the purpose of our existence. This path holds the symbols for death and change which brings new control. It crosses the Abyss by the "Gate of Death," but the so-called Angel of Death always comes in a friendly guise. It is the path of the Dark Mother—she who brings enlightenment to darkness through discipline. It is a path of heroes, and the bridge to the Grail Castle, a bridge that is like walking on the edge of a knife initially but widens as we step forward.

STRENGTH—Path 19 *(Geburah to Chesed)*

This path has energies that stimulate the development of true spiritual strength. This card is tied to those archetypal energies that manifest conditions for the facing and removing of doubts and fears. This is the path of self-discovery through overcoming indecision. Its energies teach us not to allow others to take advantage of us. It holds an energy that stimulates the desire to overcome material and spiritual barriers. This is the path of the Knights of the Grail in their quests. It involves the rightings of wrongs, and the paying of the price in order to reap the rewards. This is the path of the peacekeepers, the defenders of the weak. It is a path that stimulates the melding of opposites and contrasts.

HERMIT—Path 20 *(Tiphareth to Chesed)*

This card releases energies in pathworking that help us to realize there is always illumination for us. It helps us to realize we are never truly alone; there is life and energy on all planes around us. It requires the leaving of worldly cares behind, leaving the security of the ego and forgetting the importance of earthly endeavor. This alone will enable us to light the way for others. This is a path of healing and illumination. It is a path of understanding that all we need do is "Ask and it shall be given . . ." The problem usually lies in the proper way to ask, and this is what these energies teach. Those who have already awakened this energy, and who have already walked this path unconsciously, know how and thus always "seem" to get what they want or need. This is the path of the strong, silent types who have the capacity to conquer all with their compassion. It teaches the application of power and new forms of the expression of energy in our life conditions.

WHEEL OF FORTUNE—Path 21 *(Netzach to Chesed)*
This card, when used with pathworking, releases the archetypal energies of honor and fame, and their rise and fall within our lives. We will know good or evil according to our desires. This path releases the energies that manifest in the teaching of the principle of synchronicity (things happening in the time and manner and means that are best for us). It is a path which teaches us that there is a flux and flow of Nature, and teaches how to place ourselves within its rhythms. This is a path that stimulates sensitivity. It is the life path of sensitive and sensible souls, and creative souls (artists, musicians, etc.). It teaches us that if we want a harvest, we must first plant the seeds.

JUSTICE—Path 22 *(Tiphareth to Geburah)*
This card ties to the archetypal energies for the feeling and hearing of our own conscience, our own inner voice. It stimulates energies with pathworking that can manifest chaos and disruption if we do not heed that inner voice. To become involved with the higher self is to know your purpose on Earth. Once we realize that we are souls first, then the higher levels open up to us. This path manifests the opportunity to learn the proper application of thoughts and action. This is a path whose energies can show the need for balance at all times. This path manifests energies to learn to blend the physical and spiritual. This is the path of karmic action and assessment. It is a path whose energies are catalystic, setting things in motion within our life that need balancing. It releases an energy for clearing the debris of our life (past and present). It is a life path that can and will stimulate, and even force, equilibrium.

HANGED MAN— Path 23 *(Hod to Geburah)*
This is a link to those archetypal energies which stimulate new perspectives upon the life path. It is aligned to those energies that involve learning to submit to the higher. It is a path that teaches tolerance and upliftment. We were not meant to focus solely upon the material; this path releases the desire to merge with universal forces. When we are totally willing to hear, the word of God will be spoken.

The archetypal energies stimulated by this card teach us that we have *chosen* this earthly experience. It is the life path of ancient initiation and the testing of character to learn and manifest our true purpose in life.

DEATH—Path 24 *(Netzach to Tiphareth)*

This card helps activate those archetypal energies that release and teach transition, sacrifice and change. Transition is part of life; it is not cessation of life. This path and its energies are filled with the imageries of death, transition and love. It manifests situations that awaken opportunities to renew the soul. It manifests situations that teach us that Death is not real. It provides an aligning of the energies of the soul with the energies of the universe. This path always involves a lesson in not resisting change, because the energy around us at such times will provide all of the strength necessary. The words, "Thy rod and thy staff shall comfort me all of the days of my life . . ." hold true for this path and its energies. The pathworking with this card manifests situations that teach us to leave the past behind. It cannot be recaptured, and trying to do so only creates a limbo within our lives.

TEMPERANCE—Path 25 *(Yesod to Tiphareth)*

This card helps align those archetypal energies that teach beauty and harmony in moderation. It holds the key to higher levels of consciousness and their safe use. Rising to a higher level can bring a rapid development of the psychic energies and senses, which can create imbalance. Balancing the spiritual and the physical and the ways in which we express them within our lives is essential. This is a life path that will stimulate those experiences which demonstrate the need to balance what has not been balanced. Through equilibrium we can discover our true purpose in life. We must try new things and still keep our feet on the ground. This path and its energies manifest conditions that will teach us this. Its mysteries can link us again with the divine.

THE DEVIL—Path 26 *(Hod to Tiphareth)*

This card, when used in pathworking, helps release those archetypal energies that test our innate abilities and teach us to use our innate power properly. It is a path that presents opportunities to overcome temptations. When used with the tarot card, this path will

manifest conditions that test those upon the quest for higher consciousness. It tests the seeker of light. Its energies can submerge us in
the material, so that we will want to change. It is a path that creates
situations that strongly teach us not to ignore the inner voice. We
must seek the spiritual, just as we seek medical help for the body
when it is in true pain. This path's energies, when activated through
the symbology of this card, will help us to contact our true needs,
especially when our life is in turmoil. It requires that we come as a little child to ask for help. It is a path to put our journey back on
course.

THE TOWER—Path 27 *(Hod to Netzach)*

When used with pathworking, this card releases those archetypal
energies that stimulate karmic reassessment. It stimulates the tearing
down of the old foundations so that newer, stronger ones can be
formed. It manifests the energies in our life for the breaking down of
outworn forms. It is a path whose energies are beneficial to all who
are striving in life and wanting to step out. It releases the archetypal
energies to change fortunes. It is a path which will reveal the false
securities of our hopes and dreams. It stimulates the energy of change
in our life, especially when clinging to old goals that could prevent us
from accepting new and wonderful opportunities in the future. If we
are feeling lost on the path of life, this card in pathworking will
release energies to tear down the walls and let new light into our
life.

THE STAR—Path 28 or Path 15 *(Yesod to Netzach /*
Tiphareth to Chokmah)

This card stimulates an awakening of energy that can tie us to
the source of all inner strength within the universe. It manifests
higher understanding in all life situations. The 28th Path is the path
of all temples and their peaceful grounds. This card can inspire us to
realize that there is always light to be drawn upon. It helps us to pierce
the darkness by submitting ourselves to the divine. It manifests
situations that confront us with our petty desires so that we can lose
them. It manifests situations that make us aware of our individuality,
and it reveals the earthly concerns that must be eliminated before
reaching out to the universe. When used on the 15th Path, it lights the
way across the Abyss, and it reveals those angelic brethren guiding
our lives to higher temples.

THE MOON—Path 29 *(Malkuth to Netzach)*

This card releases the archetypal energies that teach us to awaken greater faith and intuition. It has an energy that can draw us into contact with all those who can make us feel happy and beloved. As a life path, its energies often bring a testing of an individual's faith. Without it, we become vulnerable and can succumb to failure much more easily. This path's energies, when stimulated by this card, help us to see future possibilities so we will not lose sight of the lofty goals we came to attain in this incarnation. It helps us to realize that the blessings we receive daily are often very real but very subtle and frequently unnoticed.

THE SUN—Path 30 *(Yesod to Hod)*

This card releases the energies of the pathworking in a unique manner. This is the path of ancient lodges and mystery schools, with all of their magickal and ritual equipment. This path literally stimulates new sunshine. It releases energies that reveal our own selfishness and fears, so that we can breathe new sunshine into those dark corners. It manifests conditions that help us to realize that we have been granted a place in the universe. It creates situations and circumstances that assist in recognizing our purpose in this incarnation and why we should be thankful for it. This path can awaken joy and happiness for the future, as well as the ability to pass it on to others. It stimulates new opportunities.

JUDGMENT—Path 31 *(Malkuth to Hod)*

When this card is used in pathworking, it releases the archetypal energies to show us our links to the past and to all of mankind. This is the path of karma and of cause and effect. It releases energy that stimulates situations in which we must face responsibility and take on our divine purpose. It calls forth, through life circumstances, a realization of what our purpose is and how all situations within this life have added to that purpose. It can reveal how to deal with situations and people from the perspective of our own life purpose. It stimulates energies that force and activate greater choice in our mission in life. It can reveal unwanted ties and show that there is always a blessing of cosmic energies playing within our lives.

THE WORLD—Path 32 *(Malkuth to Yesod)*

This card releases the energy of the spiral dance of creation. The world is ever growing and gives way to the newer and better. This path has an energy that can open up new worlds, perspectives and awarenesses. It lets us know, when we activate its energies, that we are free to go in any direction. It lets you know that each day contains opportunities to grow and learn. This is a path that stimulates the release of pressures, sometimes by bringing them to a head. It manifests situations that help us recognize how insignificant many of our self-created troubles are in relation to other things within the universe. It helps us hear the voice of the higher in times of darkness and prepares the consciousness to reach out ever higher.

The tarot cards are reflections of archetypal energies, just as are the Hebrew letters, the colors, the astrological symbols, etc. They all activate the archetypal energies of the paths in their own unique way, bringing them into manifestation in our physical life. The cards, when used in pathworking, trigger a release of the more universal energies in a slightly varied manner. There are many ways for energy to express itself within our lives, and each symbol serves as a catalyst for such manifestation. Self-observation and reflection is preeminent in learning how to consciously work with such manifestations. That is the adventure of pathworking and the wonder of Life!

IMAGICKAL TECHNIQUE - Discovering the Personal Life Path

Almost all of the esoteric sciences can be applied to the Qabala. Numerology—the mysticism of numbers—is no exception. Archetypal energies manifest in many forms. They are reflected through symbols and images, colors, sounds, and numbers. All energy and all life is vibration; numbers are the mathematical correlations of those vibrations in relation to ourselves or to any aspect of our life.

Numbers are Nature's alphabet. Numerology is an ancient science that dates back almost 10,000 years B.C. The masters of the fourth root race (Atlantean Epoch) recognized that everything in nature was geometrically formed. All of the world's scriptures, such as the Vedas, the Zohar, the Torah, the Bible, Zoroaster and Buddha, and the writings of Confucius, cannot truly be understood in their most esoteric sense without an understanding of the vibration and significance of numbers.

The Masters of Israel were well versed in the Law of Vibration and how the archetypal energies were reflected in it. The twenty-two letters of the Hebrew alphabet were considered the twenty-two steps the soul had to take to mastership, and as the twenty-two paths that bridged and united all the levels of our consciousness. Each letter and its numerical correspondent indicates an initiation, a path which man must walk to develop mastership.

We all come to learn certain lessons and develop certain capacities, which bring abilities to assist us in this path. Because of the density of the physical body, it is possible to lose contact with the soul and its purpose for this incarnation. In its wisdom, a soul chooses a time and date and a name with a number and energy correspondence, which serves as a subtle reminder. They act upon us unconsciously, creating situations in which we undergo the lessons we have chosen. We are not controlled by them, but becoming aware of them can increase our understanding of what we have come to do. They can tell us why we have appeared on this planet at this time, what lessons we have to teach ourselves, and how to use the tools we brought to assist us in overcoming obstacles.

Every letter has a numerical value which denotes the vibrational quality of the energy playing within our life. They provide clues to the characteristics, the desires, the abilities, and tests we encounter. This is not a study of numerology per se, but it will deal with how we can apply some very simple and basic numerological techniques to the Qabalistic Tree of Life to show us three things primarily:

1. The path we have chosen to walk in this incarnation.
2. The sephira or level of consciousness we have chosen to work with and develop most strongly.
3. The abilities and energies of the path that will assist us in accomplishing what we came to do (the path we have previously awakened, with all its inherent energies, and brought with us into this lifetime).

Our names and birthdates can be translated into numbers which are correlated to specific energies of the Tree of Life. Specifically, they can be correlated to the individual sephira and the tarot cards that reflect a specific path we have come to bridge more fully. If we know which tarot card relates specifically to our birthdate and name at birth, we can discern which of the paths on the Tree we have come to work with more strongly in this lifetime, and we will understand many of the experiences we have had.

Our *birthdate* is our dominant vibration. It is the keynote of our life essence. It can reflect which level of consciousness we must stimulate to realize true happiness and success, and it can indicate exactly which path, with all of its tests and initiations, we must walk to achieve mastership.

Our birthdate corresponds to our life path, our destiny, our School of Life lesson: what we have come to learn within this lifetime. It is the lesson that the soul wants to complete here on Earth, and the path of experience needed for our further evolvement. It indicates the path we walk, the virtues and vices we will more frequently encounter, and what we are ultimately striving for.

The birthdate gives two powerful keys to our unfoldment. It will tell us the sephira, that level of our consciousness which can reveal and illumine our life aspects most fully. At this sephira we find the archangel who will serve as the predominant teacher and source for illumination. The second key involves translating the birthdate to a specific path on the Tree to determine where and how our tests and initiations will occur. This involves translating the birthdate into a corresponding tarot trump, which can then serve as a symbol for bridging to the archetypal energies that are overseeing our initiation in this lifetime. Remember that the sephira brings *illumination, but the path activates that illumination.* Both can be determined from the birthdate.

To discover the sephira and the specific path, one must reduce the birthdate to numbers. The digits are added individually. The month is the number of the month in the year: January = 1, February = 2, March = 3, etc.

JULY I5, 1952 = 7-15-1952 = 7+1+5+1+9+5+2 = 30

When the total is achieved, reduce it by adding the individual digits within the total until they are 9 or less:

30 = 3+0 = 3

In this case *3* represents the sephira which the individual has come to awaken and use to bring greater *illumination*. It is within the energies of the third sephira that one will find the archangelic teachers to help teach. It is at this level of consciousness that assimilation of the life experiences will most strongly occur. (Reading and meditating more about the individual sephira will yield much to the individual about his or her life experiences!)

Number	Sephira
1	Kether
2	Chokmah
3	Binah
4	Chesed
5	Geburah
6	Tiphareth
7	Netzach
8	Hod
9	Yesod
10(1)	Malkuth

(Malkuth and Kether can be either 1 or 10. Both should be explored, as the individual will often work from both at different times within his or her life.)

To determine the specific path on the Tree of Life, the birthdate must be correlated to a tarot card. In this case the birthdate is reduced in the same manner as above, but instead of continuing to reduce until 9 or less, the birthdate is reduced until 22 or less:

$$July\ 15, 1952 = 7\text{-}15\text{-}1952 = 7+1+5+1+9+5+2 = 30 = 3+0 = 3$$

$$August\ 17, 1949 = 8\text{-}17\text{-}1949 = 8+1+7+1+9+4+9 = 39 = 3+9 = 12$$

By using the table on the following page, we can determine the specific path we have come to walk in this lifetime, with all of its inherent lessons!

Correspondences

No.	Card	Path
1	Magician	Binah to Kether
2	High Priestess	Tiphareth to Kether
3	Empress	Binah to Chokmah
4	Emperor	Tiphareth to Chokmah / Yesod to Netzach
5	Hierophant	Chesed to Chokmah
6	Lovers	Tiphareth to Binah
7	Chariot	Geburah to Binah
8	Strength	Geburah to Chesed
9	Hermit	Tiphareth to Chesed
10	Wheel of Fortune	Netzach to Chesed
11	Justice	Tiphareth to Geburah
12	Hanged Man	Hod to Geburah
13	Death	Netzach to Tiphareth
14	Temperance	Yesod to Tiphareth
15	The Devil	Hod to Tiphareth
16	The Tower	Hod to Netzach
17	The Star	Yesod to Netzach / Tiphareth to Chokmah
18	The Moon	Malkuth to Netzach
19	The Sun	Yesod to Hod
20	Judgment	Malkuth to Hod
21	The World	Malkuth to Yesod
22	The Fool	Chokmah to Kether

By using this table, one can see that the two examples (July 15, 1952 and August 17, 1949) can be applied to the tarot cards and their corresponding paths on the Tree of Life:

July 15, 1952 = 3 = Empress = Binah to Chokmah
August 17 1949 = 12 = The Hanged Man = Hod to Geburah

We can now discern which paths and energies will play upon us most strongly within our lives. We can begin to explore more fully that path which we have chosen to walk towards mastership in this lifetime! Meditation and the imagickal techniques for accessing these paths will reveal much concerning the circumstances of our life, especially in relation to how far off we may be from our original intentions. They can also reveal how best to get back on the right track. Above all others these techniques should be repeated periodically, for just such purposes.

One other method that can reveal even further insights into the tasks we have chosen to master within this lifetime is reflected in the path (and its corresponding sephira) that is associated with the sign of the zodiac under which we were born. It is not as specific as the path of the actual birthdate, but its energies will be reflected within our life to varying degrees. Remember that we use the Qabala—the sephiroth and the paths of wisdom—to expand our awareness of who we are and what we can do. We use it for revelation and transformation. Connecting them all, finding and exploring all the various correspondences, will provide much to assist us in the great alchemical change!

Determining the Soul's Expression

Just as the birthdate can reveal which sephiroth and paths we have come to work through in this lifetime, the full name at birth can also be correlated to the Tree of Life. Our name at birth is a compilation of the motives, knowledge and abilities that we bring with us into this incarnation to assist us in walking the path we have chosen. It reflects the archetypal energies that express themselves through us, so that we can most positively achieve what we have set upon.

When converted to a path on the Tree of Life, the name will reveal the energies we are most likely already expressing—that which we find the easiest to do. It can indicate the grade or soul level achieved in the past, along with the abilities most easily manifested. It is the reflection of our outer nature, and it tells us where we can place our natural talents to most effectively walk our individual paths.

Just as the date of birth can be correlated to the tarot trump and a particular path upon the Tree, so can the name of the individual. There are many methods of transposing the names into numbers and thus to the tarot. The most common is the following, which correlates all the letters of the alphabet to one of the nine basic digits (the number ten being counted as the number one). In this way, just as with the birthdate, the full name (as it appears upon the birth certificate) will reveal the energies of a sephira which you can access more easily, and the energies which you will be able to express more powerfully. It can also be used in relation to a specific path which reveals the energies and work you will have to put forth to express this sephira most fully within this life.

Using the table below, convert your full name at birth to numbers. Add them individually and reduce until they are 10 or less to determine which sephira's energies you are most capable of expressing. Then reduce it to 22 or less and, using the chart on page 185, find the initiation path you have taken in the past, and which will assist you in this incarnation's work.

1	2	3	4	5	6	7	8	9
A	B	C	D	E	F	G	H	I
J	K	L	M	N	O	P	Q	R
S	T	U	V	W	X	Y	Z	

John Alan Doe

1685 1315 465 = 1+6+8+5+1+3+1+5+4+6+5 = 45 =9

#9 = YESOD
#9 = THE HERMIT = PATH OF TIPHARETH TO CHESED

The energies of this sephira and this path should be the easiest to awaken and experience, assisting us in our present incarnational tests and initiations.

If desired the present name can be converted to the Hebrew alphabet. It will often elicit a different path. There are numerological texts that can show how to do this; it is then just a matter of relating that to the tarot trump and their corresponding path upon the Tree. An entire numerological analysis can be correlated to the Tree. They are all simply methods of self-exploration and realization.

The archetypal energies play subtly in all aspects of ourselves and our lives. These techniques will make us more cognizant and watchful of how they are playing. We are becoming the completely responsible being, demonstrating to ourselves and our world that everything has significance. As we learn this, we begin to understand that we are much more than what we have ever anticipated. We are creative beings with the capability of spiritualizing our lives and all of the material world. We can create greater light within our world by shining light into all corners, chasing back the shadows and revealing the wonders that exist within life and the divine expression of life in ourselves!

chapter six

Dancing the Tree of Life

Just as he who dances in the body . . . acquires the right to share in the round dance, so he who dances in the spirit acquires the right to dance in the round of creation.

—ST. AMBROSE

The singer's soul abides in her throat.
But the dancer's soul abides in her whole body.

—KAHLIL GIBRAN

As music is God's song, dance is God's silent voice . . .

—LOUISE MATTLAGE

Working with the Qabalistic Tree of Life is a creative process. That is why sound, music and dance must be an essential part of it; music and dance make us more alive and touch us on other levels than just the physical. They form a bridge between heaven and Earth that we can all learn to use within our day-to-day lives.

Dance is preeminent in ancient magickal ritual. It was used to awaken and stir the forces and energies. It was, and still is, a way to link the mental realms with the physical. It can be used to transport the dancer from the physical reality to more ethereal ones—from the profane to the sacred. It is a metaphor of life and the process of manifestation. Thought creates within the mental world, leading to actions in the physical. We think and then we act.

The purpose of any physical ritual behavior is to direct and focus the consciousness. Our physical beings have a unique capacity for blocking our evolutionary process. Directed physical behavior, such as dance, can overcome this tendency, and help us to align our physical responses with our spiritual goals. It enables our physical energies to hold contact with our higher forces.

189

Dance fuses the hemispheres of the brain, linking right and left—the intuitive with the rational. Through dance movements and gestures, the essence of music is absorbed into the physical and then experienced on subtler levels. The central nervous system and the neuro-muscular systems transform the musical rhythms into a movement pattern. We become driven by it and are led away from the familiar focus of the everyday world. In the past, individuals would surrender to and be possessed by it; today it is important that we enter in full consciousness and actually learn to ride the rhythms to the inner world, with our wills intact.

Isadora Duncan evolved a theory of the physiological process of dance. She insisted that movement and breathing are inseparable. And to the ancients, life was breath. All movement is carried aloft and then returned to Earth through inhalation and exhalation. The movements change the breathing, and thus change the bridges to other levels of consciousness. To take it a step further, by aligning physical movements consciously, we can reach newer and deeper levels of consciousness.

The purpose of ritual dance is to make the world of energies and powers physical. We attempt to re-express these energies upon the physical plane, so that as unique individuals we learn to utilize them in the manner most suitable for us.

All dance is gesture, and we each have gestures that are uniquely our own. They give us color and enhancement. Gesture is related to the human condition in its creation of a desired appearance without truly representing it. Gestures serve to link the outer man with the inner, and to bridge us to our divine selves.

The modern concepts of dance for the average individual have changed dramatically over the centuries. Dance was part of the ancient mysteries, and its substance was the realm of magic, enchantment and ancient powers which lived within caves, forests and all of creation. It was the sacred instrument of worship, prayer and true magic, whether utilized within temple worship or in the invoking of rain.

The role of magic within dance has been diminished by our modern, materialistic thought processes. Actual energies are created or awakened in all forms of dance, even in the modern social dances. In these, magnetic energies are stimulated, but we have moved to touching "romantic" realms rather than the sacred realms.

The ancients recognized the possibility of such changes and so stressed continual watchfulness and control over the dance energies. They recognized the therapeutic and educational value of dance, but they focused upon its sacred aspect because they knew that all movement invoked very subtle and powerful energies. They recognized that the male and female participants were not just dancers, but priests and priestesses. As such, there was a need for greater awareness and control of these energies.

Sacred dance was a means of transcending our humanity. The dancer could gain control over normally automatic responses by evoking emotions and energies and then channeling them through the dance. In this manner, transcendence over these lower energies could be achieved. Sacred dance was an art that could fire man's vitality and revive depleted energies. It involved improvisation and individual creativity. Every movement and gesture was linked to the purpose of the dance.

All human activity is a kind of dance and ritual, but it is time to re-tap the ancient approaches to dance ritual. Non-believers will have little understanding of the true ritual power of dance. For many the techniques will simply be a form of spiritual window-shopping. The dervishes will only be dancers. The Catholic mass becomes little more than a spectacle. These individuals must be reminded that religious ritual of any kind is not—nor should it ever be—performed for its own sake. (This may, in fact, be the primary problem of the weekly mass.) It should be performed as a way of reaching another level of being, as a way of releasing spiritual meaning into our lives. Ritual is not meant to be performed for audiences, which is a profanation in many ways. And to simply adopt the outer appearances of ritual is to start the process of death.

True sacred dance is very ancient. It is the outer expression of the inner spirit. The modern process of dancing the Tree of Life is not to just re-enact ancient mysteries. Our energies have changed too much for it to be effective or useful. We are also somewhat disassociated with much of the true esoteric teachings of the ancients. We must become priests and priestesses of New Age dance. That requires us to remember that energies are *not* created by the dance but simply invoked and challenged by it. It also requires that we remember that the energies invoked function less through our talent for dancing than through our participation! It enhances the ability to envision a second world—the major source of our esoteric knowledge.

The Tree is an ancient symbol for the axis of the world. The

entire world—heaven and Earth—spins upon it. Dancing the Tree of
Life is a way of setting the world in motion. We have our roots in the
Earth (the underworld), but like a tree, our branches can spread and
reach heavenward. Dancing the Tree (climbing the tree) is equated
with the passing from one plane of being to another. Traditionally,
the Tree (like all gateways) is guarded by a dragon or monster which
must be overcome before the treasure can be attained—before the
fruit can be picked. Esoterically, this is the overcoming of our lower
selves. This does not mean that we slay or kill the dragon. We must
harness and control our dragons—our energies. They are a part of us
while we are in the physical, but we can learn to control them and
redirect their energies in a creative manner to enhance our lives. This
is where the power of dance in ritual finds its greatest creativity. The
sacred dance provides a means for confronting and harnessing our
dragon energies for creative expression within our lives. This is the
key to the great alchemical change. It is not the killing of negative
energies. It is the transmutation of them within our lives!

BASIC DYNAMICS:

Most recently in our history, we find religious dancing taking
place within churches and temples; but many earlier groups created
"temples" by marking off sacred circles for the dance on the Earth
itself. One common theme was the imitation of angels dancing in
"heavenly rings" about the throne of God. This led to many of the circle dances which will be discussed later within this chapter, which
create a resonance, or sympathetic vibration (harmony), within the
participants.

Sacred dance helps us to transcend humanity. It is this aspect
that has been neglected for centuries, and yet which we are all capable
of reawakening. It is more than just a symbolic expression of an
individual's personal beliefs. In many cases, such as in the ancient
Kachina rites, the participants become sacred reflections of the powers
of the universe. A basic premise behind all esoteric teaching is that
we are the microcosm—a reflection of the macrocosm, or universe.
We have all of the energies of the universe within us. Sacred dance
was a means of stimulating them and bringing them out of the deeper
levels of our consciousness.

At the root of most ceremonial use of dance was sympathetic
magic. The movements and gestures create thoughtforms, vortices of
energy, fusing thought and action. The ancients understood that

dance, by its ability to invoke energy upon the physical plane, could shape the circumstances of nature simply by focusing that contagious quality of energy. It comes down to that Hermetic Principle discussed in chapter 1—"As above, so below; as below, so above." What we do on one level affects all other levels. The stronger we focus our energies and concentration, the stronger and greater will be the effect. This is what makes dance so powerful!

Religious or sacred dancing has been a functioning part of every society and civilization throughout the world. The shamans and priests used music and dance to induce a trance state. They utilized round or "circle" dances to imitate the path of the Sun. Chain dances were used to link the male and female energies, to bind both heaven and Earth, and to stimulate fertility. There were sword dances and thread-and-rope dances, as with the threads of Ariadne, the threads leading the dancer to the secret of knowledge throughout the maze of life. In all dances, intense feelings and the bodily movements were related.

In India the *devadasis* were the sacred dancing girls. They were married to the gods, and their dances represented the life of the gods they were married to. Egypt was a great dancing center. Its ancient dancers are even depicted within the hieroglyphics. The sacred mystery teachings were danced within the temples. The Nile and Cadiz were the greatest centers of ancient dancing. Cadiz was the sacred dancing school in Spain; it was also Egyptian in character. The Greek and the Roman mystery schools were strong in ritual dance. It formed— along with music—an essential part of their magickal and healing arts in the Orphic, Eleusinian and Bacchic mysteries. The snakelike winding of the Greek farandole dance of Provence symbolized the journey to the middle of the labyrinth—the pattern of the passage of the dead to the land of the afterlife. This was a common theme in many areas of the world. The dances were themes meant to stimulate multiple responses on a multitude of levels for the people.

The garments then, as they are today, were secondary to the movements. They can be discarded. Dances for higher states of consciousness are simple, personal and passionate. They do not and should not require great space. When a pattern is created or arranged for specific effects, it can create an illusion of great space, power and time. *Remember, we are fusing the mental and the physical.* It is not the talent but the participation that invokes the energy. The degree to which it is invoked is determined by the significance one can associate with the movements! Every gesture and movement is symbolic. The more meaning we attach to them, the deeper the level of consciousness and the greater the release of power.

Allow for individual expression. Do not necessarily allow the movements to become rote. Those movements and dances described within this book provide starting points. They are not the be-all and end-all for everyone. The process of evolvement requires that we assimilate, re-synthesize and adapt energies to what works for us as individuals. In essence, you are attempting to choreograph your own evolution, the awakening of your own unique energies. Yes, there are certain things that we can utilize and which serve as a foundation for us, but we must build from that point.

There are many ways of working out the dynamics of a dance that will open up the levels of consciousness that we know as the sephiroth in the Qabalistic Tree of Life.

Dancing Magic Circles

Then shall thou dance in a ring together with the angels, around Him who is without beginning or end.

—CLEMENT OF ALEXANDRIA

The fact that the sephiroth are depicted upon the Tree of Life as circles gives many clues to the use of circles for opening up those levels of consciousness to us. Even in the above quote one can find the significance for dancing the Tree of Life. The "dance in a ring" can reflect the various sephiroth, and the "around Him" can reflect the awakening of the God-force that is most active within that particular sephira, or level of consciousness, that can occur through the proper use of circle dancing.

The circle is a very powerful symbol and motion in both the physical and spiritual realms. It is a perfect symbol. It has no end and no beginning. We can start correctly anywhere within our evolutionary cycle. The movement in circles always brings to mind the turning of wheels (as in the wheel of life) and the movement of the Sun and planets. It is wholeness and the time cycles of the universe. It seals in and it seals out. The circle separates the inner from the outer; when moving in circular spirals, we can move from the outer into the inner realms or vice versa.

Making or dancing a circle is an act of creation. It is the marking off of sacred ground. When a circle dance is performed, the individual creates a sacred space within the mind (a place between the worlds, a point in which they intersect and play). The creation or marking off of a circle in Wiccan beliefs is sometimes referred to as "raising a cone of power." The circling creates a vortex of energy that is amplified by the combined wills of the participants.

The center of the circle is a point of focus. All dance—particularly circle dances—is a series of rhythmic steps around a central point, be it an altar, a fire, an individual or an idea. The dancing adds energy to the point within the circle—the *bindu*. The circle dance around the bindu creates a vortex of energy, while sealing out extraneous energies that could interfere with the ultimate purpose of the dance. By placing a symbol within the center and dancing around it, it can be protected; this also activates energies that symbolized the quest for the achievement of what was symbolized.

The circle dance is a sacred drama, employing physical motion to alter the mind and consciousness of the human being (audience or participant). It is a means to awaken deeper consciousness through physically enforced concentration. In the physical spiral motion, the individual is also mentally spiraling to other levels of consciousness.

Hints:

1. Take time to meditate upon the bindu before the dance itself. Remember that you are a being with latent power within your consciousness. Visualize yourself as being part of the spiral dance since the beginning of time. You are participating—and have been—since time immemorial, whether conscious of it or not.

2. Remember that every dance is actually two, an outer and an inner. The dance itself integrates these.

3. The dancing induces electrical changes within the human body, as it becomes saturated with the repetitive process of the steps.

4. If working with a group, keep the distances properly and start slowly. Coordinate the efforts to increase the harmony of the entire group.

5. Symmetry of steps is important and is powerfully effective, although it is not always necessary. As the circular movement unfolds, try a rhythm that is two steps forward and one step back. This particular movement is very effective in altering consciousness. It can even induce trance. (Forward—back, in—out, heaven—Earth.)

6. Have a definite beginning and a definite end. A traditional beginning and end is the taking of three steps toward the center of the circle, bowing, and then proceeding with the dance. At the end, the individual or group takes three steps back from the center of the circle and bows.

7. The speed of the movements is variable, according to the purpose of the ritual or the individual. How large a circle to make is also up to individual preference and discretion. Actual physical space available is usually the determining factor.

8. There is often great question about which way to move, clockwise or counterclockwise. *Clockwise*, or deosil, movement activates the energy. It is masculine and solar in its effects. It has a centrifugal effect, pulling the energy from the inside to the outside. It draws from the spiritual to the physical for what we need. It stimulates power.

   Counterclockwise, or widdershin, movement is inward or receptive in its energizing. It draws our outer consciousness into the inner. It activates the feminine and lunar energies. It can be used to awaken a greater sense of timelessness, opening the power of the past, present and future together.

9. As the steps of the dance unfold, there should be mental concentration upon the bringing of inner energies into the outer world or vice versa. This is why steps should be simplified. If the steps are too complicated, proper visualization of the effects will be limited.

10. Hand movements are also important during the dancing of the circle. Hand movements and gestures have been known as the true universal language. To the ancient Hermeticists, *every action should have a specific purpose and significance.* All should be organized; every gesture should have its symbolic significance in alignment with the purpose of the dance. There should be no idleness of movement.

The hands in an upward (palms raised) position is a gesture of receptivity. The palms downward indicates more of an activating energy flow—pure force. Palms up—form. Palms down—force. Form and force together (one palm up and the other down) create stress for growth. We cannot have one without the other.

Certain sephiroth on the Tree of Life are more receptive in their energy operations; others are more activating. The chart which follows can be a guideline for hand positions when performing circle dances to activate the specific sephiroth.

Sephira	Force/ Form	Palm Position	No. of Rotations
Kether	Both	Right down, left up	One
Chokmah	Force	Both down	Two
Binah	Form	Both up	Three
Chesed	Form	Both up	Four
Geburah	Force	Both down	Five
Tiphareth	Both	Right down, left up	Six
Netzach	Force	Both down	Seven
Hod	Form	Both up	Eight
Yesod	Both	Right down, left up	Nine
Malkuth	Both	Right down, left up	Ten

With the palms down, the energy radiates outward. With palms in a raised position, the energy is drawn within. When alternated, right palm down and the left up, there occurs a balance between form and force in the flow of energy activated by the hand movements. This balance occurs naturally with those sephiroth of the Middle Pillar.

11. There is often some question as to how many circular rotations to make to activate the energies of the sephiroth when circle dancing. This varies, but by using the chart above, the most simple way of determining and remembering it (while giving it appropriate significance) is by the numerological correspondence associated with the particular sephira. For example, for the sephira Hod the individual or group would dance the circle eight times.

12. Visualizing the color of the sephira, and accumulating and filling the circle with it while dancing the rotations, intensifies the effects.

13. If the sephira is one of *force*, then the dance should be performed in a deosil or clockwise direction. If the sephira is one of *form*, then it should be performed in a widdershins or counterclockwise direction. These clockwise and counterclockwise movements should bring to mind the workings of the machinery of the universe, which you as the dancer are setting in motion.

    If the sephira is one of those of the Middle Pillar combining force and form, the direction can be determined by the specific purpose. If it is a group dance, the group can be divided into two sets of performers—a circle within a circle. One group would dance clockwise, and the second counterclockwise. This intensely amplifies the energy invocation.

14. After the dance itself, there should be time for the assimilation of the energy by the individuals within the group. The simplest technique is for the individuals to step inside the magic circle that has been marked out by the dance. There the individuals assume a meditational pose, absorbing the energy and experiencing it being set in motion to manifest, according to its purpose within the physical life.

    Assuming one of the positions or *attitudes* as described below is an effective means of enhancing this. Remember that we are using the physical movements to stimulate specific responses. The more significance we give them, the more they can work for us.

Physical Attitudes:
1. **Prostrate**—This is grounding of the energies activated by the dance. With outstretched arms, it becomes serpentine (as in the Serpent of Wisdom within the Tree of Life). The prostrate position can also be semi-prostrate, as in the yoga position of the cat's stretch, with arms outstretched and the knees tucked under. Womblike in appearance, the dancer gives birth to new energies through dance.
   a. It is a position of personal negation—an acceptance of divine authority.

    b. It is an excellent position to use when reaching for the objective at the bindu or center of the sephirotic circle.

2. **Kneeling**—This position, when done on both knees, represents the human ascent toward divinity while still attached to the Earth. When assumed on one knee, it indicates an increase in freedom—partial resurrection through the divine energies activated in your life by the dance. (Genuflection signifies our status in relation to those beings of the archangelic realm who work with us as guides.)

3. **Standing**—This position signifies us now able, through the energies invoked, to be upright and able to move. It signifies the emergence into a body of light, accomplished through the energies of the dance. It is also symbolic of being able to now tread the path upon higher levels. We can climb the Tree to even greater heights.

4. **Sitting or Resting**—This position is one of outer quiet with great inner activity—the activity of the levels of consciousness stimulated by the dance. It is representative of the changing of energy from one state to the next. It is a position of closure and receptivity, especially effective for those sephiroth whose energies are *form*.

    With all of the sephiroth, any of these physical attitudes would work following the dance. The important factor is to find significance for all physical activity. Through the physical movements, gestures, and postures, we are learning to transcend the physical and link it with the spiritual.

5. Having completed the raising of the energy through the dance, you then assimilate and focus it through the meditation. This then brings us to the point of releasing it to work for you within your physical life. Before leaving the meditational pose or physical attitude, give thanks to the universe, in advance, for its manifestation into your life. Step back to the edge of the magic circle, and dance one rotation in the *opposite* direction. This opens the circle, releasing it to begin its work for you. Bow to the bindu, take three steps backward, and your ritual is completed.

Review:

1. Choose the sephira which contains energies you wish to awaken within you.
2. Decide on the particular effects within your life you wish this energy to bring about.
3. Set the atmosphere with candles, fragrances, etc. Take three steps to the center, where you have mentally placed your desire. Bow.
4. Begin the circle dance rotations (two steps forward and one step back).
   - The number of rotations is determined by the number of the sephira.
   - Make sure you have determined the proper direction to dance.
   - As you dance the magic circle, begin to see the appropriate color build within the circle.
5. Complete the rotations, step into the circle and assume the meditative, physical posture.
6. Meditate upon the objective, as if it is already working for you. Visualize and know that it is real. Hold the meditation until the realization of its fulfillment permeates your being.
7. Offer a prayer of thanksgiving for its manifestation in advance.
8. Move back to the circle's edge and dance one rotation in the opposite direction to release the energy to work for you. As you do this last rotation, see and feel the color and energy pouring forth to fulfill itself for you.
9. Bow to the center again and take three steps backward.

Spinning the Tree into Existence

A powerful technique for using circular movements to awaken the energies within us and the Tree of Life is "creating the vortex." The energies that we are trying to access operate at a higher vibration than physical energies. With spinning movements, we speed up our own energy centers, our chakras, so that we can more easily and consciously access the energies.

Our chakras mediate all energy going into and out of the physical body, and even though they are not part of the physical body, they are intimately connected to it, linking our more subtle energies to our physical consciousness. If we wish to access and ground higher vibrational energies, these centers need to operate and function more fully and completely. One effective way of speeding up our own vortices or chakras is through whirling motions.

Whirling helps to loosen the etheric webs so that the energy flowing into and out of the physical body and consciousness is stronger and more vital. It has a vitalizing effect and when combined with proper visualizations enhances meditation and work with the Qabala.

Whirling can be taken to extremes, as is done by some of the "whirling dervishes." When it is taken to extremes, the effects are detrimental. The chakras become overstimulated and thus imbalanced. This releases an imbalanced amount of psychic energy, which is often taken as a spiritual experience. It can so loosen the etheric body from the physical that it allows free access by other energies and entities without your control.

Whirling as is taught here is effective in speeding up the energy centers to elicit an easier access to levels of energy and consciousness that are not normally so accessible. Remember that dance is used in a controlled manner to achieve the energies of the spiritual—and more is not necessarily better. Just because you may feel the effects after a certain number of revolutions does not mean that increasing the revolutions will increase the effects. Some feel when they have used this technique for a while that the effect is lost. They do not seem to feel it as strongly as they did initially. This is usually a positive sign of growth. It indicates that your energy has grown, and your vibrational rate of the past has now increased and is *maintaining* a higher rate. *This is not an indication to increase the revolutions to try and recapture those first feelings.*

In essence, the individual has become acclimated to the higher vibrational rate, which is now the norm. Yes, we do want to continue to increase our energy, but this is more likely to involve a change in techniques altogether rather than an increase in the speed of the old techniques. We may still wish to use the old techniques, if only for the mind set they create in preparing to use the energies. They will align the physical so that the energies can be more fully experienced.

Creating the Vortex

1. Stand erect with arms outstretched.
2. Focus your attention on the appropriate sephira. Know how many revolutions are necessary to activate the energy of the sephira (e.g., Netzach = eight).
3. Hold the palms in the appropriate position.
4. Visualize yourself in the middle of a sacred circle. You can even create your own by walking a small area around you. As you do so visualize it filled with the color of the sephira with which you will be working.
5. In this area you will be invoking the energy of the sephira, so that you can more consciously activate it.
6. Visualize yourself as the magickal image for the sephira. Feel the energy start to come alive. Know that while assuming this image with this exercise, you become the magician. You will create energy where there had been none.
7. Tone the God-name for the sephira. This is a call to attention, and it activates all aspects of your being. Offer a prayer to the fulfillment of your purpose.
8. Visualize the archangel of the sphere standing guard over your activities and commence spinning the appropriate revolutions.
9. At their completion, assume one of the physical postures and meditate upon the energies of the sephira that are *now* active within your life. If you wish to take this even further, you can now visualize yourself entering into the Tree of Life and the appropriate inner temple, as you have already learned to do.
10. The spinning should *always* be done in a clockwise manner. Doing it counterclockwise can activate the *qlipoth*, or negative energies of the Tree. The clockwise movement also speeds up the activities of our own chakras, so they can more easily mediate the higher energies. The natural direction for the rotation of the chakras is clockwise.
11. If dizziness becomes too strong, stop immediately. The number of revolutions is a guideline. With practice, the body will be able to handle the revolutions without the discomfort. With practice, you can learn to activate the energies

of any sephira with only one revolution. You are learning to become the magician/alchemist. The important factor for now is doing something physical to correspond to the more ethereal energies you are accessing. As your own energy centers become acclimated to working with higher vibrations, the dizziness will no longer be a factor.

12. One can also "spin the entire Tree into existence" using this technique. You begin with one revolution—with proper visualizations—for Kether, move right to Chokmah and two revolutions, then on to Binah and three revolutions, etc. Assume that magickal images and visualizing the colors will bring the entire Tree of Life energies into play within the physical. This is an excellent exercise as a prelude to deeper work with the Tree, and it provides excellent practice in visualization and the assumption of "God-forms" and magickal images. It facilitates being able to do it at will.

13. Lighting the appropriate colored candle and incense enhances the effects.

14. This is also adaptable to pathworking:
    - Begin with creating a vortex for the sephira in which you will start the pathworking. Pause, move into the revolutions and visualizations for the second sephira of the path. At this point assume the physical attitude for meditation. See the colors and energies of both vortices mix and mingle. Enter into the Tree and begin the pathworking meditation as you have learned.
    - You can also begin with the revolution for the first sephira of the path. Next, assume the physical attitude for the meditation. Enter into the Tree and go through the pathworking. At the end, to ground the energies, create the vortex for the second sephira of the path.

15. As in all of the exercises, we combine visualization, sound (use of the God-names) and a physical action to imprint the mind with seeds for greater response and awareness. We create a mind-set through the physical so we can more fully touch the spiritual.

Dancing is the gesture of the whole body. It allies the body and soul. It is the creation of the energy, not just the conscious awareness of it—although the latter is what leads to the former. It induces electrical changes in the body which induce specific states of awareness. We are using purposeful physical behavior to activate very real spiritual energies, so we must learn to dance with intention. Dancing raises the appropriate energies, aligns the physical with the corresponding spiritual, complements the intention and grounds the energy so we can more fully and easily experience it and then integrate it.

By more consciously using dance we activate a very powerful force. We have discussed previously the hemispheres of the brain and the abilities that each possesses in its own right. Each hemisphere contains a force that we can learn to use. There is a third force that we have access to, and it is the force that is created when the other two are integrated. It is a force that is released from the heart and its very core. It goes beyond personal expression. It aligns our energies and rhythms with those of the cosmos. It aligns our soul with the cosmic soul. We become the true microcosm!

As we apply certain physical elements to spiritual concepts, and as we utilize physical postures and movements to enhance and invoke that which is beyond the physical, we are creating our own dance. We are creating a new world, a new consciousness and a new transformation.

Postures of the Tree

There are physical movements and postures that not only correspond to the levels of the Qabalistic Tree of Life but also reflect those energies, drawing them down into our physical environments, where they express themselves into our lives. We can learn to use specific physical movements and postures to create a mind-set that enables easier access to the energies within the Tree of Life.

Many times the student of metaphysics has difficulty achieving results through meditative exercises and work. It seems they put in much time just trying to receive something. Working with the physical movements will deliver results much more quickly and effectively. When a person finally sits down to meditate, he or she may still have on their mind that last phone call, the argument with the boss, the trouble the kids were in all day, etc. These kinds of mundane energies can block access to the energies of the Tree of Life.

The physical movements enable the person to move in consciousness from the outer world and all of its hassles to the inner much more fluidly. It creates a mindset. The physical activity forces the mind to shift gears; it must then concentrate on the movements or gestures. The movements and postures described in this next section are not exercises and are not in any way meant to be looked upon as an exercise program. They are physical movements that help us to make that transition from the outer to the inner and back again fluidly and more easily.

Gestures, postures and movements express the inexpressible. They utilize both aspects of the brain, especially when we are aware of their significances. They are direct and potent ways of communicating with the deities that lie within us, and they aid us in concentration so that we can utilize our highest capacities. The more meaning we can ascribe to them, the more they become empowered.

The Eastern world has recognized this for ages. Fortunately, there is a growing integration of Eastern and Western philosophies and techniques. There are methods that we can apply specifically to Western forms of mysticism. The yoga movements and postures are simply outer expressions which represent inner degrees of consciousness.

Yoga asanas are designed to be meditations in and of themselves, leading to greater depths. Using them in relation to the Western Qabalistic tradition reinforces the idea that there truly is "nothing new under the Sun." There are simply different variations. All gods are aspects of the same god, and we each have a responsibility of finding the method or combination of methods which best awaken the divine within ourselves.

In yoga, *kriya* is a movement, asana, mudra or exercise to produce an altered state of consciousness. There is an outer kriya which involves asanas and mudras (postures and gestures)—basic physical expressions. And there is the inner aspect as well that was only reflected through the asanas. In dancing the Tree of Life, we are doing the same thing. We are learning to apply physical expressions to inner realities. We are utilizing physical exercises to awaken spiritual energies. This is the importance of the following asanas, as they can be applied to the Qabalistic Tree of Life. They are simple physical movements and positions that reflect inner levels of consciousness, while simultaneously

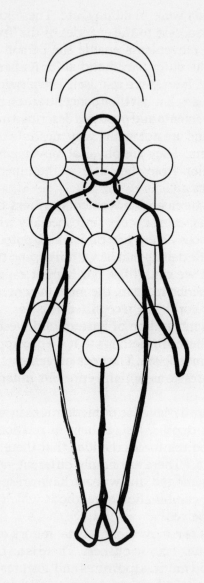

The Tree of Life Within the Human Body

206

releasing those inner latent energies and circulating them in a precise manner so that you can experience and utilize them to their fullest.

Postures are a language for communicating with the divinity that lies within us. Many of the yoga postures arose from a ritual mimicking of animals and nature to establish a magickal contact. We can use them in other ways to help us stimulate the energies on all levels within the Tree of Life.

The postures activate and circulate the energies of the sephiroth in specific ways, all of which can be correlated to the levels of our consciousness. They are creating a form for the force to manifest. They serve as a bridge to energies of our self often hidden from us. They assist in our visualization, and they help us to release energy for the transformations we are seeking.

The positions and movements are kept simple throughout the rest of this text, but it must be understood that even more techniques and methods of "Dancing the Tree" exist. The positions described are firm but pleasant, and will develop a stable, healthy connection to the energy of the sephira, and enable us to attune to it more easily for its release within our physical life. The more difficult positions and movements for you (and they do vary from individual to individual) indicate levels of consciousness that are more difficult for you to access and control. We can all do some variation, which means that we can at least access some aspect of the sephira and its energies within us. Remember the Law of Correspondence? No aspect is entirely inaccessible; and the more we work with them, the easier they become and the more energy is released to us. Even our consciousness "muscles" need to be loosened up.

Specific movements and postures are described that activate the energies of each sephira—each level of our consciousness. By doing one of each, we can activate all of the energies of the Tree of Life for ourselves. This is an especially effective preparation before any major meditation or ritual. The postures can be done before and after the meditational work. Doing it before will help open up that level of consciousness more fully. Doing it after the meditation closes the energy down and grounds it into the physical. This can be done with any particular sephira by itself, or with the entire Tree. Each must find the best way to work with them as individuals.

Balancing Pillars

The movements for balance are especially effective before and after meditation upon any level of the Tree. It enables a balanced experiencing of the energies. The right and left legs symbolize the right and left Pillars of the Tree of Life. We must learn to bring energy down into manifestation along each of the Pillars in a balanced manner. The postures help develop this ability. If we have more difficulty balancing on one leg than on the other, then the weaker leg will indicate that it is more difficult for you to balance the energies of the sephiroth associated with it as they apply to corresponding areas of your life:

Right Leg = Pillar of Severity = Binah, Geburah & Hod
Left Leg = Pillar of Mercy = Chokmah, Chesed & Netzach
Both Legs = Middle Pillar = Malkuth, Yesod, Tiphareth, Kether
(as well as Daath)

The first of these, as depicted on the following page, is the pose of the dancer. This is what we are becoming—the dancer of the Tree of Life! We are learning to choreograph our life and our resources for greater manifestation. In postures B and C, we are learning to balance the flow of energies down the Pillars of the Tree of Life represented by our legs. Many people have difficulty balancing upon one foot and leg. This is significant! Using again the Law of Correspondence, an inability to maintain balance in the physical would reflect an inability to balance the more subtle spiritual energies of the Tree of Life.

As we increase our ability to balance upon one leg, we increase our ability to balance our spiritual energies and consciousness as well. Most people find it easier to balance upon one leg than the other. This is also significant! It indicates the ability to balance the energies of one Pillar (and its levels of consciousness) more easily than the other. This then gives clues as to where we should concentrate some extra work. Remember that the Qabala will show us our greatest strengths and our greatest weaknesses, but we must be able to become cognizant of all aspects of our being and connect them. Again, as discussed earlier, this is a significant reason for working with pathworking!

A.

This position enables you to awaken the energies of the Pillars so that you can become the Dancer in the Tree of Life.

B.

C.

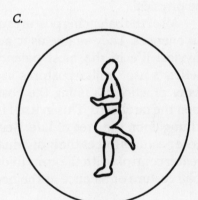

Postures which balance the Pillar energies of the Tree.

D.

E.

Middle Pillar of Balance.

Grounding the energies of all three Pillars, before touching the specific sephiroth.

In trying to discern which Pillar and its corresponding sephiroth are associated with which leg in the human body, one must see oneself as though backing into the Tree of Life diagram. The Middle Pillar becomes the spine. The left leg becomes the Pillar of Mercy, including Chokmah, Chesed and Netzach. The right leg then becomes the Pillar of Severity, including Binah, Geburah and Hod.

Postures D and E are for balancing and grounding the energies of the Middle Pillar and the two side Pillars. Position D brings all three Pillars into alignment and balance; position E grounds it all into the physical.

All of the balancing postures and movements train us in focusing our energies. They enable us to activate the flow of energy into our physical life in the most balanced manner possible. Many Hermeticists use similar postures in developing this kind of balance. Many practice assuming the post of the Hanged Man as depicted upon the tarot card. This in itself is appropriate, for the Hanged Man is hung upon the Tree of Life. Keeping the arms folded during all of these postures forces the individual to concentrate and work for even greater control. With the arms folded across the chest, we have a symbolic gesture of balance at the heart of our growth and evolution!

MALKUTH

Malkuth is at the foot of the Tree of Life. The exercises and movements associated with it stimulate the energies of the chakras within the feet. Many times, these chakras are ignored or given little credit. It is in fact the chakras in the arches of the feet that ground us and tie us to the energy of the Earth and all of its forces. Implied within this is the recognition that the Earth and its energies are what we must learn to use and control to assist us within our evolutionary spiral. If we are to activate the energies of the Tree of Life and bring them into play within our lives, then these centers must be more fully activated. We are trying to become a living Tree of Life, with our head in the heavens and our feet upon the ground. If our feet are not upon the ground, we are not a Tree; rather we become a tumbleweed when we set these energies in motion. We are trying to integrate all of our energies, and that means we must also integrate the forces of Earth with the forces of heaven.

In the past, students of metaphysics have focused strongly upon the seven major chakras and their effects and aspects within the evolutionary process. The modern-day student of the mysteries needs to become aware that there are actually Twelve Major Centers of Light to be awakened and utilized if we are to release our highest capacities.

The number twelve has always had much symbolism attached to it. The twelve centers, or major chakras of the body, can be likened to the twelve lights surrounding the manger, the twelve signs of the zodiac, etc. In the ancient Greek mysteries, twelve was the holy number. And two of the twelve centers are found within the arches of the feet. They involved helping man to become initiated into the Earth's mysteries and all of its energies.

Since Malkuth is at the "foot" of the Tree, the movements start with activating our own "foot" energies. Plants and trees grow from the bottom to the top. In the Eastern philosophies there is a belief that heaven is achieved through the feet, and through learning to connect our energies with the energies of the Earth to help propel us to new growth.

Position A, sometimes referred to as "Butterfly," is very important (page 212). It brings the chakras of both feet together. By focusing our attention upon them in this position, we help activate them. As with *all* the movements and postures, this creates electrical changes in the body, which in turn facilitate tapping the level of consciousness that is associated with it. In position B we bend forward, holding the feet, focusing our attention and energies even more strongly upon their activation. While doing this, think of yourself as a butterfly. A butterfly breaks free of the cocoon in order to fly free. Malkuth is where we begin to learn this.

There is no set time to hold these positions; each individual must work that out. When you "feel" that your chakras in the feet are activated, then move on to the next. A good test is to stand up and feel the Earth with your feet. Bend them, flex them—forward, back, side to side. Pretend you are walking while paying attention to your feet and their connection to the ground. How lightly can you touch the ground and still feel it? Can you hold your foot above the ground and feel the pull of gravity upon it? We are trying to increase our awareness of the Earth and its energies in connection to us.

In movement C, raise yourself up on your toes, hold and lower yourself into a squat position, remaining on your toes. Do not force the squat. Go only as far as is comfortable. Malkuth is part of the Middle

Malkuth

A.

B.

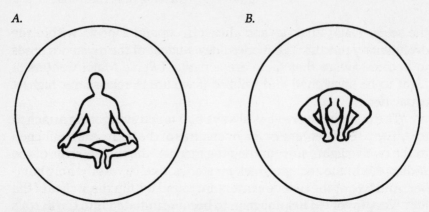

Activating the chakras in the feet so we can more fully work with Malkuth, at the foot of the Tree of Life.

C.

D.

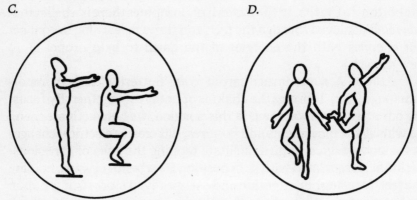

Acknowledging the energies of Malkuth in the Middle Pillar; and as the point of origin for dancing the Tree of Life.

E.

All that we need to grow and learn rests within the Kingdom of Earth (Malkuth).

Before coming to a rest, one can walk a square in a count of four, with each step at an angle or corner of the square, representing the energies in Malkuth that form the base of the Tree of Life.

Pillar. By raising up on the toes and then squatting down, we are raising our energies through Malkuth and bringing them down to Earth in a balanced manner. Movement should be slow and deliberate. Remember also that the more significance we can attach to the movements, the more they will do for us. Our higher self communicates to us through symbology, but communication must be two-way. We have to be able to respond. These movements and postures are symbols we send to the higher consciousness, because symbology is the only language it knows.

In movement D, we balance ourselves on each leg—feeling it, drawing it up into the dancer position. Through Malkuth we enter the entire Tree, including both pillars and their sephiroth. With this movement we acknowledge that all energies end in Malkuth, and that we can explore all worlds through Malkuth. All that we need rests within the Earth/Malkuth, and thus we also rest (position E), balanced for our work.

YESOD

Yesod is the foundation. It is sometimes considered the doorway to the higher energies of the Tree of Life. It is associated on a physical level with the sacrum. Western humanity in general is very tightly hipped. We are not as flexible in the spine and hips as are other peoples throughout the world. We have tended to lock our energies in. On one level these energies are sexual, but on their highest and truest level these energies are our basic life force. With these movements, we release the life force without it becoming sexual. At this level we are dealing with primal life force, not sexuality, so we want to have as much fun as possible with the movements. Life should be a celebration, and with these movements we are celebrating the release of our life force for greater, more beneficial expression within our lives.

With movements A and B (page 214) we circle the hips in a crescent, or half-circle. This is, of course, symbolic of the Moon energies associated with the sephira of Yesod. Slowly we begin to widen the circle into a "full Moon." The head should be loose and free; the spine and hips should be allowed to open up. Have fun with the movements. We are simply freeing up the energy locked in the sacrum, linking it with its corresponding level of consciousness.

Yesod

A.

B.

In positions and movements A and B, we begin the process of freeing the blocked sexual/life force energy within our foundation (Yesod). We must remember that this is life force we are freeing and not treat it as sexual energy. We circle and half-circle (crescent Moon shapes) with the hips. Allow them to swing free and full. This technique will also deepen dreams and awaken psychic ability. Keep the head free and the whole spine loose, allowing the hips to gradually open up, wider and wider.

C.

D.

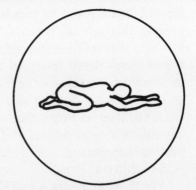

Place dominant hand on forehead and weaker on sacrum. As you push the head back, you also push the hips forward. Lift head and then bow, sanctifying the sexual/life force.

The Child's Pose balances the sacral center and gives reverence to its energy.

214

Once the hips have opened up, place the dominant hand upon the forehead and the other upon the sacrum itself, as in diagram C. We are taking the released energies of Yesod and the sacrum and using them to activate our higher abilities. We are taking life-force energies, usually expressed through sexuality, and directing them for higher forms of creativity. Push the head back and push the hips forward slowly and deliberately. Take side-to-side steps while making this gesture. We are activating this energy to use it in any direction we desire. We control where, when, how much, etc. of this energy we express. All of this is inherent within the movements.

Finally, we end the dance with a Child's Pose. You are on your knees, with arms stretched out and head down. This is a humbling and reverential posture. It says that you recognize the divinity within all energy. You are acknowledging the divine source of the creative life force within you.

This reverential aspect is very important if we are to tap that level of consciousness known as Yesod in the most balanced manner. Yes, it does release energy, but unless it is treated with reverence, it manifests as an unbalanced expression, getting off track, slipping out of the Middle Pillar into an unbalanced manifestation of Netzach in the Pillar of Mercy. The vice or unbalanced expression of Netzach is lust. Again, we begin to see the interplay between one level of consciousness and the next, and we can begin to understand the need to treat each one individually until we are more aware of how they truly function.

The reverential aspect in this movement helps us to awaken greater independent expression of our own creative life force. We each are unique and have a unique way of experiencing the universe and its energies. Recognizing the divine spark inherent within our energies helps us to lay that new foundation and begin the process of becoming an independently creative life essence within the universe.

HOD

Hod is the sphere of Mercury. It is knowledge and communication. It is quick, abrupt movement and consciousness. Within it can be found the treasures of wisdom and knowledge and the applying of these in the material world. On a physical level, it is associated with

Hod

A.

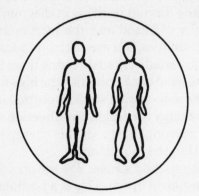

The Chaplin fun-walk and pigeon-toed movement are very stimulating to the solar plexus chakra, which helps link us to the level of our consciousness known as Hod.

B.

Hod is at the base of the Pillar of Severity. Knowledge lifts us up and plants us firm-ly in our paths, symbolized by these movements.

C.

The Cobra is the epitome of the Hod postures. We become the Serpent of knowledge, seeing where it is that we yet have to go, lifting our eyes and our lives to the higher.

the solar plexus chakra, which controls rational thinking. One of its primary symbols is that of the serpent (as in the caduceus), representing knowledge and wisdom on its lower level that will help us to reach the higher.

The movements associated with diagram A (opposite) should be quick and abrupt. Mercury moves fast. While performing these movements, one should be able to feel the pull in the solar plexus area as the physical movements themselves tighten the stomach muscles in that area of the body. Initially, stand with the toes about forty-five degrees apart, heels touching. Then walk in small circles, taking steps of about forty-five-degree angles, which will look like Charlie Chaplin movements. This Chaplin fun-walk gives the appearance of jerky, abrupt movements—Mercury-like. It also strongly activates the energy of the solar plexus. Then switch the position of the heels and toes, with toes together and heels apart. You will look pigeon-toed. Again, walk in small circles. You will feel the solar plexus, which will enable you then to more fully access that level of consciousness most closely associated with it—Hod! Have fun with it!

In diagram B, we see a picture that is symbolic of the position of Hod upon the Tree of Life. It is at the base of the Pillar of Severity. The squat position on the toes symbolizes the energy of Hod at the base (squat) of its own pillar. Then, in a slow, very deliberate movement, imitate a serpent motion to bring yourself to a standing position, with heels firm and flat upon the ground. Do this several times. Learning raises us up and builds a firm foundation for even greater expressions of energy.

The last movement is the cobra posture of yoga. The serpent is the serpent of knowledge and wisdom that is available to us at that level of consciousness known as Hod. This posture helps open that level of our consciousness even more strongly. Lie flat on the ground, face down. See yourself as a snake lying there. Slowly lift your head to see more clearly, to raise to the higher. Place elbows under you, rising and lifting the head even higher. Finally, with head back, looking up as high as possible, stretch the arms up and hold the position of the cobra, poised. Remember, knowledge lets us see what we still have ahead of us and beyond us and shows us the way to achieve it.

NETZACH

Netzach is the green sphere of Venus. It is the sphere of love and attraction, and the sphere of nature and emotions. It is the sphere of sexual energy that draws others to us with all the blessings that can come through other people. The movements associated with Netzach help us activate the level of our consciousness that helps us to attract love and quick rewards. This is not a thinking level of consciousness, but a feeling one.

Netzach is very important to dancing the Tree of Life. It is the center of art and creativity. Haniel, the archangel to whom we have access at this level of our consciousness, is sometimes considered the patroness of the arts. When we dance the Tree of Life through any of these movements, we are using an art form to work with the energies of the Tree. We are using the energies of Netzach to open up the entire Tree. The movements reflect the microcosm of the entire Tree.

We can do this with other levels as well. We also are learning to work with the Tree from an intellectual aspect, approaching it from the level of Hod. We are learning to be free in our approach to the energies within us, learning to express them and ground them in a balanced and yet creative manner. We are consciously (Hod) using specific movements and dance forms (Netzach) to access greater levels of energies. Using both balances us more fully, touches us more intimately, as the two meet in the middle. The Pillar of Mercy, with its base in Netzach, and the Pillar of Severity, with its base in Hod, meet through the conscious use of movement in the Middle Pillar, with its base in Malkuth (our physical life and consciousness).

Netzach is the sphere of nature, and nature is free-flowing, which is how the initial movements (A) should also be (opposite page). Move slowly and freely, swinging the arms and hands as if coaxing an invisible person into your presence. This is often how Venus affects us astrologically; we are mimicking it. The eyes should also coax. In essence, through the dance, we are coaxing and inviting into our lives those things we treasure and love, be it people or things. We are activating those energies within our consciousness which can bring them to us! It means also that you are putting yourself into the "flow" of nature, so that it can bring you that which you treasure and love, at the time which is most beneficial.

Humans are not always in synch with nature and the rhythms of the universe. This free-flowing movement enables us to start

Netzach

A.

Movements should be slow and expressive, as if coaxing new energy into your life. Arms and hands are invoking with love and joy. All movements and gestures should be inviting, as if pulling life to you. It is as if you are sending out magnetic energy, attracting life to you. You are drawing the fruits you need out of the Tree.

B.

This posture has you open, spread, ready to bring into you that which you need and want. From the upright position, sway side-to-side, moving your arms as if pulling energy into your life in the physical.

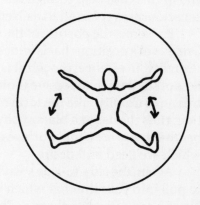

C.

The Triangle posture is very effective. Focus on the extended hand with your eyes up. We are invoking, coaxing energy and new growth to us. It also reflects that all of the energies we invite to us through Netzach from elsewhere on the Tree are to the right and above, or below and to the right (Malkuth—hand on the foot).

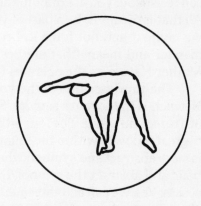

realigning ourselves with the inflow and outflow of natural tides in the universe and in our lives.

The eyes are also important. Tantra teaches different types of "gazes," in conjunction with releasing specific energies. One of these is called the "conjuring" or "coaxing" gaze, in which the eyes are turned to the right and upward while holding the breath. This is significant for Netzach. In the Tree, Netzach is placed at the bottom of the left-hand Pillar. This means that all the rest of the energies that can be manifested through that level of our consciousness are positioned either to the right or above upon the Tree of Life. The eyes also have nerve structures that are unique to the body and similar to the brain. Particular eye movements stimulate specific brain responses, and in this case help to align our energy patterns to that level of our consciousness referred to as Netzach.

For some, the posture of the second movement may be difficult. One sits in a position that is wide open, and which for many speaks of sexuality. In essence, though, it is a posture that symbolizes the openness of the person to receive the treasures they love. For most people, treasures usually take the form of a physical and tangible manifestation; thus the use of a blatant physical posture. But we must remember that these are simply bridges to help us manifest in our lives that which we need and desire.

Again, the side-to-side swaying is important, using the arms as if to pull into your life that which you love. Venus is the love goddess. No one can resist her charms. This movement is saying that nothing can resist you; you are drawing all the treasures of life into your own. All that is meant to be a part of your life and your world can be so if we invite it and not force it. Let nature bring it to you in the time, manner and means that are best for you. We are learning to trust Mother Nature as she operates fully within our lives.

The third position is the yoga posture known as the Triangle. Netzach is the seventh sephira. Seven is numerologically comprised of a three and a four. The four is the base, and the three is the Triangle, of greater power within the foundation of physical life. This position is more abstract and symbolic than the other two; and the more symbolic and abstract the symbol, the higher the level of energy we can access. Yes, we can activate much energy on a mundane level, but we also need to go beyond that. This posture opens the door to experiencing the energies of Netzach on an even higher level.

Through Netzach we coax and invoke all that we love from

everywhere in the universe. This is symbolized by the posture of the Triangle. Everything on the Tree of Life is, as mentioned, either above to the right or below and to the right of Netzach. This posture has the hand extended to the right (for everything we invite from that side of the Tree). It also has the eyes focused up to invite all that is above Netzach in the Tree. The posture also takes the energies it invites and grounds them into manifestation into the physical, as with the hand upon the foot.

This can be used specifically when linking and inviting energies from another particular sephira. For example, if new teachers or learnings are desired, alter the extended hand to point to the appropriate level of the Tree, in this case Hod, and visualize it being drawn to you, as in a ball of orange or whatever the appropriate color may be.

Netzach is that which we love and desire, and physical movement is a powerful way of drawing it to us. Shamans have used similar techniques in the past and present, such as in the inviting of rain. It must be remembered, though, that the universe is a cosmic reservoir of abundance, and this technique should never be used to interfere with the free will of another. Even that which we desire must be balanced, or it becomes a lust—be it for another person or for more material.

TIPHARETH

Tiphareth is at the heart of the Tree of Life. In the human body it is associated with the heart and the heart chakra. Tiphareth is the center of the Christ energy in the universe and within ourselves. It is the little child, the sacrificed God and the King. From Tiphareth one can reach out to all other levels within the Tree. It is the balancing center, the healing center for the physical and for the spiritual. When we bring its energies to play within our lives more actively, there results greater health and greater devotion to God.

Tiphareth is located in the middle of the Middle Pillar, which has much significance and power. It balances, as does our own heart chakra. The heart chakra has three chakras below and three above. It is by activating fully the heart chakra that we can begin to more fully open the upper chakras for even greater spirituality within our lives. It is here that we learn to sacrifice the lower for the higher, but only so that our own light may shine more strongly within the world. It is at this level of our consciousness that we stop looking for the Divine Light to shine down *upon* us and learn to bring to life our own light, so that the divine can shine out *from* us!

The movements and postures are designed to effectively stimulate the heart chakra and its corresponding level of consciousness. This in turn releases healing energies into our lives, first so we can see what needs to be healed, and second so we can heal it. They are energizing movements, and once they have been done a number of times, you will not quite feel balanced until you have done them again. This is because of the stimulating effect they have on the heart chakra. Sometimes we become acclimated to our imbalances, and thus may even deny we are in such a condition until we feel ourselves back in balance. Then we recognize the condition we had ignored.

The first exercise, "Activating the Inner Sun," is a good one to do periodically throughout the day. It keeps the heart chakra energy active. It can be done from any position and in any place—at the office or at home. With your dominant hand (we will use the right), rub the area of the heart in small circles. This stimulates the thymus gland, the heart rhythms and the entire heart chakra. It is soothing to the emotions and calms and balances the inner systems.

Next, take the right hand and draw the energy of the heart (inner Sun) to the head to activate the higher levels of consciousness. With the left hand placed over the heart, pause and contemplate the linking of the divine love with divine thought. Then draw the right hand back down and place it over the left upon the heart. This is a very calming gesture. A good confirmation of its actual effect is to place the hand over the heart to feel the heart beat before you do this exercise; then feel the heart beat at the end. You will notice a difference!

The next exercise is taken partially from oriental tai chi and adapted for these purposes. There are different breathing techniques utilized in tai chi. Two such techniques are the Sun and Moon breaths. With the Sun breath, you exhale slowly, extending the arms forward in front of the chest, with the palms of the hands facing outward. We are pushing the energy of the inner Sun out into our auric fields. The Moon breath is an inhalation, drawing the arms and energy into you with the palms of the hands facing inward. Take a few moments, practicing both. You will feel the energy moving out and drawing in. It is very invigorating.

During this version of it, as depicted on the following page, we are trying to radiate our energy in six directions (Tiphareth being the

Tiphareth

A. Activating the Inner Sun
—*Massage the area of the heart chakra with the right hand (circular motions).*
—*Place left hand over heart, and with the right hand bring the energy of the heart and inner sun to the head.*
—*Bring right hand down on top of the left over the heart area.*

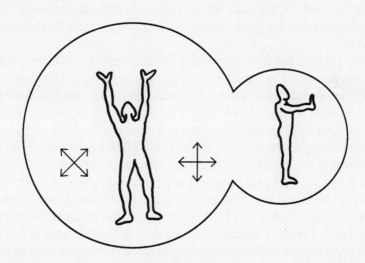

B. The Solar Breath
—*As you exhale, slowly push arms out in the six different directions. You are becoming a living Sun, radiating from the heart in all directions.*

sixth sephira): up, down, to both sides and at diagonals, and finally forward. (Or north, south, east, west, etc.) It is done with six basic movements, exhaling audibly with each. The arms raise up, pushing the energy up and out. Then they move down, pushing the energy down and out. Next, the right arm is extended out to the right and the left arm to the left. After each movement, bring the arms together, with the hands in prayer position at the heart. Inhale to gather the energy in the heart area before radiating it outward.

Next the arms are moved in a diagonal position, with one hand pushing energy diagonally down and the other diagonally up, moving in unison with each other. Then they are switched. The one that moved diagonally down now radiates the energy diagonally up, moving in unison with each other. Then they are switched. The one that moved diagonally down now radiates the energy diagonally up, etc. The hands move back to prayer position at the heart for the final and sixth movement. The arms extend with palms facing out, and the Sun within you bursts into radiant light around you. Visualize it, feel it and know it is real! You have become the Sun!

The yoga exercise on the following pages is known as the "Sun Salutation." It is a series of movements that pays reverence and tribute to the Sun of the World and to the Sun within—macrocosm and microcosm. It consists of twelve basic movements—one solar year—but it must be done twice, for the right and left legs (diagrams D and I).

Stand facing the Sun or the east, from where the Sun rises. Circle your arms out and bring them into prayer position at the chest. You are acknowledging the sacredness outside of you and within you, which is what this whole series is for. Next (B) extend your arms and head up and back, looking toward the heavens and the stars (suns) that exist there and light up our night sky. Then slowly bend forward (C), bringing the hands down to the outside of the feet to touch the ground. Do not feel you have to keep your legs straight. Bend them and squat if necessary. You are bringing the Sun and light from the heavens to the Earth. It has filled your hands and you are passing it on to the Earth through them. In this case, the hands become the side pillars and the legs the middle pillar by which you were able to reach the Sun.

Next step back with the right leg (D). The head raises up, always looking toward the Sun. We are bringing the energy into motion with this, but only so that we can look at the Sun even more. As long as our

The Sun Salutation

A.

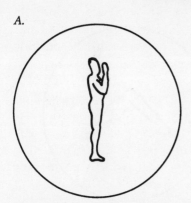

Circle arms into prayer position at the Christ center.

B.

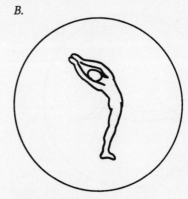

Acknowledge stars (suns) in heavens.

C.

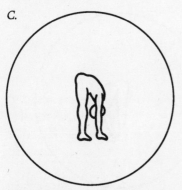

Bring the energy of the Sun to the Earth with the hands.

D.

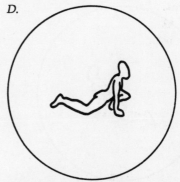

Leg steps back; head raises up—the face is always toward the Sun.

E.

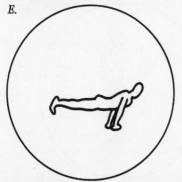

You must learn to let the Sun support you and give you strength.

F.

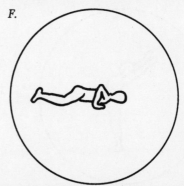

Our light—our Sun—is limited before the Light of Lights.

G.

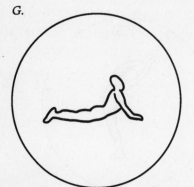

We begin to rise—like the cobra and the sun.

H.

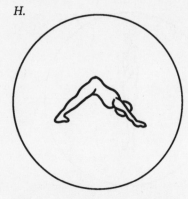

We lift ourselves from the Earth.

I.

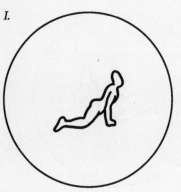

Leg steps forward between the pillars of arms, face to Sun.

J.

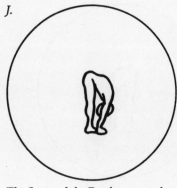

The Sun and the Earth are together again in you and through you.

K.

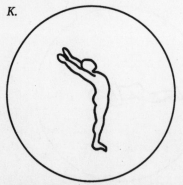

Acknowledge the Sun and stars throughout the universe.

L.

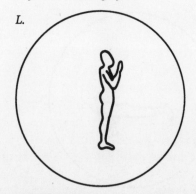

Your own Christ/Sun Center is alive within you!

face is towards the Sun, there will be no dark. Feel the Sun upon your face!

Step back with the other foot (E). You are now supported on your hands and feet. Keep the head up, toward the Sun. If you cannot support yourself this way, use your knees. This movement is to help us remember that we must attain the strength and support of the Higher Light within our lives and allow it to support us. At times, while in the physical, it may be the only strength and support we may have—*but it is always enough.*

Next, lower your knees and chest while raising the buttocks into the air (F). This position is very humbling. Through it we acknowledge that our own light, no matter how great we think it is, is humbled before the Light of Lights.

We now assume the cobra pose as we did in the sephira of Hod. In this posture (G), we are like a snake that has basked in the Sun and must now rise up to its own work. So we lift ourselves (H), pulling up from the involutionary, gravitational pull of the Earth to the evolutionary, spiritual force of the Sun.

We become active again, so we step forward with the right leg (I), bringing it up between the pillars of the arms. We then unite within ourselves the forces of the Sun and the Earth, side by side, pillar by pillar (J). The Sun and the Earth forces are operating in you and through you.

You raise yourself up, lifting yourself and your energy to the heavens (K) to place your own Sun energy among the stars and suns of the sky, there to rest and shine (L).

This completes half of the salutation. It must then be repeated, using the left leg to step back (D) and then to step forward as in step (I). Both sides must be done, or the Inner Sun will not be balanced. Both sides align the Pillars, bringing them into balance and life in the Middle in Tiphareth. This activates strong electrical changes within the body, enabling powerful contact with that level of our consciousness that we know as Tiphareth!

For some, the moves may seem too much and too complicated, but we must remember that Tiphareth is at the heart of the Tree. It is the center to which we are striving so that we can then bridge to even higher levels still!

GEBURAH

Geburah is Mars energy. It is strength, courage and will. It is the warrior and the protector. It is the energy for the tearing down of the old. Through this level of our consciousness, we can stimulate energy to enact changes of any kind. It can be used to awaken critical judgment and for the attaining of information on the discord, however it may be manifesting, within our lives.

The movements are intended to stimulate greater feelings of strength and courage, and an awareness of innate power and energy. As with all energy, to be used properly, it must be disciplined and regimented. Its symbol is the chariot and the charioteer, who has control of the horses and their powerful strength. This is why the Horse Stance (diagram B opposite) is appropriate.

The first of the movements is "Marching to Mars" (A). Its function is to awaken the Mars energy and strength that is inherent within each of us. It is not a physical strength as much as a realization that we have an unlimited source of energy that we can utilize. Marching has always been a way for military groups to harness and discipline the energy and strength of a group. In this exercise, we are activating the energy of the Earth to more willfully direct it for higher functions. Thus it begins by raising up on the toes and beginning a tapping cadence with the heels: up, down, up, down. We tap the heels in a cadence of five (Geburah being the fifth sephira), which stimulates changes in the physical body.

Five is the number for the pentagram, a symbol of tremendous energy. It activates energy in a specific pattern for work upon the physical. The tapping says that we are activating the energy to enact changes within our physical life.

As the heels tap, slowly raise the arms upward in a pumping motion in the same rhythm as the heel taps. It is as if they are being pumped upward by the energy released through the heels upon the Earth, like an air compressor. The hands are together so that the energy is controlled. Interlacing the fingers even further strengthens it. An interlaced set of fingers turns the hands into an instrument of war and strength.

When they reach the uppermost point above the head, separate the hands and swing them down and around, back to the chest, as if gathering in even more energy to concentrate. After the fifth sequence of these moves, begin marching in movements that are angular and

Geburah

A. Marching to Mars
—Raising up on the toes, begin tapping the heels against the Earth in a cadence of five.
—As heels tap, slowly raise arms upward in the same rhythm, as if being pumped up like an air compressor.
—On count of five the arms are circled down to the chest and begin pumping even stronger energy.
—After the fifth sequence, begin marching around the circle, pumping the arms and legs for even greater energy.

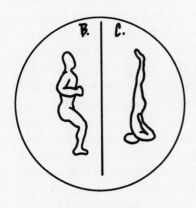
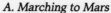

B. The Horse Stance
—Any typical martial arts stance is good. This is one of balance and strength with the energy pulled in, waiting to be set forth. Kick out as if kicking off what is no longer needed.

C. The Shoulder Stand
—This yoga posture is strengthening to the shoulders, associated with Geburah.

D. Reverse March
—A variation of (A). Heels begin cadence once more.
—Arms are circled out from the chest to an above-the-head position (gathering the Mars energy together).
—As the heels tap a cadence of five, the hands and arms are brought down to the chest.
—Do this five times.

not circular. Mars energy is sharp and direct. Pump the arms while marching, and either keep the hands in a fisted position or the fingers straight, extended and stiff.

Come to a rest in the Horse Stance (B). This is a common martial arts position. There is a slight bend in the knees, giving them flexibility. The fists are palm up and pulled back along the side of the ribs. You are balanced squarely upon both legs and should be able to move in any direction with ease. Lean forward, backward and side to side in this position to test your balance. Then begin kicking in all directions, to the sides, in front. Imagine you are kicking off the things you do not want in your life. Make the moves exaggerated but controlled. As you do this, see yourself ridding yourself of the things in your life you do not wish. Remember that Kamael, the Archangel of Geburah, defends the weak and helps us slay the dragons of our life. Visualizing Kamael behind you as you do this, giving energy to your kicks, is quite effective. Also, visualizing yourself as the magickal image for Geburah—the Mighty Warrior with his Chariot—gives it great power. Remember we are creating a mind set through physical actions to facilitate the accessing of that level of consciousness that corresponds to the energy of the physical. After the kicking, return to the Horse Stance again.

At this point, move into the "Reverse March" (D). Raise up on your toes and begin the cadence with the heels once more. Circle the arms upward from the Horse Stance to a clasped position above the head, pulling the energy down in rhythm with the tapping of the heels. As the heels tap the cadence of five, the hands and arms are brought down to the chest. They then circle out and up, to be brought down again to the cadence of five. After five repetitions of this, allow them to rest at the chest and proceed into the meditation you have chosen in relation to Geburah. You will have created the necessary changes in the energy patterns of the physical to attune it more to the metaphysical aspects of Geburah.

One can also use a shoulder stand or variations of the Plow of yoga as depicted in (C). This position is energizing and strengthening to the shoulders, which are in that area of the physical body associated with Geburah.

Find what works best for you. We are using the movements to bridge the mundane brain and consciousness to the more cosmic. Controlling how we do that is important. It is also an aspect of balanced Geburah energy!

CHESED

Chesed is the sphere of mercy and abundance. It is Jupiter. It is the seat of the Round Table. It is where we truly learn about our own quests for the Holy Grail and about all that we will need and have to achieve the quest. It is the level of our consciousness which lets us know that the universe is ruled with glory and magnificence. It lets us know that the majesty of God operates in all men and thus all men have access to everything which demonstrates that majesty.

Touching this level of our consciousness awakens a greater sense of obedience to the higher calling. It provides the energies to enable us to make the gains and opportunities beneficial to us. It awakens the realization of the abundance of the universe that exists for us all.

In order to tap that abundance, we must be willing to receive it. Unfortunately, we have developed the concept that being poor is the only way of being spiritual. We have developed a misproportioned martyr aspect that denies us abundance. If we have children, we want them to have all that they can. Yes, they may have to earn it, but they need to know that it is out there for them. We need to realize the same thing. We are the kings and queens of our own unique kingdoms, and that means that everything within it is already ours; and if it is ours, then we have the right to use it without feeling guilty.

Mercy is the quality of Chesed, and it begins at home. We have to have enough mercy toward ourselves to allow us to have all we need within our lives. Suffering is only good for the soul if it teaches us how not to suffer again. We must be willing to forgive and not punish ourselves by denying the abundance that is *our* right. Yes, it can become obsessive if unbalanced, but denying ourselves what is ours to begin with is imbalance as well.

Through Chesed we learn how to receive from the universe. We learn to share in the abundance of it so that we can do more to manifest the majesty and glory of God upon the Earth. Everything is available to us, but we must realize and be willing to accept it.

A king has much wealth in many forms, and a good king shares and distributes that wealth in many ways to those within his kingdom. The magickal image for this level of our consciousness is a crowned and mighty king, which is what we are trying to realize ourselves. We need to become that crowned and mighty king.

The exercises in this section deal with opening up that level of consciousness which allows us to share in the abundance of the

Chesed

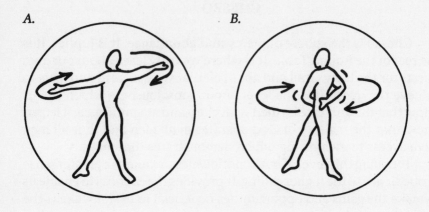

A.

B.

"Ropes of Abundance"
Figures A and B are movements that imitate the threads and ropes of life and how they are all tied together. The movements are circular, swinging the arms out and back around you, tying everything in the universe to you. You are not separate from anything; you are tied to the abundance of it all. The swinging frees us to receive that which we want, opening us to receive from the universe.

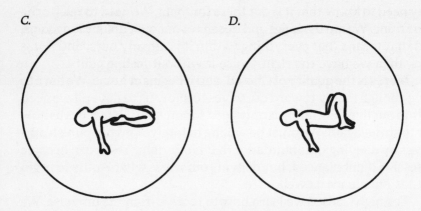

C.

D.

"Modified Fish"
This yoga position (C), as in its even more modified position (D), takes our legs away from us (tucking them under) so we have no choice but to depend upon and receive from the universe, from the heavens. We draw our true wealth from the heavens, not the Earth, and this position places us so that we have no choice but to receive, a task that is difficult for many people. Some people complain about the "uncomfortableness" of the position, and most of the time, it is because on some level they do not know how to receive. If (C) is too uncomfortable, position (D) can be used.

kingdoms of Heaven and Earth. The first movements, (A and B opposite), are called the "Ropes of Abundance." Myths and legends from all over the world speak of threads that bind all things within the universe. They are connected to us and we to them. These movements are the setting in motion of the threads and ropes that tie us and link us to the abundance of the universe.

The movements are circular, swinging the arms in a wide, expansive manner, setting off ripples of energy around you to all corners of the universe. As we swing back, wrapping the arms around us, we are pulling on the ropes to bring to us the spiritual and physical abundance of the universe. We are linked to all things, and we are learning to claim our ties to it all. The swinging frees you and opens you to receive what you want and what you need.

In the next position (C), we tuck our legs back under us and lay back, open to receive from the universe. In essence we are taking our limiting, earthly ideas and conceptions of abundance out of the way (tucking the legs back) so that we must open ourselves to receive from the heavens and their unlimited supply. We draw our true wealth from the heavens anyway, not the Earth, and this places us in a position in which we must receive. This is difficult for many to do, but this position almost forces an opening of that level of consciousness which will enable us to receive from the abundant universe.

Some people complain about the uncomfortableness of position (C), and this is significant. Probably on some level the individual is made uncomfortable by receiving. Maybe they are the type of individual who does nothing but give to others, and won't take "charity" from outside. Maybe they refuse compliments. Maybe they only accept the big things and give no importance to the need to accept the small gifts, be they a compliment or an act of kindness. By doing this exercise in conjunction with the "Ropes of Abundance," the person will receive from the universe within the week. These gifts may be small—compliments, little gifts, opportunities, etc.—but it is important to accept them. Receive them thankfully. If we refuse to receive the small things, the universe certainly won't waste its energy on the larger. Let the universe know that you wish to share in its abundance. Accept everything it gives to you.

For those who find position (C) impossible or too uncomfortable, position (D) can be used until you become flexible enough to share even more in the universe.

All of these help us to open that level of consciousness that enables us to receive, so that we can expand our devotion and work. Gifts and opportunities come in many shapes and forms, and we must become as cognizant of them as possible, every day. Then we can know the magnificence of Chesed!

BINAH

Binah is the archetypal mother. It is the womb from which physical life takes form. It is understanding which brings light into the dark. Its energies are not easy to access on their highest level, as it is part of the Supernal Triangle of the Tree of Life. Because of this, the movements and postures are less intricate and yet more abstract. They are simpler, and yet their significance is more complex. More can be read into the simple movements of Binah, Chokmah and Kether than into any of the other levels on the Tree of Life. We are beginning to work more closely with the pure essence of energy, which is not as easily defineable as in the lower levels of consciousness. This does not make them any more divine or powerful, but rather more difficult at times to relate to and work with.

Binah is understanding on all levels and the silence that is necessary if we are to understand in the fullest manner possible. In the first two postures, we acknowledge the female energy in the universe. By placing our hand upon the womb and the heart, we are acknowledging that most of us will only be able to understand the working of the female energies in our lives upon the lower levels: through the creative process of giving birth through the womb and through the giving of love from our hearts (Binah being reflected down through the Tree of Life).

The circular rotations of the head (page 235) release the energy of Binah, which is associated with the chakras of the head (particularly the third eye, which it shares with Chokmah). This released energy is then free to come to life more within our physical awareness, through the heart and the womb. The rotations of the trunk loosen the heart and the womb so they can more freely and fully express this archetypal energy. This series of movements is concluded by leaning forward. This is the giving birth of the energies throughout the Tree for greater expression—the coming out of the womb. We have circulated the energies, and now they must be given expression.

Binah

With left hand on the womb and the right upon the heart (two female centers), slowly circle the head clockwise three times. This is followed by a slow circling of the trunk three times. Then the body leans forward, with a small soft gesture, signifying a coming forth from the womb. With the male, the hand positions are reversed as are the directions for the rotations of head and trunk.

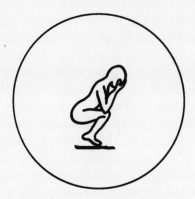

"Old Tibetan Meditation Pose"
The individual takes a squatting position with the elbows resting upon the knees. The thumbs of the individual are placed in the inner corners of the eye, and the fingers of the hands are placed together in prayer position, forming a triangle over the third-eye area of the forehead. This position is then held. The length of time depends upon the individual.

The rotations number three, both for the head and the trunk. The forward movement is done only once. (Again this is just a guideline.) Three is the number of creativity and birth; and three is the number for Binah.

The positions of the hands will vary from individual to individual, particularly from females to males. Binah is a female sephira, a level of consciousness that works most fully with the feminine energies. A female performing these movements will do the circles in a clockwise direction, which moves energy out. This is significant, because the female already has the feminine energy awakened within her; it needs only to be set free. For the male, the movements will be in a counterclockwise position, and the hand placements will be reversed as well. The male is outside of the female energy of Binah; it is not as natural to him. Circling in a counterclockwise direction draws the female energy into him, activating it more strongly. Allow the movements and hand placements to be natural and comfortable; if it feels better to rotate clockwise, do so. If it feels better to keep the right hand upon the heart and the left upon the womb, then do so as well. Remember that we are trying to work and activate the expression of our energies in our own unique manner. These movements are to assist in linking with the corresponding level of our consciousness for its greatest expression.

The last posture is sometimes called the "Old Tibetan Meditation Pose." In this posture, the individual squats first. Squatting was the proper position of giving birth in many ancient and even many contemporary rural societies. In a squatting position, the force of gravity facilitated the birthing process. In this meditation position, we are trying to give birth to clearer understanding.

The elbows rest upon the knees (Binah rests on top of the Pillar of Severity), and the thumbs of the individuals are placed in the inner corners of the eyes. Technically, this is the medial end of the eyebrow. This is a very powerful acupuncture and acupressure point on the urinary bladder meridian. It is a point used to stimulate the eyes for the relief of headaches and glaucoma and even for facial paralysis. It is stimulating to the brow chakra, or the third eye.

The fingers of the hands are brought together in prayer fashion over the forehead, forming a triangle over the third eye area. The triangle is associated with the womb (the yoni in Eastern philosophies). It is a symbol for Binah. The triangle intensifies the energy of that which it surrounds (as in pyramid energy, etc.). The thumbs activate the third eye, and the fingers in a triangle over the area intensify it. Meditating in this position gives cleared insight and understanding (Binah). When one comes out of this pose, everything is physically clearer. It seems brighter, more distinct—sharper! We have energized our sight—physically and spiritually. We can now more easily tap our consciousness for higher understanding of other aspects of our life and begin to see how to give birth to even brighter light within it!

CHOKMAH

Chokmah is the archetypal father. It is the initiator. It is that level of our consciousness which sets things in motion. When linked with Binah, the archetypal female, new birth and life results. Chokmah is pure force pouring forth to manifest in myriad ways as it makes its way into our physical life. It is energy before energy takes a form of expression.

In movement A (page 238), stand with your eyes closed, your head hanging down. Brush your hands over your head, waking up the energy to set it in motion. Brush the hands slowly over the top of the head and the eyes. The hair hangs down. (As the energy of Chokmah asserts itself, it overflows to form Binah.) The eyes open slowly; again the energy is awakened and set in motion for greater manifestation.

Chokmah sets the wheels of life and the stars in motion within our lives. It opens a realization of our hidden abilities and energies, so that we can learn to start motion within our lives. The eyes slowly open, giving us this realization. We begin to see how the heavens, the universe and our own energies (the universe in miniature) operate on all levels.

Next we assume the position of the "half wheel." Sometimes it is called a "back bend" or a variation of the back bend. In it we are becoming the wheel of life. We are setting our energies and abilities into motion, getting things rolling. This posture links us with the angelic realms associated with this level of our consciousness. These are the *auphanim*, or the "whirling forces."

Our faces and eyes are lifted up to Kether and beyond. This is to remind us of the spiritual experience associated with tapping this level of our consciousness—"a vision of god face to face." We look up to know how to best set our energy in motion!

Chokmah

Using the hands to sweep gently across the eyes as if to clear the sight is very effective. Cloudy gray is the color for Chokmah—the light hidden within the clouds. This motion moves the clouds away so the energy and light can manifest.

We awaken our energies by brushing our hands over our head. Our hair hangs down, the energies overflowing down to the rest of the tree. Our eyes open and lift upward, a growing realization of our hidden energies being brought to life and set in motion for greater manifestation.

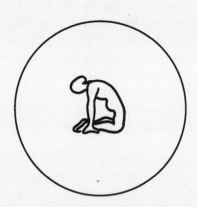

"Half Wheel"

Chokmah sets the wheels of our energies in motion. We are becoming the wheel of life to initiate new energies into our life and to understand the workings of the wheels of the universe as they play upon us and through us. Our eyes look ever upward for the vision of God face to face, so we can know how best to use our energies with the highest wisdom (Chokmah).

KETHER

Kether is the top of the Tree. It was the first to manifest out of the nothingness and is the last that we touch before we enter into that nothingness (that which we cannot know at all while in the physical). It is here that life and death meet. It is here that they become truly one and the same thing, and where we draw all sustenance for everything within our life. It is here that we can experience the unlimited reservoir of the divine operating in the universe.

Kether is not the end of our journey. It simply represents the end of a stage before the next level is undertaken. The Kether of one level of experience becomes the Malkuth of the next. One Tree of Life always leads upward into another—a Tree within a Tree within a Tree (refer to page 68). In essence this is the climbing of Jacob's Ladder. Each rung leads to the next higher rung. Kether on one level of experience becomes the first step to an entirely new level of consciousness and the manifestation of our energies within it. The lower always bridges to the higher.

In position A (page 240) we are at the top of the Tree. We are reaching up and out from Kether into that which we cannot truly and fully know of while in the physical. Hold this position, even when tired. At this level, we are training ourselves to draw our focus away from the physical to the spiritual. Do not scratch; do not acknowledge any itches. We are transcending the physical, looking where there is no ache, no pain, no itching, no scratching.

Slowly draw the arms downward, pulling the energy of the divine down into the physical to awaken new life and new strength to stimulate new energies of change and transition, and to be able to leave the past and go on to the future.

This means you must be able to put to rest that which is no longer beneficial. For this, assume the corpse pose (B). We die to one level of being only so we can be born to a new. In this pose, the energy we pulled down in essence raised us to become a part of the nothingness. Nothing is the space we wish to enter here. Visualize yourself free, floating in nothingness—no aches or pains. You are shedding the old before the new is once more taken upon yourself.

From the corpse pose, roll to your side to assume a fetal position. Out of death comes new life. We die to Kether to be born again to Malkuth. We come back into manifestation fresh, stronger, and ready to be born and to grow to yet greater heights.

Kether

You are standing upon Jacob's Ladder, the top of the Tree, looking out into the nothingness, the source of all your essence. Hold the position, even when tired. We are trying to stretch our awareness from the physical to the spiritual. You are attempting to transcend the physical.

A.

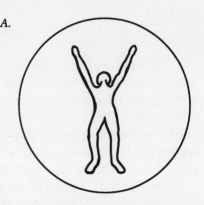

Slowly the arms lower, and the body lowers itself into a corpse pose. We die to one life that we may have a new. We are attempting to become a part of the nothingness beyond Kether—beyond the physical.

B.

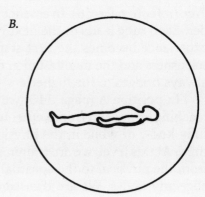

C.

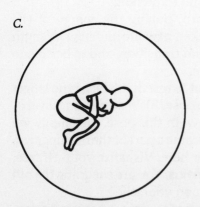

D.

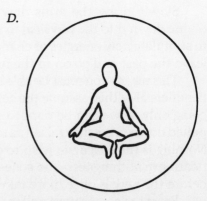

Out of the nothingness, we are born again, coming back into life.

The Kether of one Tree becomes the Malkuth of the next, and we start the next spiral up!

240

From the fetal position, sit up (D) with the arches of the feet together, activating our new essence and stronger energy in Malkuth. The Kether of one Tree of Life becomes the Malkuth for the next higher. We are never lower than we have been before and we always go higher each time thereafter. Evolution is an ever-upward spiral. Acknowledge the feet and the energies of the feet chakras, for Kether has released new creativity for new steps in your journey of life!

Variations:

1. Use the incense and candles to set the atmosphere.

2. Pause before each set of dance movements. Reflect upon their significance. Reflect upon the energies of the sephiroth that you are attempting to release through these movements.

3. Assume the magickal image as described in chapter 3 prior to performing the postures and movements. This augments the effects, enabling you to more fully access the thoughtform energy associated with the path. *Be the image, dancing the movements!*

4. Begin with the balancing movements for the Tree of Life energies before performing those of the specific sephiroth. End with them as well, to ground the energies activated by the dance.

5. The exercises can be used as meditations themselves or as a prelude to meditations, creating the proper mind-set for tapping the various levels of consciousness.

6. If used as a prelude to pathworking or meditation, the exercises should always follow as well, in order to make sure that the energies triggered are balanced into your physical life.

7. These exercises can be used as an aid to pathworking techniques described in the previous two chapters. Start with the first sephira of the path. Perform the balancing movements and move directly

into the dance movements for that sephira. Next, utilizing the Tibetan Walk to Knowhere (description to follow), make a transition into the dance movements for the second sephira of the path. Then move into the specific pathworking meditation:

Balancing Movements ➝ Dance movements of the first sephira ➝ Tibetan Walk to Knowhere ➝ Dance movements of second sephira ➝ Pathworking meditation ➝ Balancing movements

Tibetan Walk to Knowhere

The Tibetan Walk to Knowhere is a series of steps whose purpose is to induce an altered state of consciousness. It involves repetition of a set rhythm of steps: four steps forward and four steps backward. Forward, back. Inner, outer.

The steps should be taken with full attention in a sure, slow and deliberate manner. With each step, place the heel down first and then the toes. This serves as an unconscious reminder to maintain a sure footing in your journey in life and upon the path you are now treading. The number of forward and backward movements varies. One method is to use the number of steps based upon the number of the path you are working. The path from Malkuth to Yesod—path 32—then would take thirty-two forward and backward steps. To some this may seem a lot, but we must keep in mind that it initially takes more work to induce the altered state necessary to access the energies, especially at the bottom of the Tree.

Visualizing yourself as the magickal image of the beginning sephira is also empowering. As you walk this path, visualize yourself stepping on the appropriate color. Allow yourself to find your own rhythm for the steps. As you step about halfway through the series, visualize yourself merging and becoming the magickal image of the second sephira of the path. Now you are a combination of both magickal images, with the inherent power of both! This is tremendously powerful and energizing. It releases the energies of the path more intensely into the physical. It also helps you to develop concentration and creative imagination that can be used even more greatly for your benefit in the future.

MUSIC FOR THE TREE

Sephira	Corresponding Music/Composers
Malkuth	Anything of the home and hearth; Brahms' *Lullaby*; Dvorak; Puccini.
Yesod	Handel's *Water Music*; A Chopin *Nocturne* (anything that evokes deep feelings).
Hod	Woodwinds and horns; Mozart; Gershwin (rhythmic variety); Bach; Mozart's *Magic Flute*.
Netzach	Beethoven's *Pastoral Symphony*; Zamfir; Schumann; Mendelssohn.
Tiphareth	Handel's *Messiah*; Haydn's *Creation*; Pachelbel's *Canon in D*; Berlioz; sacred hymns.
Geburah	Marches of any kind; strong rhythms; Wagner's *Ride of the Valkyries*; Verdi's *Grand March*; *Pomp and Circumstance*.
Chesed	Franck's *Panis Angelicus*; Beethoven's *Fifth Symphony*; Tchaikovsky.
Binah	Bach-Gounod, *Ave Maria*; Schubert's *Ave Maria*; Brahms' *Lullaby*; Debussy's *Clair de Lune*.
Chokmah	Haydn's *Trumpet Concerto*; Rachmaninoff; Haydn's *Creation*; Vivaldi.
Kether	Wagner's *Pilgrim's Chorus*; Theme from *2001: A Space Odyssey*; Pachelbel's *Canon in D*.

*Playing these or other pieces of music
that you choose in relation to the sephiroth
adds even greater depth and power to the dance!*

Dancing to the Stars

In more ancient times, the people and students of the spiritual sciences were very cognizant of the play of the heavenly energies upon the Earth and upon humanity. The imprints of the stars were a part of their life and their mind. If we are to truly awaken our highest consciousness and employ it fully within our world, we also need to become more cognizant of this. We need to re-imprint upon our physical brain the energies of the stars. The work with the Qabala and the dance movements can facilitate this for us.

We can use physical movement associated with the Qabala to imprint upon our brain the movement and operations of the stars and planets. This will enable us to become more aware of their subtle and often ignored influences.

In the Qabala, we use symbols and gestures to awaken levels of our consciousness and link them together for greater use. There are constellations and planetary energies used as correspondences which enable us to decipher and understand the energies of our consciousness. These star and planet patterns are associated with both the sephiroth and the paths linked to them. We can use the constellation patterns to more fully bridge the levels of our consciousness by activating deeper levels of our subconscious, which is still capable of responding to those stellar influences.

On pages 248-250 are the constellations and glyphs associated with the paths on the Tree of Life. These constellations and astrological glyphs serve as doorways to explore levels of our consciousness that otherwise could not be as easily explored. If we apply physical movements that mimic those symbols and constellation patterns, we not only bring to life more intensely the energies associated with them, but we also bring out of our subconscious archives that ephemeral memory and attunement to the stars.

Stepping off the constellations associated with the various paths of the Qabala, and stepping off physically the astrological glyphs, heightens the consciousness associated with the pathworking. It enables you to become more sensitive to celestial movements and position within your life and to how such energies can be played upon while in the physical. It heightens our awareness of how astrological configurations influence and affect us on levels often not recognized. It awakens us to their gravitational influences on physical, emotional, mental and spiritual levels.

By physically dancing the constellations, we place ourselves in alignment with their rhythms, enabling them to work more fully for us and align our personal energies with the universal flow. The movements reflect the energies that will be released through the pathworking; thus they give the pathworking greater power. Focusing upon the pathworking and dance at the appropriate time of the year for the astrological sign will elicit even greater benefits to the individual. If only working the twelve paths associated with the astrological signs, an individual can dance to the heavens in the course of one year!

This opens a broad avenue for aligning the physical with the celestial. Ultimately, one could learn to dance the entire astrological chart, enhancing those aspects that are more beneficial. This can be used to smooth over those aspects of the astrological chart which are more difficult to handle in the physical. The movements of stars are so intimately connected to life in the physical that great strides could be made on any level by anyone wishing to choreograph it.

Technique #1:

1. Choose the path you will be working and review the energies associated with it.

2. Set the atmosphere—candles, fragrances, music, etc.

3. Perform the balancing postures to activate the Tree in the physical.

4. Perform the dance movements for the first sephira of the path, assuming the magickal image.

5. Step off the outline of the constellation in the area where you are performing the pathworking. (Use the guidelines and charts on the following three pages.) You may simply walk them, dance them, or spin around the area in the astronomical or astrological configuration. As you do so, see its outline being formed upon the floor in the appropriate color for the path. For example, if you are performing a pathworking for the 24th Path (Netzach to Tiphareth), you would dance an outline of the constellation of

Scorpio upon the floor in the color of green-blue.

6. Perform the dance movements for the second sephira of the path.

7. Assume one of the meditational attitudes, and begin your meditational part of the pathworking ritual (entering into the Tree, etc.).

8. Conclude with the balancing postures to ground and balance the energies stimulated into play by this pathworking.

Technique #2:

1. Choose the path and review the energies associated with it.

2. Set the atmosphere.

3. Perform the balancing postures to bring the Tree into life.

4. Assume the magickal image; perform the dance for the first sephira of the path.

5. Assume the meditational posture or attitude and begin the pathworking meditation. When you visualize yourself walking the path within the meditation, see the path as winding around to the second sephira in a pattern of the constellation or astrological glyph.

6. Complete the meditation.

7. Assume the magickal image of the second sephira and perform the dance.

8. Conclude as always with the balancing postures.

Technique #3:

This is an excellent outdoor pathworking ritual. If you can find an area (pasture, field, woods, etc.), it is a very effective technique, accelerating the play of the path's energies into your life.

1. Choose the path you wish to perform outdoors (any can be used). Review the energies associated with it.

2. Having arrived at your outdoor location, perform the balancing postures to activate your inner Tree of Life. If you can perform this in an outdoor area by a tree, it is even more powerful.

3. Assume the magickal image and perform the dance for the beginning sephira of the path.

4. Assume the meditational posture, and visualize yourself entering into the Tree of Life, and into the inner Temple. Allow yourself to be greeted by the archangel. Create an astral doorway leading onto the path and the second sephira, in its appropriate color.

5. Open your eyes and rise. Now you are going to walk in that field or woods. You are physically walking the path. Walk in the pattern of the appropriate constellation or astrological glyph. Feel yourself in the presence of the archangels. Carry on mental conversations with them. Reflect upon how you wish the energies of this path to play in your life. Be open.

6. Halfway through your "stroll to the stars," encounter the archangel of the second sephira. Know that you are now in the company of both.

7. Continue the walk until you have reached the end of the outline for the constellation or glyph. Assume a meditative pose, and meditate upon entering into the second sephira of the path, thereby completing the pathworking.

8. Perform the balancing postures to ground and balance the energies activated.

This is especially effective in a wooded area. The trees become antennae to link the play of celestial energies more acutely to the physical. The effect can be further enhanced by periodically intoning the God-names associated with the two sephiroth of the path.

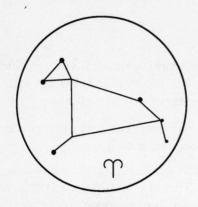

ARIES
(Path 15—Tiphareth/Chokmah)

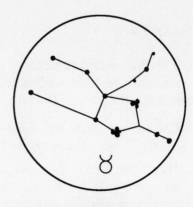

TAURUS
(Path 16—Chesed/Chokmah)

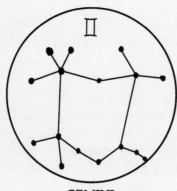

GEMINI
(Path 17—Tiphareth/Binah)

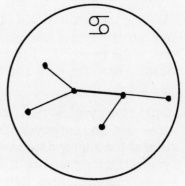

CANCER
(Path 18—Geburah/Binah)

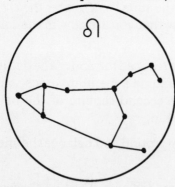

LEO
(Path 19—Geburah/Chesed)

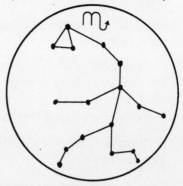

VIRGO
(Path 20—Tiphareth/Chesed)

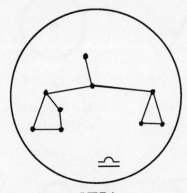

LIBRA
(Path 22—Tiphareth/Geburah)

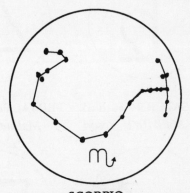

SCORPIO
(Path 24—Netzach/Tiphareth)

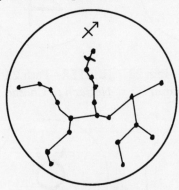

SAGITTARIUS
(Path 25—Yesod/Tiphareth)

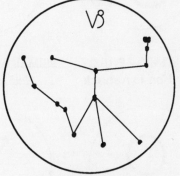

CAPRICORN
(Path 26—Hod/Tiphareth)

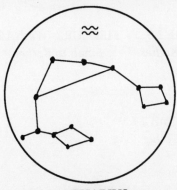

AQUARIUS
(Path 28—Yesod/Netzach)

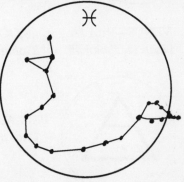

PISCES
(Path 29—Malkuth/Netzach)

SATURN—Path 32
Malkuth to Yesod

PRIMAL FIRE—Path 31
Malkuth to Hod

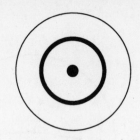

SUN—Path 30
Yesod to Hod

MARS—Path 27
Hod to Netzach

PRIMAL WATER—Path 23
Hod to Geburah

JUPITER—Path 21
Netzach to Chesed

VENUS—Path 14
Binah to Chokmah

MOON—Path 13
Tiphareth to Kether

MERCURY—Path 12
Binah to Kether

PRIMAL AIR—Path 11
Chokmah to Kether

Technique #4:

As discussed earlier, the path associated with your astrological sign holds much significance in your life lessons, as does the path of the planet that rules your astrological sign. The element of your sign (Air, Fire, Water or Earth) can give even further revelations.

One method of working with the dance and the Tree is to focus on these three aspects and paths each month. For example, work the paths for Cancer, the Moon and Water during June and July, when the sign of Cancer is most active in the year. In a year's period, you have basically danced the celestial energies into greater activity. This also helps you in learning to use and control them according to the universal rhythms so that they work more effectively for you.

A variation of this can be employed to activate energies around your birthday. Three aspects of the astrological chart which are very powerful are our Sun sign, the rising sign or Ascendant, and the Moon sign. A very powerful method of reactivating those forces in our life for the coming year is to pathwork their associated paths for one week ahead of your birthday.

1. Seven days prior to your birthday, perform the pathworking for your Sun sign. Two days later, perform the pathworking for your rising sign, and two days later, that for your Moon sign.

2. The next day is your birthday, and it is a time to meditate on that which you want to manifest in the coming year.

3. The birthday is a powerful time in a person's life. The inherent potentialities of our physical life are more active. Using the pathworkings will bring those energies into even greater manifestation.

4. You can also do this with the Sun sign, the ruling planet and the element as previously described. Either way, we are using three aspects—three paths—and three is the creative number. It is the birth-giving vibration in the universe, which is more than significant for what we are doing.

It is also a good idea to occasionally dance the movements for the constellation associated with your astrological sign. This keeps you in touch with your basic energy pattern; it is usually when we lose this link when imbalance manifests. This keeps us grounded and in a position to more easily evolve into new energies.

Theater of the Tree

One can go so far as to choreograph an entire free dance movement in relation to the various sephiroth. In many ways this is similar to the mystery plays of more ancient times. The ritual enactment of specific energies and scenes to release the corresponding energies within an individual, as well as to link them to more spiritual essences, is very effective. It can be accomplished by an individual or by a group.

Hidden within the various movements are messages and teachings. We are trying to allow the Tree of Life to become a teacher to us, and to communicate with us. Our higher levels of consciousness communicate to us through symbols, and if we wish to strengthen the connection and make it a two-way communication (to where we can call upon it at any time), then we need to learn to use symbols as well.

This is where a role-playing dance becomes beneficial. Role playing activates the physical energy to give impetus to that which we are trying to set in motion on a mental or spiritual level. We use movement and role assumption to tap levels of consciousness more strongly, so that the bridge between them and our normal waking consciousness is clear and free.

Steps to the Theater of Dance:

1. Choose the subject matter for your dance, based upon which sephira or level of consciousness you wish to access. This is also based upon what you hope to accomplish with the energies you set in motion.

2. Review the energies inherent within that sephira/level of consciousness. What kind of powers can be awakened and by what symbols? Use the Table of Correspondences from chapter 1 to assist you; or you can use the predecessor to this work (*Simplified Magic: A Beginner's Guide to the New Age Qabala*) to familiarize yourself with the basic energies.

3. Reflect on the symbolism.

4. Mentally construct a narrative, as if you were trying to explain to another the energies you hope to access through this sephira.

5. How would you act it out or demonstrate it if you could not speak? This is the preparation for physical expression. It provides focus.

6. Take this mental narrative and shorten it to two or three symbolic movements or gestures.

7. Visualize the area in which you will be working, as if filled with the color of the sephira.

8. Slowly and methodically set the scene and atmosphere and perform any initial ritual activities to stimulate the proper mindset. Then, with deliberate motion, go through the movements you have chosen for five to ten minutes.

9. Allow yourself to assume a meditative posture and meditate upon the energy you have awakened. Visualize how it is going to express itself in your life. See yourself experiencing it in real life situations in the coming week.

10. Give thanks to the universe and yourself for the manifestation of this energy into your life.

Sample Exercise

We will use the sephira of Geburah. This is Mars energy. It is that level of our consciousness linked to courage, strength, etc. It is energy that we can use to fight our dragons. Choose an aspect of your life that needs more courage, energy or strength. See yourself as if you were confronting that situation with the right energy and courage. Now act it out with gesture and movement. We all play-acted as children, but now we are going to do it in specific ways to release archetypal energies into our life.

You may feel silly initially, but that will pass. We are simply breaking down barriers. When we were children, we could act out anything. We all played "make-believe." What we are doing now is using this same process; but we are first infusing it with symbols that trigger specific physical manifestations. We are using it with a controlled, concentrated focus to create new conditions or opportunities for new conditions.

After you have "made believe" a few times, acting out the use of greater strength to change a condition in your life, take time to create simple movements to symbolize this. Create movements that reflect being confronted. Create movements that show you drawing upon great inner reserves of strength. Create movements that reflect your facing up to the confrontation and coming out on top. See yourself fighting and defeating the dragon in your life.

After getting the movements firmly in mind, set a time to perform your dance ritual. In meditation beforehand, visualize yourself in the actual situation, and not just fighting the symbolic dragon.

Hints:

1. Take at least a week to set up and perform the ritual. By focusing and developing it over this period, the subconscious can release more energy to be actualized during the ritual.

2. By taking a week, you build a thoughtform of positive energy that facilitates its manifestation.

3. By taking a week, you are able to work on it exclusively without excluding other responsibilities. It only takes 15 to 30 minutes a day to bring greater abundance, fulfillment and joy into our lives. We dissipate our energies through so many things and people; we owe it to ourselves to spend at least this much time every day doing something creative for ourselves.

Choose the Situation to Change ➞ *Choose the Sephiroth* ➞ *Then Create the Theme!!!*

4. Use simple movements and expressions—ones that can be repeated.

5. You are learning to activate and use all of your own energies. You are applying mental correlations to spiritual energies, so they can manifest physically within your life.

6. There is no right or wrong way of using this technique; but it should not be used to interfere with the free will of another.

7. Each sephira has energies and qualities that can either be awakened or overcome. (Malkuth can become a dance reflecting a coming to a decision, or Geburah can become a dance that reveals your facing a challenge with courage.)

8. Use proper and appropriate movements. Work them in phrases.

9. The speed of the movements can vary. For Geburah, the movements may be more regimented and stronger, while the movements for Chesed may be wide and expansive. (Every dancer and every person has movements in which he or she feels particularly at home. We all have levels within the Tree to which it will be easier to gain access than others. We do not want to lock ourselves into them alone. We want to change them for each sephira. We want to explore new vistas and new techniques. We want to stretch and expand our abilities. This helps us to grow.)

10. Every movement should have a purpose, symbolic or otherwise.

11. Rhythm and music add a powerful element to dance. Music can be chosen to reflect the sephiroth (refer to the list on page 243).

12. The dance can be joined with words or narration. The narration can be a prelude. Poetry that reflects the same energy can be utilized. Seed thoughts, words and sounds can be inserted and intoned at various points within the dance. God-names injected into the dance properly— instinctively—are particularly effective.

Other Considerations

For all of the movements, there can be developed male and female gestures, postures, etc., which the individual should learn to explore. We are all combinations of masculine and feminine energies, as are the sephiroth upon the Tree of Life. One can, if so inclined, even choreograph a more androgynous movement and dance for each of the sephiroth—one that is a balance of male and female.

Regarding clothing and attire: celebrational clothing always helps place the dance participant in the proper mindset for the position to be activated on the Tree. Wearing colored clothes according to the color of the sephira is effective. It can get expensive, and if nothing else, use clothing that is simple and of white, black or gray shadings. Clothing can be as much a part of the dance as the movements. The possibilities are only as limited as we allow them to be!

Group Work

Group work and ritual dance requires more organization. It is important to keep in mind, though, that in group work it is the group energy and not the individual's that is the key to successfully invoking and awakening the energy. With groups, an intensified and amplified energy and experience is the purpose. There may be a central figure, but it is the group and its collective, synergistic strength which will give the ritual of dance its true power. Group dance, like group ritual, is only as powerful as its weakest member.

Circle dances and spiraling motions lend themselves easily to group movements. The more bodies there are participating, the less complex should be the movements. Holding to rotations that correspond to the number of the particular sephira is a simple way of performing group movements. With groups, the more linear the movements, the greater the power will be that is invoked. *Simplicity is a must! Confusion in the movements will create confused and disruptive energy.*

One common group-working occurs frequently in forms of Wiccan ritual. A Wiccan group or coven is traditionally made up of 13 people. This is an effective number for choreographing dances and movements to invoke and stimulate the energies of the Tree of Life:

> 10 members of the group = one for each sephira
> 1 acting priest/priestess = the Middle Pillar
> (the Sushumna or central Nerve channel)
> 1 member = Pillar of Severity
> (feminine or Moon energy—Ida)
> 1 member = Pillar of Mercy
> (masculine or solar energy of the Tree of Life—Pingala)

One can also work out group movements for each individual sephiroth, leaving the above Tree formation for a beginning and an end:

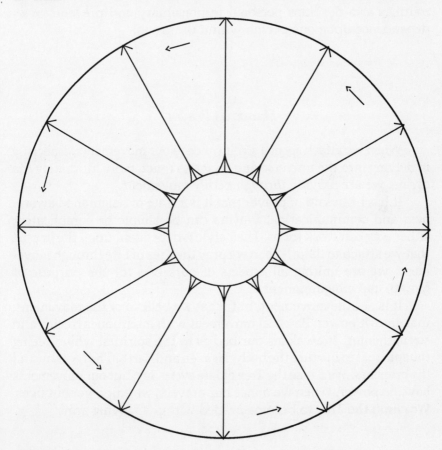

In the example on page 257, the sphere of Chokmah is danced. One of the symbols for Chokmah is the sphere of the zodiac, as depicted. Using this symbol, the group can learn to set the energy in motion. Each member would be assigned a spoke and all would begin in the inner circle. One member would stay within that circle as the hub. In unison, the group members flow to the outer edge and then back, in and out, each time moving to the next wedge, until they have made a complete circle—setting the zodiac in motion.

Similar movements can be worked out for each of the other sephiroth as well. It is a good exercise in working with the symbology and makes an excellent teaching tool for those class situations in which students are learning to apply their own energies and correspondences to the Tree of Life. It enables them to make connections. Having the different individuals of the group work out their own routines also develops personal responsibility and prevents overdependence upon one person within the group!

Dance as Prayer

When we attach special significance to our movements, especially in delving into the universe and trying to touch more intimately the divine, we are *praying through bodily movement*.

It has been said of prayer that it is a state of heightened awareness and communication. Prayers can be simple or complicated; either way can work for us. Their style is dependent upon the import that we attach to them. When we pray the Tree of Life through movement, we are uniting all aspects of ourselves for the purpose of growth and enlightenment.

It is not the movement, but what we believe of the movement, that gives it power. Physical movement with intention is freeing and strengthening. It awakens our bodies to the spiritual while freeing the spiritual to nurture the body. Heaven and Earth. The roots and all the branches. We dance the Tree of Life every day, but our movements have no power. When we dance our prayers, we empower our lives. We climb the Tree to become nestled within its loving arms!

chapter seven

Validating Your Experience

Test all things and hold fast to that which is true.

—ST. PAUL

All of the methods in this book deal with learning to open the doors that are closed. It does not matter who closed them; what is important is that we allowed them to close. We do have the ability to open the doors that will shed light into the dark corners of our life, so that we can see exactly what needs to be cleaned up.

Much has been written about meditation and its various practices and uses. There are, in fact, as many methods of meditation as there are people. As to which method or combination of methods is best, no one can answer that but the individual. What is important is that the method chosen be one that is active. It is not enough to simply quiet the mind and allow pleasant images to arise. Over time, this can lead to self-deception. We need to act upon what we are stimulating. We operate predominantly within the physical dimension, and thus all energies activated on other levels need to be grounded into the physical. It is only by working with various methods, and by experimenting and practicing, that one can determine the best method for growth. There are quick methods to open up psychic energies, but they will not propel one along the path to higher destiny or evolution. Only by bridging the psychic energy with the spiritual archetypes beyond does true growth occur.

The imagickal techniques are not only truly "magick." They may seem so to the uninformed or unenlightened, but they are simply techniques for using our tools in accordance with the divine natural laws of the universe. They can help us to solve problems, achieve goals, open ourselves to our highest capabilities and re-instill the

259

color and joy of life. This does not mean that we do not have to put forth effort. We do—spiritual, mental, emotional *and* physical effort. But it does mean that we can change our lives for the better at any time.

It is work, as any active form of growth is, but that work can be enjoyable. As is often said, it is not the destination, but rather the trip or journey itself which holds the true treasures. If we are to maximize the effects of our work, we must actively work to use whatever knowledge, inspiration and awareness comes to us through these techniques.

When we close our eyes and withdraw our senses from the world around us, we enter another realm entirely. It is more fleeting and fluid than our physical world, and it operates within what some people may consider strange laws. But as different as it is, *it is as real as our world in the physical. Its energies have the ability to touch our physical lives and enhance them, or play chaotically upon them. It all lies with us!*

Many wish to touch such realms because of the "power" that they can then demonstrate. This, in and of itself, is not wrong, but it is limiting what we can do. "Astral" power and enhanced psychic ability, which unfold naturally as we begin to grow in knowledge and experience, can be developed and used by anyone. The awakening and use of it requires no more higher morality than does the development of greater physical strength. Neither does having the ability reflect high moral character, any more than having great physical strength would reflect it. The astral and psychic senses exist within us all, and anytime we begin to open up to other perceptions, it becomes active. It is an energy and ability that can be developed, but not as an end in itself. Its purpose is to bridge the consciousness to even more spiritual heights.

Attainment of "astral" power* as an end in itself leads to what is described in the East as the *laukika* method of development. The abilities and powers obtained are only for the present personality,

---

* Miscellaneous Astral Phenomena:

1. Disintegration	7. Spirit lights
2. Apportation	8. Levitation
3. Materialization	9. Fire-handling
4. Clairsentience	10. Psychic Healings
5. Clairvoyance	11. Other
6. Spirit communication	

Almost all astral phenomena involve increased sensitivity to vibrations of the astral plane and learning to direct and handle them. (It must be remembered that the development of mediumship is *not* a power. It is a condition.)

and because true spiritual safeguards are not employed, it is highly likely that the powers will be misused. If we are to ingrain the ability on the soul for eternity, we must follow the proper discipline and will, and constantly be using discrimination and discernment.

Discrimination is the first lesson in the school of the Tree of Life (Malkuth), and it is the last thing we will be tested upon. Kether at the top of the Tree becomes the Malkuth for the next Tree, so we always come back to discrimination. Part of discrimination requires that we learn to strongly close the doors behind us when we touch the more ethereal realms so that only the energies you consciously activate play within your life. This way, you can discern them more completely.

The entire purpose of working with the Tree of Life and the techniques within this book is to increase our awareness of the interplay of other planes and dimensions upon our physical life so we can learn to control them. This involves removing the "tunnel vision" approach to life and overcoming security only within the five senses. It is the sixth—the astral—that helps expand our awareness.

We must learn to use the altered state to recognize and understand how energies are playing in all aspects of our life. We must use it to increase our own energies and capacities, as well as to distinguish them from outside energies.

Most importantly, we must learn to synthesize the inner realm experiences with the outer physical reality. There must be time set aside on a regular basis in which we evaluate the physical life circumstances and experiences with those that we set in motion through the various techniques within this book. Otherwise we are simply dabbling for "psychic thrills."

We must begin to look at the patterns of our life. Begin with those inherent capabilities of your past and your present-day proficiency at them. Look for the overall patterns within your life and the lives of those with whom you are connected. Are you repeating the same situations, experiences, etc.? Retrain yourself to look at life and people from all levels. Keep in mind that *nothing* is insignificant. Look for the connections. What irritates you the most? What pleases you the most? Ask question after question. What is the relationship? The lesson? If we do not ask the question, we will not get the answers.

Once we begin to recognize the patterns and what we are consciously setting in motion, we need to utilize all of the latitude available to us. We always have *choice*! We can choose to continue to repeat the pattern or to change it. We can choose to perceive it from new levels, identify and analyze and utilize it, or we can choose to ignore it. We are trying to identify how energies operate, so that we can re-direct those energies in specific ways to create new patterns of existence.

Working with the Tree of Life means opening up the intuition and ability to perceive your life in new dimensions. You will no longer be able to perceive people or things from a limited scope. Everything is affected by you, and everything affects you!

The control of the environment begins with the control of the self. Until we cease to be influenced haphazardly by surrounding conditions, we cannot hope to exercise mental or spiritual influence over them. We are energy systems, operating in many dimensions, but if we are unaware of how extraneous energies (no matter how subtle) are affecting us, we will end up with lives that do not click. There will be disharmony and unfulfillment. This may manifest in our lives as a physical illness, stress or the loss of a job. Our own individual energies are being affected, consciously and unconsciously, and unless we learn to recognize and control this, and redirect our energies, our lives will become more complicated and even more unfulfilling.

When we open ourselves to the subtle planes and dimensions, such as through the Qabala, we are learning how they operate and how they affect us. It is of equal importance to learn not only to activate those energies, but also to close them down and protect ourselves for those times when we cannot be as cognizant and "watchful" as we would desire.

As we work with these energies, we do develop our own "magickal body." As this energy band around us becomes even more sensitive, it becomes more necessary to protect and close off the energies that could otherwise create imbalances. One method of enclosing ourselves in a seal of protection on a "magickal" level is through the dream and sleep state.

The Tree Within our Dreams

There are many methods of activating greater consciousness in the dream state. One technique in Tantra is that of visualizing the

Sanskrit symbol for OM (𝐳) in a scarlet, brilliant red in the area of the throat as one drops off to sleep. The symbol of the Om activates our creative expression and brings it to greater wakefulness in all areas of our life. When used at night, it activates greater dream activity and consciousness within the dreams.

This same kind of stimulation can be applied through the symbol of the Tree of Life, especially for those who are actively working with the Qabala. Instead of visualizing the symbol of the OM in the throat chakra, one visualizes the symbol of the Tree of Life in vibrant red. Visualizing oneself within the diagram—or enclosed within the protective branches of your own Tree of Life—will stimulate dreams that reveal information about your own pathworking and will more strongly protect the energies you have opened so that they remain and work for you in the dream.

When we begin to work with the Tree of Life regularly and more consciously, there occurs a greater stimulation of dream activity. As much attention needs to be placed upon it as does attention upon our normal day-to-day activities in relation to our Qabalistic work. Things of which we were not conscious can be clarified through the dreams or even elaborated upon. Energies released do not always play themselves out in a physical action that is overt. The energies of the Tree may simply affect emotional or mental conditions. These are often reflected within the dreams. We need to perceive all influences in order to work with and counteract or enhance them.

Putting it into Perspective

Many people claim that because they have visions and contacts, and because they know that all knowledge lies within, there is no reason to use strong techniques of protection. The truth is that the knowledge of techniques of protection in higher-consciousness exploration enables one to keep the visions unimpaired, and protects us against many dangers of which one may be unaware. It is easy to fall into misusing the energies awakened through the techniques of this work. It is easy to express them in an unbalanced manner. Development and unfoldment releases energies that can affect the mind, leading to difficulties if care is not taken.

The increased sensitivity alone can render the individual suspicious and quarrelsome. It can result in a form of hyper-sensitivity with a loss of discrimination.

One is not trying to dominate the universe, but to learn to work within its natural rhythms. Those who "dabble" with a little bit of knowledge and experience are the ones most likely to find themselves in difficulty.

Ways to Recognize Imbalances and Difficulties:

1. You may find yourself becoming self-centered. Other things in your life (including people) may seem to be more intrusive.
2. You may find yourself motivated more and more by greed, lust and a desire for knowledge and power.
3. You may find yourself always wanting to be out in front of everyone else. This includes wanting to let others know just how knowlegeable you are; and may also include feelings of knowing better than anyone else.
4. You may find yourself working with speedier and less troublesome methods of developing psychic faculties.
5. You may find yourself expressing the energy and force in misplaced manners (i.e., using the energies for sexual gratification.) This may also involve the use of out-of-date methods to attain the effects.
6. You may develop premature trance, premature in that you do not have the development of accurate intuition and clairvoyance to test and discriminate what and who works through you.
7. You may display much hypersensitivity in any area of your life.

Contact with non-physical states of existence has a very powerful effect upon man. It tends to draw the living away from the plane of objective, physical life—which is where we should be primarily focused. This occurs even when the highest energies are contacted. This is why integration with the physical is always of great import. It is also why we must always work to maintain the health of the physical body (proper diet, exercise) so that we stay grounded.

Work with spiritual energies does not imply neglect of the physical. It is the physical vehicle that will give expression to the energies we activate. If the physical is imbalanced, then the expression of the spiritual will be as well. This is also why we must learn to strongly close the gates behind us, so that we can learn to express in a balanced manner the energies we have activated, and not have to balance those which were released by our touching the subtler realms.

IMAGICKAL TECHNIQUE: The Qabalistic Cross

The Qabalistic cross should be used before any meditational, imagickal or ritual work. It stabilizes the aura and protects. It should also be used to close meditational work. It helps close and seal off the other planes and grounds you back into the physical one. With time and practice, one can become more conscious of the overshadowing presence of our own higher divine genius.

Stand straight (this can also be done in seated position), feet together, shoulders back and arms at your side. Face east if possible.

1. Take several deep breaths from the diaphragm. As you inhale and exhale slowly, visualize yourself growing and expanding into the heavens. Do this until you can see yourself standing upon the Earth itself, with the entire universe surrounding you.

2. With the thumb (Spirit), the first finger (Fire) and the middle finger (Earth), touch the forehead between the eyes and tone slowly the Hebrew word "Ateh" (ahh—toh). Give equal emphasis to each syllable, and visualize the sound carrying to the ends of the universe. In English, it translates as "Thine is."

3. Bring the thumb and fingers slowly down, as if drawing the light of the universe down through the body. Touch the center of the chest and tone the word "Malkuth" (mahl—kooth). This means "the kingdom."

4. Bring the hand to the right shoulder and tone the words "Ve Geburah" (vuh—guh—buhr—ahh). This translates as "the power."

5. Move the thumb and fingers across the body to the left shoulder, and tone the words "Ve Gedulah" (vuh—guh—duhl—lahh) which means "and the glory."

6. Raise both arms to the side, bow head and bring the hands to a folded, prayer position at the chest, fingers pointing upward. Tone slowly the words "Le-Olam Amen." This means "forever, Amen."

> Thine is
> the kingdom
> and the power
> and the glory
> forever, Amen.

This is the ending phrase of the "Lord's Prayer," only one of many indications of the Qabala as an intimate part of true Christianity.

The visualization that goes with this to enhance its effects is to see a brilliant, crystalline white light descending from on high, through one's head, down through the feet and into the heart of the planet. The light extends vertically through the body to infinity in both directions. Then one visualizes a brilliant shaft of light—the cross shaft—from shoulder to shoulder, extending in both directions horizontally into infinity. As you make the cross, touching each point on the body, visualize the brilliant explosion of light, engulfing each of the four points, filling the body and then extending into the lines of light.

Vibrate or tone the names and words strongly. If need be, tone them several times. This not only improves concentration, but it can help you to formulate the cross more clearly and vividly in your mind. You want the cross to be so brilliant that it is blinding in its intensity and actually lights up the universe. You become a cross of light within the universe and on all dimensions.

When vibrating these words or any of the God-names, keep in mind that they are holy and should be said with great reverence for the power and energy they invoke. The deity names, mentioned elsewhere, are names for the forces that the One Great Power in the universe manifests. They are holy and they deserve only the greatest respect and reverence!

Keep in mind, when visualizing and vibrating, the idea of divine white brilliance, because the vibrations attract a certain force to you. The nature of the force attracted rests largely on the condition your mind is in. Thus, we want to always focus on the highest, most brilliant and the most divine! As you breathe in, breathe in the brilliance. As you slowly emit the breath, slowly pronounce the words. See them as vibrating and ringing throughout the universe with glory and power. At the end, visualize yourself assuming normal size and absorbing the brilliance into yourself as you return, to become a part of the light for the physical world in which you live!

IMAGICKAL TECHNIQUE: Banishing Ritual of the Pentagram

This simple ritual involves using the power of the God-names associated with the Tree of Life and the power of the archangels for protective purposes. It is protection against impure magnetism. It cleanses the aura, as well as the environment in which it is performed, entirely. It builds a field of positive, protective, brilliant energy around you and your environment, so that nothing negative can penetrate. It can be used to get rid of obsessive thoughts, protects against psychic attack, shields one against lower astral entities, dissipates negative thoughtforms and closes the doors of other dimensions. It cleanses the aura of negativity that we accumulate throughout the day from others. It helps seal the aura, the home, and the temple from negativity.

The banishing ritual should be practiced by everyone within the metaphysical or spiritual field. Those doing ritual work, or those just beginning to open up to other energies and other dimensions, should practice it every day to build a force field around them to prevent intrusion that is negative and unwanted. It builds a ring of fire energy (a force field); studded in the four directions with five-pointed stars of flames. The more this technique is used, the more protective it becomes. It instantly dissolves negativity before it can reach us or after we have been touched by it.

Initially, it should be practiced every day. It should *always* be done at the close of a ritual or an imagickal working, for these open doors to planes that may not close entirely, even with an official closing to the ceremony or ritual. Until we become more knowledgeable, we may not recognize that the doors are still cracked. Thus you may have energies enter and bleed through that have no business being present. The Banishing Ritual prevents this, for with its power and energy, *only* the highest and truest vibrations can pass through the field of fire, unless we invite it or give it an opportunity.

This is a powerful tool that removes unwanted mental and astral entities, and obsessive thoughts, from the aura and environment. Once its power is established, the sphere of sensation is purified, exalted and made impenetrable to any disturbing influence. With such an aura, one can go anywhere, do almost anything, and meet entities without fear or anxiety of being assailed. One must realize, though, that it is not a cure-all for a lack of temperance, patience or common sense; and one must not try to rush enfoldment by invoking forces not fully comprehended.

1. Face east and make the Qabalistic cross. Then step forward with the left foot, symbolic of "entering within."

2. Using a ritual dagger, a stick of lighted incense or by just using your first finger (Fire finger), draw in the air before you a banishing pentagram, keeping the arm extended:

Top of Head

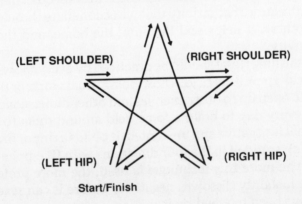

(LEFT SHOULDER)   (RIGHT SHOULDER)

(LEFT HIP)   (RIGHT HIP)

Start/Finish

Begin at the left hip and draw a line in the air before you to a point just above your head. We are inscribing in the air a line of fire blue. This is much like the process of creating the astral doorways. Without stopping, continue the line down to the right hip. From the right hip, inscribe the line in the air to just outside the left shoulder, and then draw the fire line across the front of you to the right shoulder. From the right shoulder, bring the line back down to the left hip, where you started. You have inscribed a fiery blue pentagram in the air before you. The lines should be continuous, with all five points connecting. (See the diagram on the opposite page.)

Thrust the finger into the heart of the pentagram and tone the God-name Yod He Vau He (yod—heh—vaw—heh) slowly and fully. Keep the finger pointing in the center throughout the process. Visualize and feel the pentagram expand and explode with an intense blue heat and energy, engulfing you, your aura and all of your surroundings. Know that it is instantly dissolving and vaporizing all negativity. Visualize the pentagram continuing to grow, its heat and fire cleansing all of the east. It then remains in the east, burning strongly with purity, permanence and strength.

3. Still holding the arm and finger extended, rotate toward the south. Visualize the finger inscribing with fire an arc of blue flame from the center of the pentagram in the east to a point in the south. See this as the beginning of a protective wall or ring of flame. When completed, it will seal you within a ring of purity, while sealing out negativity and impurity.

    Drop the finger to a point outside the left hip, and just as you did in the east, inscribe before you a flaming pentagram in the south. Thrust the finger into the heart and vibrate the God-name Adonai (ahh—doh—nye). Visualize the same effects as in step number two—with even further burning, purifying and cleansing.

4. Still extending the finger to the center of the pentagram in the south, rotate to the west, visualizing the arc of flame being formed between the point in the south and a point in the west. Inscribe a pentagram in the west. Thrust your fire finger into the center and vibrate Eheieh (eh—huh—yeh). Visualize and feel the effects.

5. Holding the finger and arm straight out, rotate to the north.

Visualize and inscribe the continuing arc and then inscribe a pentagram before you. Thrust your finger into the center and intone Agla (ahh—gah—lah). This is not a God-name as the others were. This is an abbreviation for the words "Ateh Gedulah Le-Olam Adonai." This translates to "Thou art mighty for ever, O Lord."

6. Still extending the arm, turn to the east, completing the circle of flame and fire. This is the protective ring of fire, studded in the four directions with flaming pentagrams. They burn upon the ethers and within your universe. Drop your arm from the center of the point in the east and relax. Take several deep breaths, experiencing the purified air.

7. Still facing east, outstretch your arms to the side in the form of a cross and tone: "Before me—Raphael!" (rah—phah—el). Vibrate it slowly, one syllable at a time. This is the name of the archangel of the east. Visualize a tremendous column of gold and blue light forming before you. Visualize this column materializing into a powerful being with wings that fan the air, causing a rush of fire and air which revitalizes the forces of your aura. It is contact with great healing and protection. He is facing away from you, guarding against any intrusion into your space.

8. With arms still outstretched, say, "Behind me—Gabriel!" (gah—bree—el). Visualize a tremendous column of blue-green light forming behind you. See it and feel it form into a figure of those same colors with silver flashes of light and tremendous swirls of colors upon his wings. He is electrical in nature, and you can feel it. He is like the battery to the universe, and from him comes the basis of all vision. His back is to you as he guards the west.

9. Arms still outstretched, say: "At my right hand—Michael!" (mee—chah—el/the ch is gutteral as in loch ness). Visualize a column of intense pure red light, blazing with all the reds of fire itself. See it change into a mighty winged being with sword upraised, crushing a dragon beneath his feet. He handles and purges dangers and unbalanced forces of any nature. His back is to you that he may more fully guard the south.

10. Then say, "At my left hand—Auriel!" (auh—ree—el). Visualize a column of light of russet and greens and browns that intensifies into a column of crystalline white. From that column emerges a giant figure. This one has the primeval light of God and manifests it upon the Earth. Auriel is considered the tallest of angels, able to see across eternity. Auriel is also concerned with the light of our teachings. This wondrous being also stands with its back to you to guard against intrusion from the north.

11. Visualize all of the archangels behind you. Feel their protection, their energies, and then say (with arms still extended): *"Before me flame the pentagrams! In the column shines the six-rayed star!"*

    "In the column" refers to the physical body, the column of light that you became with the Qabalistic cross. Visualize the six-pointed star within you and shining out from you. Its very center is located at your own heart center. It shines with blinding brilliance.

12. Visualize it all as one, and then make the Qabalistic cross again to seal and lock those energies in place for you. It will hold them firm upon the ethers!

In this banishing ritual all of the archangels face away from you, so as to guard you against anything false, unhealthy, unbalanced, impure or negative. You are encircled by them—within the ring of flaming pentagrams. Each guards and works for us in various ways. When we vibrate their names, we draw to us their essence, energy and power. Raphael and the east is for healing. Michael and the south is a source of balance and protection. Gabriel and the west is the source for higher and truer vision. Auriel and the north is a source for teachings of all kinds—especially truth! Together they guard us against all types of negativity and impurity—subtle and gross. They help us to awaken and utilize the energies of the Qabala in the safest manner possible!

The Holy of Holies

Our individual search or quest for our true essence is one that leads us down many paths. Each of these paths is like a polishing stone that cuts and facets our rawness into a priceless gem.

In more ancient times, the spiritual student underwent symbolic "faceting." Each phase of the training brought the student to a new temple which reflected new energies and manifestations of the divine within the physical world. And each time the student had to synthesize and integrate this with the past. Temple by temple, the student grew and learned until he or she was led into the last of the temples, that which is referred to as the "Holy of Holies."

This consisted of an empty chamber. No symbols. No altars. No tools. Just an empty chamber. Here the student was left alone to find the divine that existed within this temple's emptiness. Here the student learned to rely on his own higher self and his own knowledge of the innate union that exists between man and the Supreme Being. Here in the darkness of this last temple, the student learned that only he or she could bring the light and illumination to this temple. Only the student could light the lamp within the sanctuary that brings brilliance out of darkness. Here the student ceased to look for a light to shine down; but rather for that light within to shine out from him or her. Here was the lesson of the God within. Here the student learned that only s/he could initiate him/herself into the mysteries. Here were understood the words of the master who said, "At that day Ye shall know that I am in the Father and Ye in Me and I in YOU!"

appendix

Index to Weaknesses and Strengths

Sephiroth/Path	Weakness to Overcome*	Strength to Obtain
Malkuth	Laziness	Discrimination
	Greed	Discernment
	Avarice	Prosperity
	Recklessness	Common sense
	Overly reactive	Planning before acting
	Aggressive	Greater physical energy
	Lack of energy	
Yesod	Idleness	Independence
	Laziness	Confidence
	Emotional imbalance	Self-awareness
	Mental agitation	Intuition
	Vanity	Social acceptance
	Superficial arrogance	Spontaneity
	Obsessively sexual	Ambition
	Impulsiveness	Greater expansiveness
	Follower of crowds	Psychic energy & ability
		Knowledge of dreams
Hod	Deceit	Facility at learning
	Dishonesty	Truthfulness
	Impatience	Enhanced communication
	Dogmatism	Patience
	Mental cowardice	Practicality & objectivity
	Overly critical	Expanded intellect
	Separative	Eloquence
	Cold and aloof	Precision
	Planning but never manifesting	Prosperity through knowledge
		Knowledge of magic

---

* When we work with the Qabala, particularly through touching the levels of consciousness and pathwork-ing, we release energies into play within our lives so that we can overcome weaknesses and develop strengths. This can happen in a variety of ways—even opposite to what we anticipate. We may do work to obtain a release of "Patience," but what may actually manifest are situations that test our ability to be patient, in which we learn to strengthen the patience we have.

Sephiroth/Path	Weakness to Overcome	Strength to Obtain
Netzach	Lust & impurity	Unselfishness
	Overemotionalism	Creativity
	Worry over what others feel and think	Artistic energies
		Love & idealism
	Possessiveness	Warmth
	Antisocial	Expressiveness
	Superficially extroverted	Optimism
		Knowledge of relationships
	Introversion	Knowledge of Nature
	Envy & jealousy	Kingdom (Fairies and
	Social imbalance	elves . . .)
		Control of emotions
Tiphareth	Insecurity	Security
	Self-doubting	Generous
	Possessiveness	Open-hearted
	Fear & mistrust	Nurturing
	Irreverence	Reverent
	Need self-confirmation	Compassionate
	Need recognition	Healing energies
	False pride	Devotion
	Blaming others	Idealism
		Vision of beauty & success
		Glory & fame
Geburah	Anger	Courage
	Fear of others	Strength
	Self-doubt	Self-assured
	Manipulative	Confident
	Bullying	Active
	Timidity	Energy for change
	Hyperactivity	Critical judgment
	Surrendering	Learning of and dealing
	Power-seeking	with enemies
	Impulsive	Overcoming discord
	Aggressive	
	Belligerent	

Sephiroth/Path	Weakness to Overcome	Strength to Obtain
Chesed	Hypocrisy	Devotion
	False pride	Authority
	Disobedience	Idealism
	Stinginess	Abundance
	Overly conservative	Synthesis
	Overly traditional	Truth and loyalty
	Rigid	Committed
	Dogmatism	Higher callings
	Self-righteousness	Contentment
	Slowness to respond	Patient & enduring
	Needs supervision	Peace & mercy
	Smugness	
	Melancholy	
Binah	Avarice	Higher understanding
	Fear of the dark	Discipline
	Fear of the future	Patience
	Undisciplined	Higher intuition
	Introversion	Refinement of ideas
	Belittling	Strength through silence
	Inability to manifest	Confidentiality
	Impatience	Faithfulness
	Martyrdom	Nurturing
	Self-sacrificing	Understanding importance
	Overly mothering	of restrictions
	Lack of confidentiality	Understanding birth &
		death
Chokmah	Inability to manifest	Initiative
	Superstitiousness	Far-sightedness
	"Spaced-out"	Visionary
	Forgetful	Trusting of the future
	Misguidedly futuristic	Intuition
	Lateness	Inspiration
	Inefficient	Able to tune into
	Fear of the future	inner world rhythms
	Envious of others'	Devotion beyond piety
	talents	Realizing hidden
	Idolized relationships	abilities
		Understanding of zodiac

Sephiroth/Path	Weakness to Overcome	Strength to Obtain
Kether	Negative self-image	Creative imagination
	Daydreamy	Power of transformation
	Seeking sympathy	Ability to bring order
	Erotic imagination	Charming
	Shame	Sense of wonder
	Illusions	Instinctively mystical
	Self-denial	Facilitator of change
	Conflict with reality	Revealor of light
	Need to feel popular and indispensible	Spiritual fires
	Feels misunderstood	
	Lack of sympathy & tenderness	

(When it comes to the weaknesses and strengths of the paths, we must keep in mind that they also include the weaknesses and strengths of the individual sephira as well as their own unique manifestations. This is what makes them such powerful tools. They manifest path energy itself plus the energy of the two individual sephiroth linked by the path!)

Path 32		
Malkuth/Yesod	Greed	Discrimination
	Idleness	Motivation
	Hidden fears	Facing of subconscious
	Despondency	fears
	Depression	Self-discipline
	Insignificance	Common sense
	Lack of discipline	Greater structure
	Lack of feeling	Strengthening of light
	Overly calculating	bodies

Path 31		
Malkuth/Hod	Emotional imbalance	Self-discovery
	Weak-willed	Strength of will
	Irresponsibility	Fortitude
	Inertia	Self-assertiveness
	Fear of change	Helpfulness & kindness
	Greed	Inspiration
	Dishonesty	
	Ruthlessness	
	Self-imposition	

Sephiroth/Path	Weakness to Overcome	Strength to Obtain
Path 30 Yesod/Hod	Selfishness Fears Half-formed ideas Idleness Dishonesty Overly rational Lack of diligence Egocentric	Recognition of purpose Joy & happiness Optimism Balanced reason & intuition Artistic inspiration Prophetic insight Productive use of vitality Development of self- mastery Power in healing Alchemy

Path 29
Malkuth/
Netzach
	Greed
	Ungoverned imagination
	Sexual obsession
	Vulnerability
	Separatism
	Family disharmony
	Excessive empathy
	Controlling of others
	   through giving
	Withdrawal
		Unselfishness
		Simplification
		Faith & optimism
		Fellowship
		Family harmony
		Personal responsibility
		Innovation
		Subtle intuition
		Ability to work with
		   animals & nature

Path 28
Yesod/Netzach
	Fear of following dreams
	Inability to study or
	   concentrate
	Pettiness
	Doubting abilities
	Fear of trying the new
	Flightiness
	Overly talkative
	Imposition of will
	Impracticality
		Hope & inspiration
		Greater will &
		   understanding
		Individuality
		Sociability
		Loyalty
		Greater learning
		Peace
		Strength to follow
		   dreams

Sephiroth/Path	Weakness to Overcome	Strength to Obtain
Path 27 Hod/Netzach	Emotional & mental conflicts	Endurance
		Courage
	Insecurity	Faith
	False security	Self-awareness
	Feelings of being lost	Strength to re-create self
	Failure to resolve conflicts	Fighting spirit
		Energy to change fortune
	Self-delusion	
Path 26 Hod/Tiphareth	Weak-willed	Strength of will
	Materiality	Generosity
	Pride	Tolerance
	Self-illusion	Pragmatism
	Domineering	Strengthened beliefs
	Selfishness	More giving
	Conceit	Trust & loyalty
	Lack of belief & pragmatism	Increased organization
		Stronger inner voice
	Demanding or dictatorial	Openness and innocence
	Secretive	
Path 25 Yesod/ Tiphareth	Temptations	Self-sufficiency
	Irresponsibility	Responsibility
	Fear to try the new	Openness to the new
	Inability to integrate & synthesize	Harmony and balance
		Boldness
	Afraid to choose	Straightforwardness
	Narrow-sightedness	Wider perspectives
	Gluttony, coarseness	Self-discovery
	False exaggeration	Moderation
Path 24 Netzach/ Tiphareth	Fear of death or change	Strength for transformation
	Resistance to change	Acceptance
	Inability to deal with grief	Assimilation of grief
	Inability to understand others' conflicts	Understanding of others' problems & conflicts
		Activation of life force
	Seductiveness	True friendship

Sephiroth/Path	Weakness to Overcome	Strength to Obtain
(Path 24 continued)		
	Misuse of friends	Desire to merge physical with spiritual
	Egotism	
	Failure to leave past	Ability to leave past behind
Path 23		
Hod/Geburah	Intolerance	New perspectives
	Depression	Tolerance
	Focus on material	Upliftment
	Dominance	Compassion
	Unproductive day-dreaming	Trust in our instincts
		Greater psychic energy
	Self-indulgence	Sensitivity
	Overly impressionable	Discernment
	Lack of compassion	Greater service
Path 22		
Tiphareth/ Geburah	Ignoring disruption & chaos	Application of thought & action
	Duality	Facing our conscience
	Unforgiving	Impartiality
	Ignoring the negative	Artistic energies
	Failure to make decisions	Sociability
	Manipulation (by self or others)	Inspiration to others
		Objective self-discernment
	Deceitfulness	Decisiveness
	Superficiality	Strength to face all consequences
	Unsociableness	
	Lack of conscience	Blending of physical & spiritual
Path 21		
Netzach/ Chesed	Inability to see choices	Maturity
	Immaturity	Greater application of effort
	Non-committal	
	Discontent	Commitment
	"Passing the buck"	Sensitivity & sensibleness
	Chronic complaining	Recognition of Divine Law within our lives
	Feelings of universal "unfairness"	
		Opening of way to the "Grail"
	Self-pity	

Sephiroth/Path	Weakness to Overcome	Strength to Obtain
Path 20 Tiphareth/ Chesed	Hypocrisy False pride Non-committal Fear of the past Too much deliberation Underhandedness Indecisiveness Improper application of power Fault-finding	Helpfulness Unassuming attitudes Dependability Unselfishness Openness to change Calmness, self-reliance Illumination Strong, silent compassion Application of power
Path 19 Geburah/ Chesed	Burnt-out attitudes Putting up false fronts Self-pride Avoidance of trials & growth Vanity Self-seeking attitude Indecision Allowing others to take advantage Cruelty	Peacekeeping ability Energy to right wrongs Ability to defend the weak Decisiveness Protectiveness Sincerity Transmutation & inner alchemy Strength to face reality
Path 18 Geburah/Binah	Instability Unwilling to carry on Energy depleted Lack of determination & hard work Lack of caring for others' needs Inability to focus in the present No self-control Hysterics & irritability	Balanced response to life Enhanced concentration Release of hidden knowledge Discipline Determination Strengthened psychic energy Self-control

Sephiroth/Path	Weakness to Overcome	Strength to Obtain

Path 17
Tiphareth/
Binah
	Lack of communication
	Lack of humor
	Inability to choose &
	  discriminate
	Imbalanced male &
	  female energies
	Rigidity
	Insensitivity
		Versatility
		Integration of male &
		  female energies
		Selectivity
		Intelligence and sensi-
		  tivity
		Strengthens inner voice
		Opens sense of humor
		Alchemy

Path 16
Chesed/
Chokmah
	Wishy-washy beliefs
	False sense of security
	Ancestral fears
	Misunderstandings
	Misplaced loyalties
	Lack of fertility
	  and productivity
	Stubbornness
	Overindulgence
		Loyalty
		Greater understanding
		Revelation of creative
		  talents
		Fertility in life
		Upliftment of soul
		Freedom for beliefs
		Kindness & compassion

Path 15
Tiphareth/
Chokmah
	Non-recognition of laws
	Disrespect for authority
	Bitterness
	Unclear focus
	Disassociation with
	  people & life
	Foolhardiness
	Egotism
	Acting without fore-
	  thought
	Highly opinionated
		Energies of vision
		Revelation of life potential
		Courage
		Ability to inspire
		Increased intuition
		Initiative
		Attunement to higher
		  orders
		Increased connection with
		  "guardians" & friends

Path 14
Binah/
Chokmah
	Disbelief
	Failure to merge with
	  creative principles
	  for prosperity
	Feeling unattractive
		Knowledge of birth
		Belief in impossible
		Merging of imagination &
		  reality
		Attractiveness

Sephiroth/Path	Weakness to Overcome	Strength to Obtain
(Path 14 continued)	Lack of femininity or understanding its function in the universe	Sentiments of love & sharing
	Lack of joy & creativity	Understanding of the feminine
	Non-appreciation for life	Joy, love & reproductive ability (physical & spiritual)
Path 13 Tiphareth/ Kether	Self-made obstacles	Faith
	Imbalanced emotions	Removal of barriers between inner & outer worlds
	Inability to see purpose in all things in life	Resourcefulness
	Overdependency on others	Security in oneself
	Lack of faith	Self-reliance
	Conflict with being alone and being lonely	Opens wealth of intuition
	Unable to be relied upon	Revelation of hidden
Path 12 Binah/Kether	Failure to recognize abilities	Nourishment
	Blocked vision	Wisdom, truth & dexterity in all aspects of life
	Communication blockages	Vision and seership
	Restlessness	Recognition of potential
	Imbalance between rational & intuitive	Magic & alchemy
	Unbalanced emotionalism	Separation of mundane & spiritual
	Unwilling to take advantage of growth opportunities	Balance of intuitive & rational
		Artistic, creative energy
		Expanded intelligence
Path 11 Chokmah/ Kether	Overcomplicated view	Innocence and trust
	Foglike perspective	Mental clarity
	Repetitive	Gregariousness
	Hyperactivity	Cooperation

Sephiroth/Path	Weakness to Overcome	Strengths to Obtain
(Path 12 continued)	Coldness Distrust	Stimulation of intellect, intuition & artistic mind Poise in the universe Wisdom teachings

bibliography

For the Qabala

Albertus, Frater. *Seven Rays of the QBL.* Weiser Publications, 1985.

Ashcroft-Nowicke, Dolores. *Shining Paths.* Aquarian Press, 1983.

Bardon, Franz. *Key to the True Quabbalah.* Dieter Ruggeberg, 1986.

Bischoff, Dr. Erich. *Kabbala.* Weiser Publications, 1985.

Case, Paul Foster. *True and Invisible Rosicrucian Order.* Weiser Publications, 1985.

Denning & Phillips. *The Magical Philosophy, Books I-V.* Llewellyn Publications, 1978.

_____.*Magical States of Consciousness.* Llewellyn Publications, 1985.

Fortune, Dion. *The Mystical Qabala.* Ernst Benn Limited, 1979.

Frank, Adolphe. *The Kabbala.* Bell Publishing, 1960.

Gray, William. *Concepts of the Qabalah.* Weiser Publications, 1982.

Halevi, Z'ev ben Shimon. *Adam and the Kabbalistic Tree.* Weiser Publications, 1985.

_____.*Work of the Kabbalist.* Weiser Publications, 1984.

Knight, Gareth. *Practical Guide to Qabalistic Symbolism.* Weiser Publications, 1978.

Reed, Ellen Cannon. *The Witches Qabala.* Llewellyn Publications, 1986.

Regardie, Israel. *A Garden of Pomegranates.* Second edition. Llewellyn Publications, 1985.

_____.*The Golden Dawn.* Llewellyn Publications, 1982.

_____.*One Year Manual.* Weiser Publications, 1981.

_____.*The Tree of Life.* Weiser Publications, 1972.

Sturzaker, D. & J. *Colour and the Kabbalah.* Weiser Publications, 1975.

Suares, Carlo. *Qabala Trilogy.* Shambhala Publications, 1983.

Waite, A. E. *The Holy Kabbalah.* University Books/Citadel Press.

Wang, Robert. *Qabalistic Tarot.* Weiser Publications, 1983.

Wippler, Migene Gonzalez. *A Kabbalah for the Modern World.* Llewellyn Publications, 1987.

For Magic and Symbolism

Buckland, Raymond. *Practical Candleburning Rituals.* Llewellyn Publications, 1982.

Cooper, J. C. *Symbolism—The Universal Language.* Aquarian Press, 1982.

Cunningham, Scott. *Cunningham's Encyclopedia of Magickal Herbs.* Llewellyn Publications, 1985.

_____.*Magical Herbalism.* Llewellyn Publications, 1983.

de Coppens, Peter Roche. *The Nature and Use of Ritual.* Llewellyn Publications, 1985.

Denning & Phillips. *Practical Guide to Creative Visualization.* Llewellyn Publications, 1980.

_____.*Psychic Self-Defense and Well-Being.* Llewellyn Publications, 1985.

Fettner, Ann Tucker. *Potpourri, Incense and Fragrant Concoctions.* Workman Publishing, 1977.

Fortune, Dion. *Applied Magic.* Aquarian Press, 1979.

Gawain, Shakti. *Creative Visualization.* Whatever Publishing, 1978.

Gray, William. *Magical Ritual Methods.* Weiser Publications, 1980.

Hall, Manly P. *Magic.* Philosophical Research Society, 1978.

Highfield, A. C. *Symbolic Weapons of Ritual Magic.* Aquarian Press, 1983.

Jung, Carl. *Archetypes and the Great Unconscious.*

_____. *The Collected Works (Vol. 18)—The Symbolic Life.* Princeton University Press, 1976.

Miller, Richard Alan. *Magickal and Ritual Use of Herbs.* Destiny Books, 1983.

Price, Shirley. *Practical Aromatherapy.* Thorsons Publishing, 1983.

Regardie, Israel. *Ceremonial Magic.* Aquarian Press, 1980.

_____.*Complete Golden Dawn System of Magic.* Falcon Press, 1984.

Sturzaker, James. *Aromatics in Ritual and Therapeutics.* Metatron Publications, 1979.

Vinci, Leo. *Candle Magic.* Aquarian Press, 1981.

Vinci, Leo. *Incense.* Aquarian Press, 1980.

Weinstein, Marion. *Positive Magic.* Phoenix Publishing, 1978.

For Metaphysical Concepts/Philosophies

Brennon, J. H. *Astral Doorways*. Aquarian Press, 1986.

David, William. *Harmonics of Sound, Color and Vibration*. DeVorss, 1980.

Davidson, Gustav. *Dictionary of Angels*. Free Press, 1967.

Drury, Neville. *Music for Inner Space*. Prism Press, 1985.

Fortune, Dion. *Aspects of Occultism*. Aquarian Press, 1986.

_____.*Esoteric Orders and Their Work*. Aquarian Press, 1982.

_____.*Practical Occultism in Daily Life*. Aquarian Press, 1981.

Hall, Manly P. *Man—Grand Symbol of the Mysteries*. Philosophical Research Society, 1972.

_____.*Secret Teachings of the Ages*. Philosophical Research Society, 1977.

Heline, Corinne. *Music—The Keynote of Human Evolution*. New Age Bible and Philosophy Center.

Hodson, Geoffrey. *The Kingdom of the Gods*. Theosophical Society, 1952.

Lewis, H. Spencer. *Mystical Life of Jesus*. Rosicrucian Press, 1944.

_____.*Secret Doctrines of Jesus*. Rosicrucian Press, 1954.

Lingerman, Hal. *Healing Energies of Music*. Theosophical Society, 1983.

Powell, A. E. *The Etheric Double*. Theosophical Society, 1983.

Richardson, Alan. *Gate of Moon*. Aquarian Press, 1984.

Schure, Edouard. *From the Sphinx to the Christ*. Harper and Row, 1970.

_____.*The Great Initiates*. Harper and Row, 1961.

Steiner, Rudolph. *An Outline of Occult Science*. Anthroposophical Press, 1972.

_____.*Esoteric Development*. Anthroposophical Society, 1982.

_____.*Knowledge of the Higher Worlds*. Anthroposophical Press, 1947.

_____.*Spiritual Hierarchies*. Anthroposophical Press, 1970.

For the Dance and Posture

Beck, Lilla and Annie Wilson. *What Colour are You?* Turnstone Press Limited; Great Britain, 1981.

Bellamak, Lu. *Dancing Prayers.* Cybury Graphics; Arizona, 1982.

Copeland, Roger and Marshall Cohen. *What is Dance?* Oxford University Press; New York, 1983.

Davies, Sir John. "Penelope Full of Dance," *Orchestra* (1596).

Douglas, Nik and Penny Slinger. *Sexual Secrets.* Destiny Books; New York, 1979.

Highwater, Jamake. *Dance—Ritual of Experience.* Alfred Van der Marck Editions; New York, 1978.

Hittleman, Richard. *Guide for the Seeker.* Bantam Books; New York, 1978.

_____.*Introduction to Yoga.* Bantam Books; New York, 1975.

_____.*Yoga—8 Steps to Health and Peace.* Bantam Books; New York, 1976.

_____.*Yoga Meditation Plan.* Bantam Books; New York, 1978.

Humphrey, Doris. *The Art of Making Dances.* Grove Press Incorporated; New York, 1980.

Johari, Harish. *Tools for Tantra.* Destiny Books; Vermont, 1986.

Joyce, Mary. *Dance Techniques for Children.* Mayfield Publication Company; California, 1984.

Kelder, Peter. *The Eye of Revelation.*

Laws, Kenneth. *The Physics of Dance.* Schirmer Books; New York, 1984.

Lawson, Joan. *Teaching Young Dancers.* Theatre Arts Books; New York, 1975.

Mattlage, Louise. *Dances of Faith.* County Press; Pennsylvania.

Sorell, Walter. *Dance Has Many Faces.* Columbia University Press; New York, 1966.

Stearn, Jesse. *Yoga, Youth and Reincarnation.* Bantam Books; New York, 1978.

Tegner, Bruce. *Kung Fu and Tai Chi.* Thor Publishing; California, 1973.

Tillyard, E. M. "The Cosmic Dance." *Elizabethan World Picture.*

Vishnudevananda, Swami. *The Complete Illustrated Book of Yoga.* Pocket Books; New York, 1960.

STAY IN TOUCH

On the following pages you will find listed, with their current prices, some of the books now available on related subjects. Your book dealer stocks most of these and will stock new titles in the Llewellyn series as they become available. We urge your patronage.

To obtain our full catalog, to keep informed about new titles as they are released and to benefit from informative articles and helpful news, you are invited to write for our bimonthly news magazine/catalog, *Llewellyn's New Worlds of Mind and Spirit*. A sample copy is free, and it will continue coming to you at no cost as long as you are an active mail customer. Or you may subscribe for just $7.00 in the U.S.A. and Canada ($20.00 overseas, first class mail). Many bookstores also have *New Worlds* available to their customers. Ask for it.

Stay in touch! In *New Worlds'* pages you will find news and features about new books, tapes and services, announcements of meetings and seminars, articles helpful to our readers, news of authors, products and services, special money-making opportunities, and much more.

Llewellyn's *New Worlds of Mind and Spirit*
P.O. Box 64383-016, St. Paul, MN 55164-0383, U.S.A.
* * *

TO ORDER BOOKS AND TAPES

If your book dealer does not have the books described on the following pages readily available, you may order them directly from the publisher by sending full price in U.S. funds, plus $3.00 for postage and handling for orders *under* $10.00; $4.00 for orders *over* $10.00. There are no postage and handling charges for orders over $50.00. Postage and handling rates are subject to change. UPS Delivery: We ship UPS whenever possible. Delivery guaranteed. Provide your street address as UPS does not deliver to P.O. Boxes. UPS to Canada requires a $50.00 minimum order. Allow 4-6 weeks for delivery. Orders outside the U.S.A. and Canada: Airmail—add retail price of book; add $5.00 for each non-book item (tapes, etc.); add $1.00 per item for surface mail.

FOR GROUP STUDY AND PURCHASE

Because there is a great deal of interest in group discussion and study of the subject matter of this book, we feel that we should encourage the adoption and use of this particular book by such groups by offering a special quantity price to group leaders or agents.

Our special quantity price for a minimum order of five copies of *Imagick* is $38.85 cash-with-order. This price includes postage and handling within the United States. Minnesota residents must add 6.5% sales tax. For additional quantities, please order in multiples of five. For Canadian and foreign orders, add postage and handling charges as above. Credit card (VISA, MasterCard, American Express) orders are accepted. Charge card orders only ($15.00 minimum order) may be phoned in free within the U.S.A. or Canada by dialing 1-800-THE-MOON. For customer service, call 1-612-291-1970. Mail orders to:

LLEWELLYN PUBLICATIONS
P.O. Box 64383-016, St. Paul, MN 55164-0383, U.S.A.

Prices subject to change without notice.

SIMPLIFIED MAGIC
A Beginner's Guide to the New Age Qabala
by Ted Andrews

In every person, the qualities essential for accelerating his or her growth and spiritual evolution are innate, but even those who recognize such potentials need an effective means of releasing them. The ancient and mystical Qabala is that means.

Simplified Magic offers a simple understanding of what the Qabala is and how it operates. It provides practical methods and techniques so that the energies and forces within the system and within ourselves can be experienced in a manner that enhances growth and releases our greater potential. A reader knowing absolutely nothing about the Qabala could apply the methods in this book with noticeable success! The Qabala is a system for personal attainment and magic that anyone can learn and put to use in his or her life. The secret is that the main glyph of the Qabala, the Tree of Life, is within you. The Tree of Life is a map to the levels of consciousness, power and magic. By learning the Qabala, you will be able to tap into these levels and bring peace, healing, power, love, light and magic into your life.

0-87542-015-X, 208 pgs., mass market, illus. **$3.95**

GODWIN'S CABALISTIC ENCYCLOPEDIA
A Complete Guide to Cabalistic Magick
by David Godwin

This is the most complete correlation of Hebrew and English ideas ever offered. It is a dictionary of Cabalism arranged, with definitions, alphabetically in Hebrew and numerically. With this book, the practicing Cabalist or student no longer needs access to a large number of books on mysticism, magic and the occult in order to trace down the basic meanings, Hebrew spellings, and enumerations of the hundreds of terms, words, and names.

This book includes: all of the two-letter root words found in Biblical Hebrew, the many names of God, the planets, the astrological signs, numerous angels, the Shem ha-Mephorash, the Spirits of the *Goetia*, the correspondences of the 32 Paths, a comparison of the Tarot and the Cabala, a guide to Hebrew pronunciation, and a complete edition of Aleister Crowley's valuable book *Sepher Sephiroth*.

Here is a book that is a must for the shelf of all magicians, Cabalists, astrologers, Tarot students, Thelemites, and those with any interest at all in the spiritual aspects of our universe.

0-87542-292-6, 528 pgs., 6 x 9, softcover **$15.00**

HOW TO HEAL WITH COLOR
by Ted Andrews

Now, for perhaps the first time, color therapy is placed within the grasp of the average individual. Anyone can learn to facilitate and accelerate the healing process on all levels with the simple color therapies in *How to Heal with Color*. Color serves as a vibrational remedy that interacts with the human energy system to stabilize physical, emotional, mental and spiritual conditions. When there is balance, we can more effectively rid ourselves of toxins, negativities and patterns that hinder our life processes.

This book provides color application guidelines that are beneficial for over 50 physical conditions and a wide variety of emotional and mental conditions. Receive simple and tangible instructions for performing "muscle testing" on yourself and others to find the most beneficial colors. Learn how to apply color therapy through touch, projection, breathing, cloth, water and candles. Learn how to use the little known but powerful color-healing system of the mystical Qabala to balance and open the psychic centers. Plus, discover simple techniques for performing long distance healings on others.

0-87542-005-2, 240 pgs., mass market, illus.   **$3.95**

HOW TO UNCOVER YOUR PAST LIVES
by Ted Andrews

Knowledge of your past lives can be extremely rewarding. It can assist you in opening to new depths within your own psychological makeup. It can provide greater insight into present circumstances with loved ones, career and health. It is also a lot of fun.

Now Ted Andrews shares with you nine different techniques that you can use to access your past lives. Between techniques, Andrews discusses issues such as karma and how it is expressed in your present life; the source of past life information; soul mates and twin souls; proving past lives; the mysteries of birth and death; animals and reincarnation; abortion and pre-mature death; and the role of reincarnation in Christianity.

To explore your past lives, you need only use one or more of the techniques offered. Complete instructions are provided for a safe and easy regression. Learn to dowse to pinpoint the years and places of your lives with great accuracy, make your own self-hypnosis tape, attune to the incoming child during pregnancy, use the Tarot and the Cabala in past life meditations, keep a past life journal and more.

0-87542-022-2, 240 pgs., mass market, illus.   **$3.95**

A KABBALAH FOR THE MODERN WORLD
by Migene Gonzalez-Wippler
The Kabbalah is the basic form of Western mysticism, and this is an excellent manual of traditional Kabbalistic Magick! It contains one of the best introductions to the Kabbalah ever written.

If you have ever been intimidated by the Kabbalah in the past, and never studied its beauty, *this is the book for you*. It clearly and plainly explains the complexities of the Kabbalah. This is an ideal book for newcomers to the study of Kabbalah or mysticism and spirituality in general.

This book covers a variety of Kabbalistic topics including: Creation, the nature of God, the soul and soul mates, the astral and other planes, the four worlds, the history of the Kabbalah, Bible interpretation and more.

A Kabbalah for the Modern World is written so clearly that it makes complex kabbalistic ideas easy to understand. This book needs to be in the library of every occultist, Pagan, Kabbalist, mystic and person involved in the New Age.

In this book Wippler shows that the ancient Kabbalists predicted the New Physics. She goes on to discuss such topics as: Planck's Quantum Theory, God and Light, Archetypes, Synchronicity, The Collective Unconscious, the Lemaitre 'Big Bang' Theory, Einstein's Theory of Relativity and much more.

There have been many books over the past several years which have compared psychological theory and the New Age Physics with various Eastern philosophies such as Taoism and Zen. But there is only one which unites psychology, physics and *Western* mysticism: Migene Gonzalez-Wippler's *A Kabbalah for the Modern World*.
0-87542-294-2, 240 pgs., 5¼ x 8, illus., softcover.   **$9.95**

THE INNER WORLD OF FITNESS
by Melita Denning
Because the artificialities and the daily hassles of routine living tend to turn our attention from the real values, *The Inner World of Fitness* leads us back by means of those natural factors in life which remain to us: air, water, sunlight, the food we eat, the world of nature, meditations, sexual love and the power of our wishes—so that through these things we can re-link ourselves in awareness to the great non-material forces of life and of being which underline them.

The unity and interaction of inner and outer, keeping body and psyche open to the great currents of life and of the natural forces, is seen as the essential secret of *youthfulness* and hence of radiant fitness. Regardless of our physical age, so long as we are within the flow of these great currents, we have the vital quality of youthfulness: but if we begin to close off or turn away from those contacts, in the same measure we begin to lose youthfulness. Also included is a metaphysical examination of AIDS.

This book will help you to experience the total energy of abundant health.
0-87542-165-2, 240 pgs., 5¼ x 8, illus., softcover   **$7.95**

HOW TO SEE AND READ THE AURA
by Ted Andrews

Everyone has an aura—the three-dimensional, shape-and-color-changing energy field that surrounds all matter. And anyone can learn to see and experience the aura more effectively. There is nothing magical about the process. It simply involves a little understanding, time, practice and perseverance.

Do some people make you feel drained? Do you find some rooms more comfortable and enjoyable to be in? Have you ever been able to sense the presence of other people before you actually heard or saw them? If so, you have experienced another person's aura. In this practical, easy-to-read manual, you receive a variety of exercises to practice alone and with partners to build your skills in aura reading and interpretation. Also, you will learn to balance your aura each day to keep it vibrant and strong so others cannot drain your vital force.

Learning to see the aura not only breaks down old barriers—it also increases sensitivity. As we develop the ability to see and feel the more subtle aspects of life, our intuition unfolds and increases, and the childlike joy and wonder of life returns.

0-87542-013-3, 160 pgs., mass market, illus. **$3.95**

HOW TO MEET & WORK WITH SPIRIT GUIDES
by Ted Andrews

We often experience spirit contact in our lives but fail to recognize it for what it is. Now you can learn to access and attune to beings such as guardian angels, nature spirits and elementals, spirit totems, archangels, gods and goddesses—as well as family and friends after their physical death.

Contact with higher soul energies strengthens the will and enlightens the mind. Through a series of simple exercises, you can safely and gradually increase your awareness of spirits and your ability to identify them. You will learn to develop an intentional and directed contact with any number of spirit beings. Discover meditations to open up your subconscious. Learn which acupressure points effectively stimulate your intuitive faculties. Find out how to form a group for spirit work, use crystal balls, perform automatic writing, attune your aura for spirit contact, use sigils to contact the great archangels and much more! Read *How to Meet and Work with Spirit Guides* and take your first steps through the corridors of life beyond the physical.

0-87542-008-7, 192 pgs., mass market, illus. **$3.95**

THE LLEWELLYN DEEP MIND TAPE
FOR CREATIVE VISUALIZATION
by Denning & Phillips

The Deep Mind Creative Visualization Tape is designed to help you attain your objectives by means of the most powerful single technique existing: Creative Visualization. You should use it to accompany your work with *The Llewellyn Practical Guide to Creative Visualization*.

The Deep Mind Creative Visualization Tape will guide you in the use of Creative Visualization to gain specific objectives. This present tape is designed to help you gain such objectives as material possessions, or the development of a talent, or for success on some specially important occasion. When you have gained your present objective, you can use this tape again whenever you feel like it, to reinforce your success, to gain other objectives, and to enter more deeply, with practice, into Creative Visualization.

The Llewellyn Practical Guide to Creative Visualization is the basic text, teaching you all the techniques you need for performing Creative Visualization effectively, and making clear also the reasons for everything you should do. You should read that helpful and inspiring book right through at least once, thoughtfully and carefully, before beginning to make practical use of this tape. So also with any other Deep Mind Creative Visualization Tapes you may choose for special purposes; in all cases you should read this *Practical Guide* through from time to time to ensure you are keeping close to all of its vital counsels and its positive affirmations.

0-87542-169-5 $9.95

Note: If you have the book, THE LLEWELLYN PRACTICAL GUIDE TO CREATIVE VISUALIZA-TION you may order this DEEP MIND TAPE by sending full price, plus $1.50 postage & handling ($7.00 overseas airmail). Or, you can order both book AND Tape for a special price of just $15.00 Postpaid in U.S.A. ($25.00 overseas airmail).

THE LLEWELLYN DEEP MIND TAPE FOR ASTRAL PROJECTION
by Denning & Phillips

This is a tool so powerful that it is offered only for use in conjunction with the above book. The authors of this book are adepts fully experienced in all levels of psychic development and training, and have designed this 90-minute cassette tape to guide the student through full relaxation and all the preparations for projection, and then—with the added dimension of the authors personally produced electronic synthesizer patterns of sound and music—they program the Deep Mind through the stages of awakening, and projection of, the astral Body of Light. And then the programming guides your safe return to normal consciousness with memory—enabling you to bridge the worlds of Body, Mind and Spirit.

The Deep Mind Tape is a powerful new technique combining guided Mind Programming with specially created sound and music to evoke deep level response in the psyche and its psychic centers for controlled development, and induction of the Out-Of-Body Experience.

0-87542-168-7, 90-minute cassette tape. $9.95

Note: If you have the book, *The Llewellyn Practical Guide to Astral Projection*, you may order this DEEP MIND TAPE by sending full price, plus $1.50 postage & handling ($7.00 overseas airmail). Or, you can order both Book AND Tape for a special price of just $15.00 Postpaid in U.S.A. ($25.00 overseas airmail).

THE LLEWELLYN PRACTICAL GUIDE TO
CREATIVE VISUALIZATION
For the Fulfillment of Your Desires
by Denning & Phillips

All things you will ever want must have their start in your mind. The average person uses very little of the full creative power that is his potentially. *If you can see it in your mind's eye you will have it!* You can have whatever you want, but there are "laws" to mental creation that must be followed. The power of the mind is not limited by the material world. *Creative Visualization* enables man to reach beyond, into the invisible world of astral and spiritual forces. Some people apply this innate power without actually knowing what they are doing, and achieve great success and happiness; most people, however, use this same power, again unknowingly, incorrectly, and experience bad luck, failure, or at best an unfulfilled life.

This book changes that. Through an easy series of progressive exercises, your mind is applied to bring desire into realization! Wealth, power, success, happiness, psychic powers, even what we call magickal power and spiritual attainment all can be yours. You can easily develop this completely natural power, and correctly apply it, for your immediate and practical benefit. Illustrated with unique, "puts-you-into-the-picture" visualization aids.

0-87542-183-0, 294 pgs., 5-1/4 x 8, illus., softcover $8.95

THE LLEWELLYN PRACTICAL GUIDE TO
ASTRAL PROJECTION
by Denning & Phillips

Your consciousness can be sent out of the body with full awareness and return with full memory. You can travel through time and space, converse with non-physical entities, obtain knowledge by nonmaterial means, and experience higher dimensions. The ability to go forth by means of the Astral Body gives the personal assurance of consciousness (and life) beyond the limitations of the physical body. The reader is led through the essential stages for the inner growth and development that will culminate in fully conscious projection and return. Not only are the practices outlined step-by-step and augmented with photographs and visualization aids, but the vital reasons for undertaking them are clearly explained. The great benefits from the various practices themselves are demonstrated in renewed physical and emotional health, mental discipline, spiritual attainment, and the development of extra faculties.

Guidance is also given to the Astral World itself, including the ecstatic experience of Astral Sex between two people who project together into this higher world where true union is consummated free of the barriers of physical bodies.

0-87542-181-4, 266 pgs., 5-1/4 x 8, illus., softcover $8.95

THE MIDDLE PILLAR
by Israel Regardie

Between the two outer pillars of the Qabalistic Tree of Life, the extremes of Mercy and Severity, stands the Middle Pillar, signifying one who has achieved equilibrium in his or her own self.

Integration of the human personality is vital to the continuance of creative life. Without it, man lives as an outsider to his own true self. By combining magic and psychology in the Middle Pillar Ritual/Exercise (a magical meditation technique), we bring into balance the opposing elements of the psyche while yet holding within their essence and allowing full expression of man's entire being.

In this book, and with this practice, you will learn to: understand the psyche through its correspondences of the Tree of Life; expand self-awareness, thereby intensifying the inner growth process; activate creative and intuitive potentials; understand the individual thought patterns which control every facet of personal behavior; and regain the sense of balance and peace of mind—the equilibrium—that everyone needs for phsyical and psychic health.

0-87542-658-1, 176 pgs., 5-1/4 x 8, softcover $8.95

A GARDEN OF POMEGRANATES
by Israel Regardie

What is the Tree of Life? It's the ground plan of the Qabalistic system—a set of symbols used since ancient times to study the Universe. The Tree of Life is a geometrical arrangement of ten sephiroth, or spheres, each of which is associated with a different archetypal idea, and 22 paths which connect the spheres.

This system of primal correspondences has been found the most efficient plan ever devised to classify and organize the characteristics of the self. Israel Regardie has written one of the best and most lucid introductions to the Qabalah.

A Garden of Pomegranates combines Regardie's own studies with his notes on the works of Aleister Crowley, A.E. Waite, Eliphas Levi and D.H. Lawrence. No longer is the wisdom of the Qabalah to be held secret! The needs of today place the burden of growth upon each and every person . . . each has to undertake the Path as his or her own responsibility, but every help is given in the most ancient and yet most modern teaching here known to humankind.

0-87542-690-5, 160 pgs., 5-1/4 x 8, softcover $8.95